Upgrading and Refurbishing the
Older Fiberglass Sailboat

Books by W. D. Booth

Selling Commercial and Industrial Construction

Upgrading and Refurbishing the Older Fiberglass Sailboat

Upgrading and Refurbishing
the Older
Fiberglass Sailboat

by

W. D. Booth

Cornell Maritime Press
Centreville, Maryland

Library of Congress Cataloging in Publication Data

Booth, W. D.
    Upgrading and refurbishing the older fiberglass
sailboat.

    Includes index.
    1. Sailboats—Maintenance and repair.   2. Fiberglass
boats—Maintenance and repair.   I. Title.
VM351.B624   1985   623.8′223′0288   84-46109
ISBN 0-87033-335-6

Manufactured in the United States of America
First edition

CONTENTS

ACKNOWLEDGMENTS

This book would not have been possible without the very willing help of a good many people, whom I would like to acknowledge and thank publicly.

For furnishing information and/or allowing pictures of their sailboats, I'm indebted to the following southern Chesapeake Bay sailors: Don Boozer, Bob Canestrari, Tom Dade, Neal Garrett, Jim Gormsen, Dave Huff, Phil Mayhew, Vernon Vann, and Jim Whitley.

Jim Gormsen is to be singled out for a special vote of thanks. Not only did he provide information as well as his boat, but took the time to read, critique, and offer advice concerning the contents of the manuscript.

I'm most grateful to: Bill Hudgins, P. E., for his explanation on how hot and cold air interact; Suzanne Winters for her assistance on cleaning sails; Myrna Powell for all the typing: and M. L. Barnett for making my snapshots presentable.

My ongoing thanks to the girl who loves to go to weather with the lee rail under, my wife Julie, who spent untold hours editing.

INTRODUCTION

So, you have decided to look into fixing up an older fiberglass sailboat, and you're beginning to wonder just what you have let yourself in for. Don't let the idea overwhelm you. If you're not afraid to get your hands dirty (matter of fact, dirty all over), what you have in mind will be easy to accomplish. There's also fun and pride in turning a sow's ear into a silk purse.

I'm going to assume that you are somewhat handy with your hands. Because if not and if you plan to pay to have the work done, then I strongly recommend you simply purchase a newer boat in better shape for a wiser return on your investment. By the term "handy," I don't mean those skills that are characteristic of people like engine mechanics and sailmakers.

Along with being able to use your hands, I'm sure that wanting to economize is the single largest factor that has made you look into this route to get your boat. It certainly was one of my main reasons for buying and refurbishing an older fiberglass sailboat. Of course, there were several other reasons: I like a boat with nice looking lines, a full keel, wide decks that really can be used to walk, sit, and lie on.

In addition, an older boat will have more fiberglass which gives you a stronger hull—and to me this is just another way of saying "safer." Granted the more fiberglass, the more weight; but to my way of thinking this is good because it gives you a more stable boat.

So money was a factor—but not the only one—and I'm sure you're taking into account all or at least some of these deciding reasons when you're thinking about this type of project.

The information contained in this book is directed at what is generally looked on as an older fiberglass sailboat, to be specific, boats turned out in the 1960s and early 1970s. The key word here is fiberglass. Fiberglass sailboats first came on the market around 1959, and by the middle 1960s fiberglass had become a major boat-building material. It still is, and has stood the test of time very well.

There are many twenty-year-old fiberglass sailboats still sailing, and just as important, still holding their value in the marketplace. There are two basic groups of these boats: the ones designed to the Cruising Club of America (CCA) handicap racing rule, and the group that is made up strictly of cruising designs.

The main difference between the CCA boats and the straight cruising designs, in my opinion, is speed. The CCA boat gave the sailor a yacht with a good turn of speed for the race course, whereas the cruising designs seem to put other priorities over hull speed. The CCA-designed boats went out of production when the racing handicap rule was changed in the early 1970s in favor of even greater speed.

I might add that while the older CCA boats are now out of production, the cruising designs are still going strong today. But, have you priced the cost of a good-looking new thirty-five-foot sailing yacht lately? Stunning and stratospheric are the words that come to mind when I see the numbers. So this takes you back to why you're reading this book.

These older fiberglass boats are very easy to spot in the marinas and boatyards, and not necessarily from a "down-at-the-heels" appearance. No, these boats will have beautiful lines, will not be too broad in the beam, and will have some overhang at the bow and stern. For the most part, if seen hauled out, the keel will be full with the rudder hung on the aft edge. They are boats that look like they were made to be at home in the water, no matter what the water was doing. These boats have a reputation for being seaworthy and safe, and just as important to the sailor, sea kindly.

Your choice of boat and reasons for buying are your own to suit your personal needs. When it comes to refurbishing your boat, it won't make one bit of difference if you're after speed and then comfort, or just want something really comfortable from which to see the world. Therefore, my aims in writing this book are to give you the *confidence* to undertake the project, ideas on what to do and how to carry them out, and, finally, how to avoid the many problems and mistakes which I learned the hard way.

There will be a great deal I'm sure that you won't be interested in doing. I'm also sure at times that my way may not be the best for you, and you will take another approach to solve the problem. But I'd like to think I got the old gray matter going for you to work out the answer to your particular problem. I want to help you get in the right frame of mind and start you thinking about all that goes into a refurbishing project and also pass on what I've learned so that you can sift through and poke around in to see what will work best for you.

When you start working on your projects, you'll quickly discover that you are constantly turning to the marine catalogs. I also suggest you look through the monthly boating magazines. There is a tremendous amount of useful information in these boating publications, so take a glance every month to see if there's anything you can use, be it detailed information on a subject or some piece of equipment. If you're like me, you will find that you have material from suppliers and manufacturers that will slowly grow until you have a sizable reference library on everything from anchors to zincs.

Just one last thought before we get into the nitty-gritty details. When you've finished and people walk by the latest "Boat of the Week Racing Machine" and stand on the dock beside your boat and say, "Now that's the way a sailboat should look," you'll know without a shadow of a doubt that it was well worth all the work.

Upgrading and Refurbishing the
Older Fiberglass Sailboat

One

TYPE OF BOAT, WHERE TO LOCATE, AND PURCHASING

The purpose of this book is refurbishing the older fiberglass sailboat. If you already own such a boat, that's fine because you're now ready to get to work. But, if you don't have an older fiberglass sailboat, the first order of business is to obtain one. In this chapter I will give you ideas and guidelines that should prove helpful when you sally forth into the used-boat marketplace.

At this point you should ask yourself two questions. *What do I want in a boat? What type and make of older fiberglass sailboat do I intend to fix up?*

Your answers to the above questions may be something like: "Oh, I think a boat in the thirty-feet range will do nicely," or "I don't know for sure, I thought I would look around and see what's out there." You must consider the amount of money you plan to spend. As a matter of fact, the money may actually be the main factor in any decision you make. There's nothing wrong with this because one of the reasons you're using this book, I assume, is to end up with a nice boat without having a fortune invested.

When it comes to money, there's really nothing I can offer that can be of assistance. Only you know your own financial situation. On the other hand, when it comes to spending it, I can give you solid help and advice so that you're getting the most possible value for your dollars.

Go back to the answers to the two questions. If your answers were something like those quoted, you're running the chance of not having the right boat to work with. The very worst thing that can happen to you after you have purchased one boat is to come across another boat that is exactly what you wanted.

The way to make sure you get the right boat and know it's the right boat is very simple. Do your homework! There are two main areas that must be addressed under the heading of homework. First, list your personal requirements, and second, list the boats that meet these personal requirements.

Now let's go back to money. You must be honest with yourself. Most of us have to live within a budget. Therefore, your first guideline is to establish how much you can afford to spend, keeping in mind you'll be putting out additional money for refurbishing. Thus the initial cost will not be the final cost.

It's difficult to determine exactly what the refurbishing cost will be at the beginning. However, I feel I should be able to provide some sort of yardstick, so I'll go out on a limb. From my experience the refurbishing cost will run in the neighborhood of ten to twenty percent of the cost of the boat. For example, if you pay twenty thousand dollars for a boat which needs attention, you'll spend between two and four thousand dollars to put it in good shape. This guideline is very general and subject to all kinds of variations, of which engine work or replacement seems to be the major unknown.

Assume you now have a price budget and are ready to list requirements. Start with the question, "What do I want in a boat?" In order to look at this question with all of its ramifications I'll break it down into seven separate divisions and discuss each in turn.

1. Overall length
2. Type of rig
3. Hull design
4. Deck layout
5. Sailing ability and locality
6. Auxiliary power
7. Accommodations below

These may seem a little basic to you. But it's important to recognize you can be undecided between a sloop and a ketch, and the pros and cons need to be investigated. Or you may not have a fixed idea on an aft or center cockpit, and some investigation will have to be done here because your decision will directly affect your other guidelines. Look at the list of general guidelines and the many questions they can generate.

Overall Length

You need to know this first because everything else builds on it. Most people want as much boat as they feel comfortable with and can afford. Start by checking the classified sections of boating publications, newspapers, and yacht brokers. In short order you will have a feel for the price range of the various lengths.

Along with establishing the overall length of the boat within your budget you may want to consider the size for manageability. For example, are you a one-person crew or a husband-wife team?

If crew is no problem, you don't have to worry about this. From my experience the usual cruising crew is a couple with occasional guest. Most of my sailing friends think that thirty-six feet is about tops for a couple to handle, and I agree. This guideline is not iron-bound by any means.

Type of Rig

What will be the best rig for you? Sloop, cutter, ketch, yawl, or schooner? One sure way to end up with a boat which is not much fun to sail is to have one with a rig that becomes an exercise in manual labor every time you go out. Take a look at your options as they relate to the types of rig you are likely to encounter in the older fiberglass sailboat.

Sloop. The sloop is the most widely used rig, offering the simplicity of a mainsail and a foresail hoisted on one mast. A very good choice up to thirty-six feet, but beyond thirty-six feet, the sails can become quite large, making them heavy and cumbersome. The single mast is an advantage in that you only have rigging necessary for the one spar which gives you a less cluttered deck when compared to boats with two masts.

Cutter. The cutter is very similar to the sloop except the mast is farther aft. This makes for a smaller mainsail, but allows for two foresails to be used at the same time. This means your total sail area is broken down into smaller, easier-to-handle increments. The cutter rig lends itself very well to reducing sail when the wind starts getting up. This rig can be used on any size boat, but I feel lends itself more to the larger boats, say over thirty-six feet.

Ketch and Yawl. Here you have boats with two masts. The tallest will be the forward one, in this case called the mainmast, with the shorter or mizzen placed aft. This applies both to the ketch and the yawl. What makes the difference between these two types of rigs is location of the mizzen and, to a lesser degree, the relationship of the mast height. The ketch will have a mainmast only a little taller than the mizzen, and the mizzen will be located forward of the steering station. The yawl, on the other hand, will have a mainmast much taller than the mizzen, and the mizzen will be located well aft behind the rudder post. At first glance a yawl can resemble a sloop with a small mast on the stern.

The advantages of two masts are smaller sails for easier handling plus the ability to tailor certain combinations of sails to fit the weather conditions. One disadvantage of two masts is the mizzen rigging will clutter up the cockpit area. The ketch and yawl rigs are used on boats of all sizes; but for the purpose of this book, you'll find these rigs on the larger boats, mostly over forty feet.

Schooner. This particular rig was used very little in the class of sailboats you'll be interested in, but nevertheless, I feel it should be included. The schooner rig can have any number of masts. For most pleasure sailboats there are two masts, the taller mainmast aft and the shorter foremast forward. In other words, the schooner is the reverse of the ketch, keeping in mind the names of the mast are different. The taller mast is always the mainmast with the other taking its name from its location. The pros and cons for the schooner rig are the same as for the ketch.

When working on your planning guidelines, you should give serious consideration to the type of rig you prefer. You'll have to weigh the good and bad points of the various rigs to determine exactly what's the best rig for you. Keep in mind that everything concerning a boat is a compromise. The sloop offers speed and ability to sail close to the wind, but the sails can be hard to handle, and the boat somewhat tender. The cutter may be your choice and you're willing to put up with the hassle of tacking two headsails. The ketch, yawl, or schooner may appeal to you because of the ease of smaller sails. All the extra rigging and not being able to sail close to the wind (as compared with the sloop) may present no problems to you.

While on rigs, I'd like to bring up roller furling. This idea has been added to many older boats so expect to see them as you look at boats. But more importantly, consider working into your guidelines roller furling as an addition to make a particular boat acceptable. For example, you've located a sloop, but feel the sails are much too large to work. Then consider roller furling to make the job easier. More will be said about roller furling later.

Hull Design

You will have to look into this area with a very critical eye. Your questions should be: do I want the more traditional full keel, or the newer fin configuration? How about the displacement? Heavy, moderate, or light? These questions will all have a direct bearing on the boat's overall performance in some manner. Let me say here, though, remember that the large majority of boats built during the 1960s and early 1970s have the more traditional hull with nice overhang fore and aft. My point is you may not have too many choices when it comes down to the bottom line with the older fiberglass sailboat.

Along with this guideline you have to consider depth, and here really take a hard look at where you'll be using the boat. If there's a problem with depth, you have the option of investigating the centerboard boat. You'll find a good selection in this category because the older designs lent themselves nicely to the centerboard. One word of caution—while the centerboard seems to offer you the best of both worlds, it's notorious for creating problems. My personal feeling about this is if you can get the needed depth in a fixed keel boat, do so, and settle for the centerboard only if there's no other way.

Deck Layout

Is the aft cockpit a must, or do I want to consider a center cockpit? How about a boat with a pilothouse? Am I willing to give up some space below to get wide side decks? You will lose space below because the wide side decks limit the width of the cabin top. How about a flush

7

deck boat? Loads of room both on deck and below, but some people do not care for the appearance. And do not overlook the choice between the tiller and the wheel.

Sailing Ability and Locality

These are very important considerations. Will the boat sail? Can she go the weather? I don't mean like an America's Cup twelve-meter boat, but she should be able to get you off a lee shore. How about speed in general? Cruising boats generally give a little in the speed department to gain in other areas, but I don't think you'll want a boat that won't get out of its own way. Think twice before you buy a boat with a reputation of taking forever to get someplace.

Along with these questions you should consider how you plan to use the boat and just as important, where. Am I mainly interested in weekending with a couple of weeks cruising in the summer? Or do I want to cruise all summer and lay it up the rest of the time? How about living on the boat permanently?

If you plan short periods on the boat, you can probably get by with less storage, but allow plenty of room for guests, whereas, longer periods of living on the boat will demand much more storage and may mean you'll have to lose some bunk space. So, how you plan to use the boat has a direct effect on the guidelines.

Next look at where you will use the boat. New England, Chesapeake Bay, or the Great Lakes? Each area will have some special weather that should be considered. A boat designed for the ocean off New England may not be the best boat for the Chesapeake Bay where the summers are hot with light air, and good ventilation is necessary in order to survive.

Auxiliary Power

You don't have much choice here. It's either gas or diesel. Nevertheless, it's important to look at this subject with the guidelines in mind. If, on one hand, you will have nothing but a diesel, that becomes one of your prime requirements when shopping around. It will save you many wasted hours to know at the outset if the boat you're considering has a diesel. There's nothing wrong with a well-cared-for gas engine; if you can accept a gas engine, your number of choices will be much wider. Don't discard completely a boat with a gas engine if everything else is to your liking. Determine the condition of the engine. If the gas engine is old and needs replacing, then consider replacing it with a diesel.

Accommodations Below

It is in this particular area that you may exercise your personality. You probably have definite ideas about what you want. You should address questions like: do I want an aft or side galley? Each kind of galley has its good and bad points; the side galley is great for cooking, but the social seating area is restricted. On the other hand, the aft galley opens up the main cabin for people, but people always seem to be getting in the way of the preparation of food. Some newer boats have a U-shaped galley which really solves both problems. However, very few of the older boats will have this layout.

Do I want a dinette arrangement or a fold down table? Are quarter berths important to me? Can I get by without a holding tank for the head? Or is a holding tank absolutely mandatory in the sailing area? How about headroom? To some this is very important. Then there's the question of storage and even a good wet locker.

I can go on and on with questions on what to consider below, but what you have to decide is what you really have to have. The little added extras are fine if you can get them, but it's extremely important for you to be honest with yourself on this subject.

First work out what is necessary, then add what you would like to have. At the same time you have to crank in all the other guidelines and start weighing the tradeoffs. And believe me, there will be tradeoffs, boats are nothing but floating compromises. For example, you want a low cabin which gives you a beautiful looking yacht, but you lose standing headroom and so which do you want? How about the boat that has everything you want on deck, but has a short waterline that cuts down some on the space below. What's really important to you?

The overall visual appearance of the boat is another aspect reflecting you as an individual. Is the overall appearance important to you? Is it a pretty boat with pleasing lines that delight the eye? To me appearance is one of the most important considerations I make about a boat.

By asking yourself these questions you'll get an idea about what you want and can develop your own guidelines to follow. For example, you really like the idea of a midship cockpit, but don't intend to make a decision until you have thoroughly investigated this type of sailboat. If you are fortunate enough to already know what you want, you can run through the requirements in short order, and decide exactly what your guidelines will be. You may already have several makes of sailboats on your list. If you're at this stage, you have a good start on getting your boat. What you need to do is to compile information in order to answer all your questions. So far your homework has been pen and paper, but now you'll have to add some legwork. You need to take a look at where you go for this sailboat information.

Yacht brokers head the list because of the tremendous amount of boat specifications at their disposal. If at all possible visit them in person. Note I said them. That means more than one, and that's exactly what you should do. If you live in an area where there are no brokers, then you'll have to use the mail or telephone. One word of advice: use the phone if possible. I feel that being able to ask questions during the conversation is well worth the expense. Be honest when talking to the broker. Tell him you're doing your homework before buying an older fiberglass sailboat, and you would appreciate any help whatever. By this time you should have some idea of the overall length of boat you're considering. This will become very important when dealing with the yacht broker, because this length will give him a category to concentrate on.

Don't feel you're imposing on the broker. He makes his money selling boats, and that means he has to have interested prospects to work with. Any good yacht broker will recognize that you're a likely prospect, and will be willing to work with you. As a matter of fact, you may have a boat that must be sold before you can buy the boat in question, and he can perhaps help you with this.

One advantage of using the yacht broker is that brokers are part of national and regional listing organizations, and will have untold numbers of boats to draw from. Best of all, they will be able to give you printed literature giving all kinds of pertinent data with pictures and layouts. Don't worry too much about cost of boats over budget here. You're seeking information at first.

Next, pore over the classified ads in boating magazines, and newspapers that cover large boating areas. Again if you don't live in one of these areas, take a trip to your newsstand on Sunday and you will find plenty to read. Go over the ads and contact the ones that look promising. You may prefer to use the mail here, and if you do, I think it's a very good idea to include a self-addressed stamped envelope with your inquiry. This is not only being courteous, but it seems to give you a speedy reply.

Another source of information will be marinas and boatyards. And just don't talk with people that work there, strike up conversations with boat owners, and let them know what you're doing. Sailors like to talk about boats, particularly theirs, so you'll probably have an opportunity to look at some nice examples.

The last general suggestion for gathering information is to draw from your own personal experience or from the experiences of a friend or acquaintance who you feel is knowledgeable about sailing. Regardless of how you go about gathering information to crank into your requirement list, assume that you now have come up with your guidelines. Say it reads something like this: 30 feet to 33 feet overall, full keel drawing no more than 5 feet, sloop rig, moderate displacement, large aft cockpit, sleeps four or more, aft galley, standing headroom if possible, prefer diesel, but will consider gas engine, sailing mostly in the Chesapeake Bay, traditional looking, and, last but not least, cost to be no more than X.

Having armed yourself with an impressive list of requirements, you can now move on to the second important area of your homework: What boat meets these guidelines and how do you locate the boat you want.

First things first: you should go back over your information to determine what make of boat or boats best fits your requirements. I hope that while you were pulling all this information together, you were also getting a feel for this or that boat, and should have a good start on what make and type of boat fits the bill. Once you've determined what you intend to look for, you need to address yourself to another point, the reputation of the manufacturer at the time the boat was built. Note I mention when the boat was built. You are looking at older fiberglass sailboats, and are, therefore, interested in what went on then, not now. I feel it's very important to be seeking a boat which has a reputation for being reasonably well constructed and durable. Frankly, it makes good business sense to be interested in a boat which will hold its value in the marketplace.

There is a possibility this particular question was answered when you were gathering data; but if not, be sure to check on it! There are, in my opinion, a good number of fiberglass sailboats built in the 1960s and early 1970s which had numerous problems show up as they grew older. One excellent source to check are boatyard owners and employees to see if the particular boat (or boats) you're interested in has a history (or histories) of repairs or troubles.

I use the word "trouble" to cover the whole range of problems, not just the major ones. For example, the joint where the deck and hull are fastened together always leaks when the boat begins to work in a heavy sea. This is a major trouble spot and, as well as being a nuisance, may indicate that the fastening system could be weak. Leaking ports, on the other hand, may seem minor, and, in most cases, they are, but if persistent could indicate the deck and cabin top are experiencing excessive movement. So consider all problems both big and small and try and find out as much as possible about them.

Another good source on this subject is to contact people who've owned a boat like the one you're considering. You may know someone locally who can help; if not, I recommend looking through the boating magazines and publications to see if they include an *"opinion section."* This section is a listing by boats where the publisher will provide contacts with the owner so that you may discuss the pros and cons of a particular boat. This is also a very good source of ideas when it comes to refurbishing. So don't hesitate to use this service.

The last thing you can do to check out the reputation of a boat is to talk to sailors and get a feel for how a certain boat has been accepted by the sailing fraternity; there's nothing like first-hand knowledge.

At last you know what to go shopping for. You want an ABC 32 as your first choice and you'll consider an XYZ 31 for your second choice. By knowing exactly what you're setting out to buy, you'll save a great deal of time, "wheel spinning," and money because in most cases it'll cost you something, if nothing but gas, to check out a boat. In addition, your mental attitude concerning the project you're planning will be positive when you know what you're doing. It's very easy to become negative when you start to flounder about without any results in sight.

Locating the boat of your choice will probably be easy. Chances are from all your information gathering you already know where one is. But if not, you can go back to your yacht broker, give him instructions, and let him go to work for you.

Go back over the boating magazines, publications, and boating-area newspapers. You'll be amazed how quickly you can look through the ads when searching for a particular type of boat. Check places that have boats for sale by owners like marinas, boatyards, yacht clubs, and sailing associations. Don't forget the old-fashioned word of mouth. Put the word out to people that you're looking for a certain kind of boat.

Unless you selected a rare boat, i.e., the case where very few were built, chances are good that you'll locate several boats of your choice. This gives you the added advantage of having the option of buying what you consider to be the best deal. I hasten to point out that by the best deal I don't necessarily mean the cheapest price. If Boat A with a new Atomic Four engine is selling for fifteen hundred dollars more than Boat B with a twelve-year-old engine, Boat A is by far the best deal in the long run in my opinion. Price is important, but don't be penny-wise and pound-foolish.

Now I want to discuss some areas about what to look for and take note of when you're inspecting a particular boat. I know you've heard that first impressions are important. Therefore, I'm cautioning you not to let this influence your first look at a boat. I'll tell a quick story involving my wife and me. A few years back we went to look at a twenty-four-foot flush deck fiberglass sailboat that was for sale at a very reasonable price. The boat looked neglected from the outside, and when we pushed the hatch back to go below, the stale air almost knocked us over. But worse yet everything was covered with mildew. I closed the hatch, and we left, never really taking a good look at what was under the mess. All we were actually seeing and smelling was a cosmetic problem which could have been cleaned up with elbow grease as a friend reminded me the next day. In other words, we let first impressions rule our judgment, and I'll always feel I missed an excellent buy. Why didn't I go back? I did some days later, but the boat had been sold shortly after we looked at it. Some person smarter than I saw through the grime.

Usually when a boat is for sale, for whatever the reason, the owner will have lost interest to a certain degree, and the boat will begin to have that neglected air about it. You will see far more of these than well kept and polished ones. The best advice I can give concerning first impressions is not to have one. Expect to see a shabby, uncared-for boat. Be surprised when you don't. Note Figures 1 through 6. By the way, this neglected appearance can work in your favor when it comes to the selling price. I'll cover this point later on.

For now let's get back to what you're looking at. Remember for the most part the apparent problems which are easily seen are cosmetic. Forget about the mildew on the overhead, the unpleasant-smelling head, and trying not to get your hands dirty. Don't even think about these things at first because there's a much more important subject to be addressed—the structural integrity of the boat.

The main structural areas to check are: bilge, bulkheads, engine mounts, hull-deck joint, chain plates, mast step location, and any rot in wood used for bulkheads and the deck core. Be sure you have a flashlight, and some sort of probe, screwdriver, or knife, and starting in the bilge, look at and under everything. You're looking for signs of fracture, breaking, movement, wear—in short, anything that shows you something has broken loose. Let's look at an example. Many of the full keel boats will have the ballast inside and located in the forward section of the bilge; if there is room often the water tank is placed behind or on top of the ballast. Both ballast and water tank will be held in place with fiberglass or a combination of wood and fiberglass. What you're checking here is the bonding which holds everything in place. I think you can quickly see that if there has been movement, it may have caused some unseen damage which could cause problems later.

Along with checking for any movement, take note of anything structural that looks like it was added or repaired after the boat was built. This may indicate a previous problem which should be investigated further. Give special attention to the keel bolts if the ballast is external.

Bulkhead bonding to the hull is a very important area to check out thoroughly. Make sure you look at the smaller ones as well as the

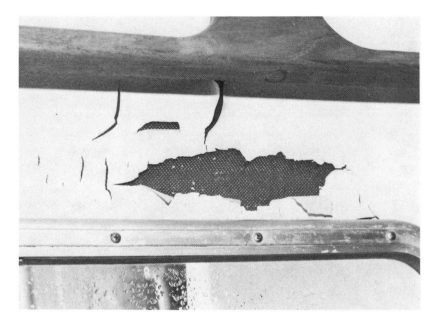

Figure 1. Paint flaking off interior cabin side

Figure 2. Mildew in galley

Figure 3. Topside in need of repairs and painting

Figure 4. Engine panel in very poor shape

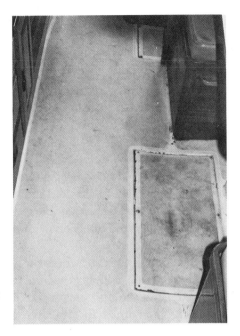

Figure 5. Dirty cabin sole

Figure 6. Old instrument opening in cockpit

larger, more obvious ones. Open lockers and peer into all the inaccessible little holes. Be ready to do some work because these lockers will have years worth of accumulated items stored which you'll have to take out and then replace.

When you check bulkhead bonding, I suggest you use more than your eyes. With your knife or even a screwdriver, make sure the bond is in fact adhering to the hull. See Figure 7. Often what looks okay is actually only lying in place with the bond broken. While here check on rot in any wood present.

Using your probe go over the engine mounts. Make sure the engine mounts are indeed bonded to the hull. After checking this, start the engine, rev it up, and again go over the mounts. Any problems not seen earlier will most likely show up when the engine puts movement on the mounts.

The next area you inspect is the joint where the hull is fastened to the deck. Mechanical fasteners will be used in many boats. The design of the contact edges of the hull and deck will depend on the builder and/or designer. This joint will also have fiberglass added, bonding the hull and deck together, hiding the fasteners and making a continuous watertight seal around the entire boat. Sounds foolproof, doesn't it? Well, I'm afraid it's not. This main joint is notorious for leaking when the boat is being sailed hard. I know of cases when leaks would occur at the dock during a heavy rain.

No matter how good the design of putting the hull and deck together is, the problems are introduced when people perform the work. It could be something as simple as a nut not being tight or screw threads stripped, and the screw left in place. But generally sloppy fiberglass workmanship is the real culprit. The fiberglass bond is supposed to make the hull and deck as one solid unit. The fasteners are to hold the two sections together while glass work is being done, and then become added structural insurance after the bonding together of the hull and deck.

Sometimes not enough layers of glass are added, or the layers are not quite in the correct position or maybe not enough resin is applied. In my opinion, there are two reasons for this: tight awkward spaces to work in, and most of the joint is unseen. Therefore, the workman has a tendency to get sloppy. When inspecting this area, expect to see some untidy glass work. What you're really looking for are broken

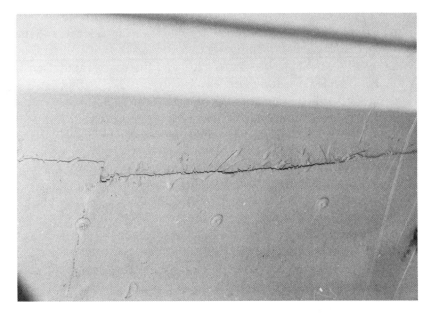

Figure 7. Broken fiberglass bulkhead bond

bonds and obvious leaks so you'll have to take your time and give these areas a good going-over.

The last structural problem to look for pertains to chain plates and mast step location. Check the chain plates to note any movement. See if the nuts are tight on the holding bolts. Check the chain plates fastened to fiberglass supports coming out of the hull. These are all-important bonding areas, and any movement at all needs to be noted.

Next the mast step. Chances are the mast will be stepped on deck. Therefore, it's vitally important to determine how the mast loads are supported, and then to check everything. What you'll look for here mainly is the deforming of the cabin top or supports under the cabin whether they are bulkheads or some types of vertical support. At the same time, go on deck and have a good look from that vantage point also.

The object of doing this inspection is to determine: first, if the boat is sound structurally in an overall sense; second, where problems exist, if at all; and third, what corrections will be necessary. If problems are found in any of the structural areas you've been advised to investigate it's not all that much trouble to repair them. That's the really beautiful part of working with a fiberglass boat; it's repairable. But if really serious problems do exist and the boat's reputation is dubious, consider passing it up. On the other hand, if the boat has held up well and has a good reputation with sailors, don't let a structural problem scare you off if everything else is to your liking. If you're not comfortable with doing the repair yourself consider having it done by people that know what they're doing. But keep in mind the price you pay should reflect the cost of this work in some fashion. While on this subject, here's some advice: It's easy to let the seller make the repairs, and chances are they will be fast and cheap, meaning you may not get a first-rate job done. So, to get a better job done, contract for the repair work after buying the boat. Of course, the price will reflect this.

The next area to investigate is the general condition of the boat below deck. Keep in mind that your goal is refurbishing, so don't start by picking everything to pieces. You're not looking at a shiny new model, but at a boat that's at least ten years old, no doubt, and shows it.

Let's get to work. Check for leaks everywhere: ports, hatches, and under every place you can reach. Next check for any rot where water may have accumulated near or next to any wood. Look at all thru-hull valves, and here you'll probably find some unsightly places because they all seem to weep on the older boats. What you want to do here is make sure they are safe. Don't worry about how they look.

The head comes next, and the thought may go through your mind, "no way that junk is staying on the boat." But take a good look. Can the head area be used after a thorough cleaning, and some paint? Or is everything (shelves, lockers, and water closet) in need of replacement?

How about the galley? Can the sink be kept? Possibly the counter top alone is enough to turn you off. Be sure to check the sink thru-hull drain.

Look at the bunk cushions carefully and think about where you and fellow voyagers will sleep. Check out exactly what is available for storage: drawers, lockers, hanging locker, shelves, under bunks, forepeak, and the one thing most of the older boats will have, the lazaret.

A very important consideration is the auxiliary engine. Ask these questions: will it run? If so, how well? Age? Any major repair work? Overhaul? If yes, try and get the name of the mechanic or yard that performed the work. What is the general appearance and condition? Is it all rusted, or painted and clean? Are wires, belts, and hoses in good shape? How about connections where wires are attached by a nut, clean or dirty? If engine will not crank, why not?

This is the one area where you may feel more comfortable with a marine engine mechanic doing the checking for you. But only go to this expense after you have decided to think seriously about buying the boat. One of the best suggestions I can make is to talk to the firm or man who has maintained the engine if at all possible. Don't hesitate to ask the owner for his records, and hope he has some because this will usually indicate an owner who has taken care of his equipment. However you choose to determine the condition of the engine, try to come up with some idea of what will have to be done to put it in acceptable shape for your intended use. I realize everything I've said about the engine has been negative so far. But, let me add that you might be lucky and come across a boat that has had a bright, shiny new power plant added.

Next inspect the electrical system: lights, instruments, any type of equipment, switch panel, and any wires you can get to. Don't expect to see new material. Remember you're thinking about buying an older boat to refurbish. Turn on everything to check exactly what does work and what does not. If there is a VHF radio, call for a radio check if possible. Take a good look at wire connections to see if there is corrosion. Check storage location and general condition of the battery, and if there is only one battery, give some consideration as to how you will go about adding a second battery.

At this point the below deck's situation should be apparent. I hope you have recorded all the pertinent information you'll need to help you make a decision, so let's now go on deck.

Your first interest is safety. Take note of everything on deck that is subject to a strain: turnbuckles, pulpits, lifelines, halyards, cleats, blocks, winches, and don't forget the tiller or wheel. First inspect to determine if anything is obviously wrong; then grab hold and give it a few good jerks. Don't be afraid you'll break something. Better now than later, and I'm speaking from personal experience. When I was checking out my present boat, I gave the tiller only a cursory examination. The only time I touched it was to lift it up so I could get to the seat lockers. Two weeks later I was moving the boat, and twenty minutes after leaving the dock, while still in heavy boat traffic, I might add, the tiller broke. I don't mean it merely cracked and could be quickly fixed with tape. I mean it broke where the tiller came out of the fitting attached to the rudder post like snapping a carrot in two.

If the boat has a wheel, be sure to inspect what is under the deck for any wear, not just what you see in the cockpit. Take note of the condition of any instruments in the cockpit as well as the compass.

Grab all the stays supporting the mast and give a good pull. Remember, you're looking for problems, broken strands in wire, bent turnbuckles, fittings showing signs of wear, etc. If the mast has wooden spreaders, use a pair of binoculars to check visually, taking special care to look at the area that is attached to the mast. Note if all screws are there and the condition of the wood as best you can. While doing this, inspect the entire mast with the glasses. Of course, the best way is to go up the mast, but you may be by yourself or don't feel like trusting the halyards at this time. On an older boat the boom may be wood so take the time to look it over for rot or loose fittings. This goes for handrails, cockpit coamings, and any other areas with wood.

While you're on the deck area, I want to caution you to pay attention to how the deck feels under your feet. A spongy or soft feeling may denote deterioration of the wood core used in the deck. Not all boats used this method, but for the ones that did, it pays to check. One or two small areas can be repaired, but if a larger area, say three or four square feet, then I suggest you pass this particular boat up.

You'll probably find it helpful to make notes as you work along the deck. Make sure you record not only safety problems and deterioration but also places that will need cosmetic work. Safety is the real purpose of your inspection of the deck; this should remain foremost from the very start. Safety problems always need to be corrected before all else.

The sails are the last area to get your attention. Now you can drag all those bags out of the lockers and have a look. But first a reminder; chances are they will look more like paint drop cloths than what you're expecting. They are going to be old, dirty, and blown out.

Any sails that are new or close to new are a real bonus, so be pleasantly surprised if you have some.

The main consideration about sails is you either use what's on the boat or replace them. There is really no way to refurbish a sail in the same sense as redoing, say, the galley area. One thing you should do is take note of any sails you plan to replace so that you can take into account the cost when you pull together your figures.

While in the deck lockers check all that loose gear: anchors, dock lines, sheets, life jackets. These storage areas tend to be like the back hall closet at home, full of any and everything.

As I'm sure you have already recognized, this inspection section is a checklist to be used in the systematic inspection of a prospective boat. These suggestions are very general in nature. The nitty-gritty details are covered in the rest of this book. Therefore, I strongly recommend you complete this book before using the inspection guidelines. Also, I would suggest you have a camera along on your inspection tour and use it. The pictures will prove very helpful.

This initial investigation of a boat's potential is where the refurbishing process starts. The next step is to analyze exactly what you have.

If possible when you analyze your notes for the first time stay on or close to the boat because it's very beneficial to be able to take a second and even a third look. What you want to do is get a feel exactly for the work to be done. You're only concerned that the galley needs all kinds of improvements, you're not going to get involved with the details; so starting with what has to be done, list all safety problems, then hull and structural integrity. You're looking at things like a badly bent backstay turnbuckle, a gate valve thru-hull that has a broken turn handle, and you're not sure if the valve is open, closed, or somewhere in between.

Next list the areas which must be addressed in order for you to use the boat. For example, engine repairs, condition of sails (maybe a new main is a must), the water closet in the head will have to have new gaskets and flapper valves, and, of course, a thorough cleaning. At this point, the boat can now be used. She may look a little down at the heels, but you're sailing.

The last section in your appraisal is the cosmetic work. Here you list all the general areas which will bring the boat literally back to life. Things like a new paint job for the hull, varnish for all the wood trim below, teak grate for the cockpit, a new counter top for the galley and table; this list can go on and on. There's always something else to add or do to a boat.

After sizing up your list, look at it from the standpoint of time and, as much as possible, money also. Now you need to seriously consider the question: Do I want this boat? You may not prefer to answer at this point because you plan to look at one or more boats, or you could have inspected enough to be able to make a decision.

So far you, or you and a knowledgeable friend, have done all the inspecting and you may have complete confidence in your, or his, ability when it comes to knowing what you're looking at. If you are hesitant about spending thousands on an older boat without an expert opinion, I strongly recommend you engage a marine surveyor. The boat will have to be hauled if in the water; even if you don't use the marine surveyor, still haul and inspect the under body, before you buy. However, you may have no choice about using a surveyor. A survey may be necesary to obtain both insurance and a loan on the boat. It can also help when negotiating by having an expert opinion concerning a particular problem. The surveyor will be able to give you a detailed written report on the seaworthiness and the condition of the systems on the boat. He won't be able to help from the viewpoint of refurbishing. That's not what marine surveying is about, but it's exactly what this book is about.

The only thing left to do is sail the boat. Sometimes this will present a problem in the winter because of ice and boatyard storage. If for whatever reason you aren't able to sail the boat, try to sail on one like it. Of course, you may already be familiar with the boat's sailing properties. At any rate, know how the boat sails before you buy.

What you've done so far is determine what boat meets your requirements, and located and inspected the boat in question. But nothing is going to happen until you put out your hard-earned money and buy it.

This leads to our next subject which could be the most important section in this book—in a word, money. Human nature being what it is, you want to pay as little as possible for whatever you buy. This is especially true when looking at the large numbers generated by big-ticket items like houses, cars, and boats. I'd like to remind you of an obvious truism—you get what you pay for and that cheap is not synonymous with a good deal.

You won't find many cheap boats that have any real potential, and I want you to be wary when you think you have one. For the most part you'll wonder how an owner could possibly expect someone to pay such a high price for an older boat. A "good deal" lies somewhere between those concepts. It takes two to make a sales agreement, so the place to begin the subject of money is with the owner. In most cases you and the owner will have already met if the boat for sale is offered by the owner directly. You will have been able to form an opinion of him while he showed you the boat, pointing out all the many reasons the asking price is reasonable. I think it's a good idea when you work on your inspection notes to include your impression of the owner. For example, did he seem a nice enough guy? Did he try to make you feel at ease? Did he point out some of the problems the boat may have? Or did he seem a little irritated when you mentioned a problem or went back to a problem that you really wanted to explore? Was he businesslike or blasé about arranging to show the boat? What does he do for a living? This question is vital, I feel, because it allows you to read between the lines. Take notice also of his appearance and what he drives. And last and always, find out why the boat is for sale. The answers to these questions should provide you with enough information to form a fair opinion of the type of owner you're dealing with.

The man who tries to put you at ease, is not afraid of problems, and seems interested in providing you with any information he can will probably be open-minded and fair during the give-and-take of negotiating. Now I don't mean to imply this type is a pushover; the owner can still be a nice guy and a good businessman at the same time. On the other hand, if the owner implies he is doing you a big favor in taking his time to show you his boat or thinks you're attacking him personally when you question him about the engine, he will more than likely be difficult to negotiate with.

The very worst owner to deal with is that fortunate fellow who doesn't need the money from selling the boat to buy another boat. If he doesn't need the money, he can afford to put a price on the boat in question and wait. Chances are he won't come out and tell you this. But seeing the expensive car in the parking lot and the fact that he has this particular boat for sale because he's bought that new fifty footer tied up at the next dock makes it very clear. So pay attention to details, and ask, if the information is not volunteered, why the boat is for sale!

There is a special category of owner I would like to mention. He's the owner of a boat you're interested in, but his boat is not advertised as being on the market. Let me give you an example. Say, while doing your homework and inspecting boats you notice one which is what you want, but it isn't for sale. From what you can see it offers potential. Don't let the fact that it has no "for sale" sign on it stop you. Make inquiries, find out the owner's name, and contact him. Use the phone or drop by the marina and try to catch the owner. Since you'll be coming on to this owner "cold turkey," tell him who you are, that you are interested in buying a boat like his, and ask if, by any chance, he would consider selling. If his answer is no, ask him if he knows of anyone who might have a boat like his for sale. Sometimes, this question can lead you to a boat that no one is aware is for sale.

Some people may feel uncomfortable about doing this. Don't be; there's nothing wrong with a pleasant, courteous contact by phone or in person. I would point out, though, if you visit the boat in hopes of catching the owner, make sure you talk to him in private.

The very worst that can happen is you will be told no. On the other hand, you can be very pleasantly surprised. I was, as this illustration will show. After doing my homework I decided a Pearson Vanguard was the boat I wanted, but I was having some difficulty locating one for sale reasonably close to home. Over lunch with several sailing friends the talk got around to my boat hunting, and led to a local Vanguard owner's name being mentioned. All my friends agreed that there was no way this boat could be bought even though it hadn't been sailed very much over the past few years and was in need of work. During that afternoon my thoughts kept coming back to the question: How do I know it's *not* for sale? That night I phoned the owner and asked if he would entertain the idea of selling. After what seemed to me the longest pause on record, he answered yes. Later he told me that two days before I had called him, he had tentatively decided to sell, but was dreading the hassle of fixing some problems and showing the boat. My phone call solved his problem. The end result was a good deal for both of us. This long shot paid off for me in a big way. Therefore, don't hesitate even if you get a negative answer. Keep trying. All the right conditions may soon be present and a deal can be made.

If you're really uncomfortable in the cut-and-thrust type of business dealings, perhaps the main advantage the yacht broker can offer is the "arm's length" transaction where you never actually meet the seller. The broker also is a valuable source of information you can use to try and obtain the best deal possible. This area will be covered again shortly. The main thought to have and understand when working with a yacht broker is his main loyalty will always be with the person who signs his check. While the broker's loyalty is to the owner, there is another agent's rule of thumb which works in favor of the buyer, "Some commission is better than no commission." Therefore the broker may consider your offer low, but he'll still be interested in presenting it to the owner.

All these details and little bits of information about the owner are leading to one place—the negotiating of a sales agreement between you the buyer and the seller of the boat.

When it comes to spending your hard earned money for a sailboat or anything else for that matter, you can never have too much information. Glean everything possible from every bit of data. Don't overlook any scrap that may seem insignificant.

A few pages back I made a point of always asking the owner why he is selling the boat. Let's see how the answers to this question help. Things like: "I want to move up and I have to sell this boat first," or "I'm being transferred and I won't be able to take the boat." How about, "I bought a new so-and-so at the boat show and I need to sell this one," the latter statement not only points out to you that the owner wants to sell but, more importantly, *has* to sell.

On the other hand answers like: "Oh, I'm getting out of boats, just don't have the time," or "I plan to get a larger boat in the near future, and I thought I'll sell this one now and take my time shopping around," tell you the owner would like to sell, but is not "under the gun."

Knowing what the owner does for a living can provide you with second-hand information that might prove useful. Suppose the owner is a residential house builder and you know the home construction market has been in shambles for the past year. The owner says he wants a larger boat, but maybe his prime aim is to get out from under

27

the one he has. This owner not only wants to sell or has to sell; it's absolutely imperative he do so.

Also if the seller is in what is recognized as a high-income position, he can wait to sell at his terms. In other words, there is no money pressure the owner has to worry about.

So far only the owner has been discussed, but it takes two to sell a boat. Let's take the buyer into consideration. What you, the buyer, must guard against is inadvertently giving the seller or yacht broker information which gives an advantage to the seller. I have a personal experience I feel will show you exactly what I mean. Some years back I owned a Cal 25. One winter to keep busy during the off hours I installed drawers, lockers, and storage units in every spare place I could find. Two years later I wanted to move up to a larger boat so I put a fair price on the Cal 25, and put her on the block.

I had already located the new boat I wanted. The only problem was money, and time. I felt I needed to buy the other boat quickly or I would miss out. Hence the price I established was reasonable, but I would take less for a quick sale. And frankly once the word was out I had my eye on another boat and was anxious to sell, I knew I would be offered less than the asking price for my Cal 25.

Several days after I advertised it, I showed my Cal 25 to a couple from out of town. As they stepped below, the wife said, "Honey, this is exactly what we're looking for; look at all the drawers and storage bins." He agreed with her. The bottom line is I did not budge off the price and the couple decided to buy. The reason I held the price firm was based solely on what was said as they stepped below. I was handed an advantage that worked in my favor.

When you and the owner are looking over the boat in question, remain pleasant but noncommital; don't ooh and ah over the things you like. The rule here is to smile, be pleasant, ask questions, take your notes, and give away nothing. If you have a friend or your wife along, keep your discussions concerning a particular subject to a minimum. After the guided tour ask the person showing the boat for a little time to inspect further in private. This is when you talk over the pros and cons.

The next step is to put to use all the information you've gained. You like the boat; it has excellent refurbishing potential. So it's time to discuss money with the seller. You know at this point the asking price. Your primary goal is to purchase this boat for as little as possible.

Let's assume you have determined the owner has to sell. Therefore he will most likely consider an offer less than the asking price. Your next step is to come up with the numbers for the offer. You may ask, "How do I do this?" No problem. One way is to take the asking price, and subtract what you think will be spent on refurbishing. Another method would be to take the obvious problems that detract from the boat's value, cost them, and subtract from the asking price. This is especially true if the problems will have to be put in working order so the boat can be used. For example, the engine will have to be overhauled, or say the mast will have to be dropped for a new backstay.

Another very good way to arrive at the offer figure is to get the opinion of someone you feel is knowledgeable in this area. At the same time you may be able to rely on your own experience and knowledge, but it will help to have a second opinion. Whenever possible compare prices with like boats, taking into consideration the condition.

This apples-to-apples comparison of like boats is an excellent method to use. The advantage is that it gives you the ability to adjust the asking price in relation to the general market price for a particular boat. For example, the boat in question has a price of twenty-eight thousand dollars. You have determined the general going price for this boat is twenty-five thousand dollars so you use this as your base asking price from which you subtract items requiring initial cost to work up the offer.

This market comparison can also work the other way and let you know that the asking price is under the general market level. One word of caution. Find out why the boat is selling below market. Is there a hidden problem that will cost you a bundle?

Now don't come out and ask the owner. He may not be aware that you consider him below the market and asking could alert him to raise the price. No, find out the answer to this question on your own. Right here is where the money spent on a marine surveyor is well worth the expense.

Once your offering price is determined and you feel like bargaining don't be afraid to take off a few thousand more and see how it is received. Remember you can always go up in price but never down, so start low and go up as necessary.

Let's consider the owner who doesn't have to sell. He can afford to wait until he gets his price without being in a bind. From experience, I've learned this seller will be hard to dicker with. One thing to be aware of when dealing with this type of owner is to note that when you make an offer under the asking price, the time element tends to drag out. The seller has your offer, but has the time to wait and see what else comes along. If your offer is not rejected out of hand, stay in touch with the seller as time passes, i.e., if you want the boat.

When you submit an offer lower than the asking price, it's very important to justify as much as you can how you came up with the numbers. Don't give the figures to the owner and say, "That's my best offer; it's all this boat's worth." You run the chance of making the fellow mad and him saying, "Well, the price is X and that's what you'll pay if you want the boat." Under these conditions I don't think there'll be much room for negotiating. Remember I mentioned that shabby appearance can work in your favor. Well here is where you use it. What you say is something like this, "I'd like to offer X for the boat and I want to explain exactly how I arrived at that figure, Mr. Owner." Then justify the offer; you'll have to do a lot of work to overcome the rundown looks, the sails need some work, and there is a cracked place on the toerail, and so on and on. These areas will cost X and subtracting them from the asking price gives the offer price. I'm the first to admit some of this justifying may be a little gray in places and the owner may not buy all that you're saying, but at least the door stays open for the two of you to negotiate a price satisfactory to both. Of course, if the asking price is within your range and you feel it's a good deal for you, then go ahead and pay the asking price.

To sum up quickly the subject of negotiating, keep in mind this list of general guidelines.

1. Know as much as possible about the seller.
2. Don't inadvertently give an advantage to the seller.
3. Check comparative prices on like boats if possible.
4. Start the offer low and work up.

Well, you have bought a boat. The only thing left to do is take ownership, so let's look at suggestions on how to go about this. No matter how much of a nice guy and honest he is, you should still conduct the changing of ownership in a businesslike fashion and that means putting it down on paper. What you're protecting yourself from is that one chance in a thousand when the owner is not what he seems or he drops out of the picture for whatever reason, and you end up dealing with another member of the family. When your offer is accepted, a deposit or binder is usually paid with the remainder changing hands later. There always seems to be something that has to be checked before the final transaction takes place, and once in a while the deal will fall through based on what was found in the inspection. This usually happens when the boat is hauled to check below the waterline. So make sure your deposit is *refundable*—and have this in writing.

If you're dealing with a yacht broker, you'll give the check to him. Make sure that the broker puts it in an escrow account so that it goes to the owner only when the sale is final.

The long-distance transaction with a private owner can pose problems. Both you and the seller are dealing with a stranger, and large sums of money are involved. Let's take an example. The boat is only an hour's drive away, but the owner lives five hundred miles away. So far everything after the marina manager showed you the boat has been done on the phone. Now it's time for papers and money to change hands, and you're a little apprehensive. One way is to have a lawyer handle the paper work. Another place to look for an acceptable go-between is your bank, especially if you are taking out a loan to buy the boat. Finally, you might meet the seller at some convenient halfway point. One piece of advice: meet some place which has a notary so papers can be witnessed. If possible, use a bank, preferably one you or the seller is familiar with. Money and the papers can then be handled in a businesslike fashion.

Before the transaction is final, make certain there are no outstanding bills to be paid. For example, if the engine overhaul has not been paid and the boat changes hands, the boatyard will come after the boat because they can get their hands on it, and you most likely will be left holding the bag. Also if there is a loan on the boat, this matter will have to be taken into consideration. Again you're back with the lawyer and the bank. And last but by no means least, take out proper insurance to go into effect the minute the boat is yours.

Once the sale is final you'll have to take care of the red tape. If the boat is documented, the Coast Guard will have to be contacted in order for the ownership to be changed. Even if the boat has a state registration, you'll have to contact the proper agency for an ownership change form.

At this point you may be in for an unpleasant surprise if you're not familiar with boat laws of your state. Some states may have a boat titling fee or tax which can amount to a sizeable sum. My state, Virginia, has just adopted this plan, so I can only speak for one state. It may be called by a different name, but the bottom line is you'll have to pay to bring in or keep your new boat in some states. I suggest you check this out with your state government, and have the information sent to you so there can be no misunderstanding over who said what on the phone.

Along with the federal and state authorities, don't forget to contact your local government. It sure will help if you know what to expect by way of taxes.

I sincerely hope all this talk about taxes has not depressed you. If so, cheer up; I have some good news. This book is about fixing up the older fiberglass sailboat, say, boats ten years old or more. The key word here is *older*. It has been my experience that the older boats are not taxed anywhere near as much as the more recent models. Seems the tax people use a blue book for boats just like it is done to determine the value of a car. With new boats added each year, the older boats are being dropped. With no benchmark as a reference point, it's sometimes difficult to place a true value on the older boat. The end result is that the taxes on the older boats are not too bad. I can speak for only one locality, but in general I feel this will be true. You might find it interesting to know there are some owners of older fiberglass sailboats who bought them primarily because of the low tax value placed on the boat. In some areas of the country I can easily see why this is an important consideration and it just may be of prime importance to you.

Well, now you have an older fiberglass sailboat to refurbish, so get organized; and this leads us to the next chapter.

Two

PLANNING AND ORGANIZING THE PROJECT

It's critical to know or at least to have some idea exactly what it is you want to accomplish when you start the refurbishing. Part of this planning also includes where you'll do the work, when you may need to get expert help, and where and how to locate the needed supplies. Let's now look at these areas in detail.

Outlining the Work

It's perfectly natural to want to do a project first which shows dramatic visual results. No matter how hard the temptation is to do this, follow your outline. For example, most of the older sailboats will have some sort of wood in the cabin sole, teak being the most popular, that shows its age, and since it's the first thing you usually see when going below, you tell yourself this is the number one job, and proceed to bring it back to life. But, then you may spend the rest of the refurbishing project trying to protect your beautiful sole from damage as you proceed with all your other projects.

This outline won't be rigid, as you will discover. It will have to be flexible because projects will be added, as you proceed, dropped, or postponed for a variety of reasons. For our purpose, the refurbishing process can be broken down into two main areas: *structural* and *cosmetic*. Everything done will fall into one or the other of these two headings.

Let's take the structural area first. This category will include any type of work which must be done to repair damaged or broken items and areas that pertain to safety or hull integrity. Examples are thru-hull fittings, bulkhead to hull bonding, questionable fuel lines, corroded battery cables, or replacing a backstay. Most of the structural work will be the kind that's not readily noticeable. You'll work all weekend and then cover up the job and only you will know what's back of the cover.

I look on the structural section as the area where the real dirty work takes place. It's not fun to do; but, it's something that has to be done, and the sooner it's done, the better. Because of this it's easy to put off these projects or even not do them, but keep in mind it's very important to have the messy dirty work completed before you start the cosmetic projects.

I'm sure you know by now what the cosmetic section will include. It will be all the projects that have to do with looks, comfort, and convenience. Some examples are boat cushions, painting the hull, adding locker space, new stove for the galley, racks to hold glasses, etc. These projects are fun to work on because in almost every case you can see the results of your labor.

Now here is the good news about the structural category. It will be nowhere near as much work as the cosmetic section. From my experience the structural work will represent only ten to twenty percent of the total whereas cosmetic projects will make up eighty to ninety percent of the whole project. I'm sure you're wondering just how I can come up with an estimate of the percentage between structural and cosmetic work. Well, let me explain it's a loose estimate. But the method I use is based on the time I think a certain job will require. When the outline is completed, I assign a time frame for each project. It takes a little experience to come somewhere within the ball park, but after you have done a few of the jobs, you'll have a much better feel for this kind of estimating. One thing you need to do is to keep a log of your time. And, the important fact is you'll spend the majority of your time on the cosmetic jobs.

For now let's consider one general work outline. The first step is to list every project that must be done and then to list every project you would like to do. Don't worry about trying to sort out the list under special topics at this point. It's important to get the list down on paper, and have it as complete as possible. When I say complete, I mean giving the projects some thought, and add anything, no matter how insignificant you may feel it is. When the general list is complete, the second step is to break it down into structural and cosmetic, beginning with structural. Don't worry about any organizing of your projects until the sublists are complete.

One word of advice concerning the structural list. Be honest and objective. Don't even think about cutting any corners with safety or hull integrity. If in doubt about any item, put it on the list, and then follow through.

Here's a personal experience which serves as a perfect example of why I emphasize this so strongly. Several years back when I was refurbishing my 1965 Pearson Vanguard, I planned to replace the thru-hull valves for the head, but the small sea cock for the engine cooling water didn't look in bad shape. By that I mean it was not weeping water, and the handle moved easily. So I hauled the boat and went to work on all the jobs that required the boat to be out of the water. Just before the boat was ready to go back in the water, I had to make one last trip to the marine supply firm. While there and for future reference, I priced the small sea cock for the engine cooling which was twenty-seven dollars. All the way back to the boatyard, about thirty miles, I had the feeling I was doing something wrong. The more I thought about it, the more I was convinced I was making a grave mistake. For the sake of twenty-seven dollars and a little work I was leaving a questionable thru-hull in the boat. And that was not only stupid but dangerous, so I turned around and returned to purchase the valve.

The first thing I did back at the boatyard was get to work replacing the sea cock so I could get it off my mind. The holding nut came off with no trouble, but the bedding compound still held the sea cock. I took hold of it with the idea of wiggling the valve around to break it away from the hull, and *snap!* With very little pressure the sea cock broke cleanly in two at the hull. It doesn't take much imagination to come up with horror stories about what might have happened. I keep this sea cock hanging behind my garage workbench as a constant reminder of what not to do.

Back to the job at hand. After doing the structural list, get busy on the cosmetic part, again not worrying about organizing anything. You now have two lists of projects you intend to pursue. Each of these lists should be treated differently as to the *scope of work* and *organization of the work.*

The scope of work principle which deals with just how much you may want to put into a particular project on your list will not have very much bearing as it pertains to the structural list. For most of the items here in the interest of safety or hull integrity provide no halfway point. Recognizing this, you concentrate on organizing the work. The prime rule is to keep in mind that you should do everything when given special conditions or when having access to a particular place on your boat. For example, when the boat is hauled, know exactly what you're going to work on and, at the same time, recognize you most likely will uncover one or more added jobs that also should be done while the boat is out of the water.

Also let me stress that while the boat is out of the water, you probably will want to organize structural and cosmetic work to be done in parallel. For example, you'll want to have the hull painted while you're taking care of the structural items. Another place where both lists will be on common ground is when the mast is dropped. This is a good time to paint the mast or perform some other cosmetic job.

Try to arrange any dirty or large project, for example, rebuilding the engine, at the top of your work list. At the same time, look ahead and plan to do everything you can that's made simple by the engine being out of the boat. It may be something as easy as adding a support for that extra drawer, which once the engine is back in place may be impossible to get to.

I've found that most of the structural work will be done when the boat is out of the water. Even though yard space and time cost money, try and do all you can while the boat is up. I'm sure you see by now that organizing the structural work is really not very complicated at all. The basic rules are:

1. Know exactly what is to be replaced and what is to be inspected, keeping in mind questionable areas most likely to require some work.
2. Plan on doing the large projects first, as well as doing work in parallel when possible. The best example of this organization is with engine work. Let's say you plan to have the boatyard rebuild the engine. So you have this started as soon as the boat is hauled and you go on to other jobs while the yard does its work. Furthermore, I've found it's a psychological lift to have the large job completed first, especially when you're doing all the work yourself.

3. Take advantage of accessibility when something is removed. When you can get into a space easily that's almost impossible to reach otherwise, it just makes good sense to do so. For example, if the fuel tank is removed to repair a leak, put on your work clothes and get into the area to inspect everything possible. More importantly, add to your list anything that should be done.

4. Plan to do all you can while in the water, recognizing, of course, in certain sections of the country boats are not kept in the water all year round. Anyway there will be jobs that do not require hauling, for example, repairing a section of rubrail or replacing a bent turnbuckle.

5. Consider the cosmetic work that you'll have to have done while the boat is hauled, and at the same time schedule the work so this will be performed after the structural work which could cause problems. The best example is painting the topsides. Wait until all the work is completed, including the bottom paint, before you do this.

Next is the cosmetic list. Here there are different rules because with structural work you do what you *have* to do, with cosmetic projects you do what you *want* to do. I'm sure you'll agree there's a great difference.

The first area to consider is *scope of work*. At this point it will be useful to consider breaking down the cosmetic list into two separate lists. What we are doing here is taking a hard sensible look at the proposed projects, and putting them in order as they pertain to your time and money situation.

Label these two sublists *present* and *future*. Take all the projects from the main cosmetic list and place them under the appropriate heading, giving each project serious thought. Keep in mind these lists are very flexible. You will probably find yourself switching a number of projects as you move along with the actual work.

Organizing these two lists is next, and here the cosmetic projects will differ from the structural jobs. Structural projects seem, for the most part, to be located all over the boat. Each area is a separate job that does not have a domino effect on another project. In other words, replacing a lifeline stanchion has nothing to do with preparing a fiberglass bulkhead bond. On the other hand, the domino effect is very much a part of the cosmetic work. You're going to have to analyze every proposed project from the viewpoint of how it fits in with other potential projects. I have a good example of what happens when you dash in without considering the domino effect. While working on my boat, I removed all the storage racks from the galley countertop area, and proceeded to refinish them. The wood was teak and the result was beautiful. I could hardly wait to get them back in the boat. Keep in mind these racks were not a small box to hold dishes but a large affair capable of holding all manner of galley stuff. It was quite a job to put everything, including the trim, back in place after I had refinished the racks. The following weekend a friend stopped by to see how I was getting along. (By the way, expect to have people visiting you while you are working since such projects are like a natural magnet to other sailors.) He took one look, complimented me on the job, and then asked how I intended to remove the old stained formica countertop since the racks were sitting on the counter. The bottom line was that I lost several hours taking the racks out again; and when you consider the time spent installing them in the first place, I lost almost an entire day, not to mention feeling a little dumb.

The rules I recommend to organize the *present* list are as follows:

1. Consider work that should be done when the boat is hauled. The best example of this again is painting the hull or maybe it's only adding your new name to the transom.
2. Unload the boat of everything. Nothing is as difficult as trying to work around piles of gear.
3. Clean the boat from stem to stern. I haven't said anything about cleaning the boat until now because there's really no need to give it a thorough going over until the dirty part of the structural work is done. Of course, you'll have to do some cleaning. It may even expose some unknown problem, but there's no need to spend the time doing a first-class job when you intend to haul the boat and make a general mess all over it.

What you will have at this point is a spick-and-span boat that's as empty as a drum. At this point all the blemishes stand out like sore thumbs, and you'll probably wonder just what it is you've gotten yourself into. Don't worry; this is as bad as it's going to get. From here on everything is an improvement.

4. Note all the outboard jobs. By this I mean the work that will be done on or near the hull. For example, there may be several leaks where the hull and deck are joined, or maybe you intend to add lockers where there now is only a shelf between the backrest and the hull. The point is, you want to plan the work so you start outboard and work into the boat.

5. Note inboard areas needing work. This will be the bunks or dinette section, locker doors, drawer fronts, and the vertical part of work places like the galley or bulkheads.

6. Consider the area right down the middle of the boat. Now you can do the cabin sole, the table, and the one place that by now is really starting to look bad from all the work—the steps or ladder leading out from below.

7. Look into putting on the final touches—what I like to think of as the icing on the cake. Here is where the new bunk cushions are put in, the new VHF radio and stereo is installed, the clock on the bulkhead, and all those items that add to a pleasant atmosphere below deck.

By now I'm sure the main purpose of organizing the cosmetic list is apparent. Plan so a completed project is out of the way of the next one. While this is easy to say and even to plan, there'll be places it simply cannot be done. When you get to this type of situation, don't worry about it; give the job some thought, and do what has to be done. But I think it's important to know ahead of time that the awkward project will present itself, and that you'll be prepared to handle it.

As for the *future* cosmetic list, it will be difficult to break it down into the same steps as outlined for the *present* list. It's obvious you'll be planning projects for the future. This necessitates having to work over and around previously completed projects. Therefore, your future list really cannot be organized in the true sense of the word. About all that can be said for it is it will allow you to have an overall plan for the ongoing refurbishing of your boat. Another positive benefit from having a future projects list is that by trying to plan the overall refurbishing, you may see it would be better to stretch a point, and shift a future job to the present list. For example, your scope of work approach is to do only what has to be done to make the boat acceptable as quickly as possible. This gives you a present list of mainly paintbrush work with no woodworking planned. On your future list you want to tear out a pipe berth and add storage bins; but when you start analyzing your projects you realize what a mess the job is going to be. So you stretch both your time frame and money to add the bins now in order for a smoother work schedule down the road. The real value of the future list is to make you think about the overall undertaking, and at the same time consider making changes that will facilitate the flow of work, which in my opinion will give better results.

Where to Do the Work

Usually problems in this area are solved or lived with, as the case may be, as the work progresses. But with a little thinking ahead, you'll save yourself time, effort, and money down the road.

Take where the boat is kept, for example. All too often the fact that the boat either stays in its slip or is in the boatyard is accepted by the owner. Any inconvenience this creates is also accepted, but ask yourself: Does it have to be this way while I'm refurbishing? You would like to answer no, but what exactly are the alternatives? Here I think I can give you some answers and ideas.

Where the boat is located can be controlled. A great many marinas and most yacht clubs with slip facilities that I'm familiar with will not allow any sort of extensive work to take place in the slip. You should check this out before you find out the hard way. I'm sure you can understand the reason. A boat undergoing extensive work can look most unsightly. Furthermore, if the owner is doing most of the work, it seems to stay that way for a long period of time. Check with the proper persons, and explain what you plan to do. If okay, then great; but if not, try to work out some other arrangement. For example, see if it's possible to do the work during the off season winter months. This can work well except in the southern regions where there is no off season.

If your marina has an odd slip out of the way, maybe you can make a swap with the slip holder for a period of time which will be acceptable both to management and the slip holder. Another point to consider if you can work it out with management is to get permission to use vacant slips close to the parking lot. Although it's a little inconvenient to slip hop, the closer the boat is to your car, the easier the work.

In the event you'll not be able to work in your regular slip, check around your area for a temporary berth. The best bet, in my opinion, is a boatyard; and just don't look at the yards that specialize in pleasure boats. There are many places that do work on small commercial boats. These yards may not look as nice as the yacht yards, but the convenience should far outweigh this. An added plus is being able to haul the boat at the same location.

When looking around for a berth to put the boat, don't hesitate to ask for help. Your dock master may not have one available, but he may know someone who does; and if this someone can't help, then ask him for assistance. It's amazing what can be located if enough people are questioned.

The northern sections of the country will have their own particular problems because of the winter weather. Therefore, during the off season you'll have to be working on a hauled-out boat in cold temperatures.

Working on a hauled-out boat brings up another thought that should be addressed. There are some boatyards which require all work to be performed by their employees, in which case I advise you to go some place else. Also there are many yards requiring that you purchase your supplies and materials through them but will allow you to do your own work. If this is the case with a particular yard you want to use, sit down with management and explain what you plan to do. Offer to buy what's practical through the yard but explain there'll be other materials you plan to purchase from other sources. In short, make a deal; and never hesitate for one moment to ask. Remember, the very worst that can happen to you is that you get a simple *no*.

The main problem with working on a boat in cold weather is that almost everything, including you, needs heat. Even if the boat is in the water, you'll have to have electric power so that the interior heat can be furnished easily with an electric heater. A small one will do nicely because it's not a large volume to heat. (While on the subject of heaters, I strongly recommend the electric heater because it has no flame nor does it give off any fumes.)

There are two things you can do to make life more bearable when working on the hauled-out boat in cold weather. One is to try and find a protected place on the storage yard from the winter winds, maybe next to a building or a stand of evergreen trees. Even being located between two larger boats is better than nothing. Anyway, get with the yard operator, and try to work out something to your benefit. The second is to wrap the boat in clear plastic polyethylene. It comes in rolls of one-hundred-feet long by twelve-to-twenty-feet wide. I recommend the hundred by twenty, six mils thick, which can be found at any good hardware store or building supply firm. The cost is around fifty dollars a roll. With this clear plastic and a few pieces of wood or plastic pipe, you can put the boat under a greenhouse. On a sunny but cold day you'll even be able to do some outside work. One word of caution: you may be in an area where there is a lot of snow and you'll need to take this into consideration.

Of course if you're fortunate enough to be able to get under a roof, even if it costs more, do it. I've found the amount of work done is directly proportional to the working conditions, so the extra cost will be worth it when compared to the results.

Safety of the slip is an important aspect often overlooked. A refurbishing project takes time. Also after the major work is completed, the boat will probably be in use while the other jobs are in progress, so the slip area will be a scene of a great deal of coming and going. Exactly how safe is this area?

Even if you stay in your regular berth during the work, have you surveyed the dock from a personal safety viewpoint? I'm sure your permanent slip and dock section is in good repair, but how about the shape of the dock if you're using a temporary slip? Take note of things like loose or deteriorated decking, or maybe some nails are working themselves out of the decking, and you'll stump your toe on one while both arms are loaded. Bring these potential problems to the attention of the proper people. Sometimes the response may not be fast enough for you, so don't hesitate to repair a minor problem yourself.

In my opinion the most dangerous place is where you climb on board the boat. This area, be it your regular slip or a temporary one, should be looked at with the idea of being able to get aboard safely with awkward items. The main problem is you're dealing with large pilings and pieces of decking that offer a very poor handhold. I have found a simple solution to this problem, but I didn't address it until I looked into why my wife always called for me to help her go aboard our boat. We were loading for a trip after moving to a new slip, and every time I found myself in the middle of something, I was called to come help her. After what seemed like the hundredth time I asked why she couldn't climb on board by herself. With icicles hanging from her words, she told me there was no way she could get a firm handhold on the piling or finger pier and until such time as I saw fit to provide her with something that gave her a firm place to grasp, I had jolly well better show up when called. Well, she had a good point. After returning from our cruise, I designed all sorts of handholds, but nothing really seemed to solve the problem, because women have small hands. Several days later while in a hardware store I saw the very thing—a garage door handle. (See Figure 8.) It works perfectly, and costs under five dollars with bolts or screws. It's without a doubt the handiest thing to have and, in my opinion, one of the safest. Frankly, I don't know how I got along without it. I strongly suggest you add a garage door handle to your permanent berth and any temporary one you may be using.

Thinking about safety is also important when the boat is in the cradle. Again, getting on and off the cradle is the main problem. A

Figure 8. Garage door handle

thirty-five-foot sailboat can have a deck easily ten feet or more off the ground. Now a ten-foot ladder climb is not too hard until you're trying to carry something with you. Why carry anything, you ask? Just pull it up after you have attached a line. Trouble is there will be items which you won't want to pull up, believe me. So it's in your best interest to make sure you have a safe method of climbing on and off the boat. The best thing is a portable set of stairs that some yacht yards are equipped with. The next best method is the plain old ladder. If the yard furnishes ladders to use, check yours out, and if it's only a little bit questionable forget it. There is one other problem with a yard ladder: Everybody will use it, and when you show up on Saturday morning, you may have to waste time finding one to use.

A ladder may be your only choice, so if the yard cannot assign you a good safe one then provide your own, something with a wide step for good footing. An aluminum one is the best bet because it's easy to handle. Paint your name on it. After you're finished for the day never leave it up where it can be damaged or worse yet damage the boat. Always stow it under the boat chained and locked to the cradle. That way it's always there when you're ready to use it. Two more points concerning the ladder. Make sure you have it padded where it rests on the boat, and always tie the top to the boat. I well remember one time on a winter Sunday when I was the only person working on a boat, and a gust of wind blew over my aluminum ladder leaving me stranded, and I mean really stranded. I had taken everthing off the boat including all sheets and lines. I had no way down except to jump, and I didn't relish the idea. In the end I used some string and a coat hanger to hook the ladder. Do yourself a favor and always tie the ladder to the boat. Never take for granted something is safe and then discover the hard way that it's not. You're the only one who's going to look after your own welfare, so do it!

Tools to Use

Since I've made the assumption that you are somewhat handy with your hands, I'll also assume that you have the usual tool box with its assorted wrenches, screwdrivers, and the like. What I want to discuss here are some additional basic tools that I feel are necessary to turn out nice looking work. My main interest now is to make you aware of them in the planning stage, and for ease of reference I'll list them.

Hand Tools.

1. Wood chisels (with sharp straight edges)
2. Keyhole saw
3. Coping saw
4. Regular hand saw
5. Putty knife
6. Utility knife
7. C clamps (2 small, 2 that open at least 6 inches)
8. Wood plane
9. Wood rasp
10. Small square
11. Wood drill bits up to one inch

Powered Hand Tools.

1. Drill motor with variable speed
2. Belt sander
3. Vibrating sander
4. Saber saw
5. Router
6. Disk sander

Shop Power Tools.

1. Radial arm saw
2. Table saw
3. Drill press

As you've undoubtedly noticed, these tools are mostly for working with wood and fiberglass, but then that's where you'll spend most of your refurbishing time. Don't dash out and buy everything on the tools list right away. My aim is to make you aware of what you should have access to. Then again you may already own most of these listed items, in which case you're in pretty good shape to get started.

I feel it's the shop tools that present the greatest problem, both in cost and working space needed. Here it may pay you to scout around and see if there is an alternative to buying these items. See if you have any friends that don't mind your coming over to do some cutting. The boatyard probably has a shop, and will be glad to do some work for you. If space at home is no problem, you can consider renting these tools for a short period of time. Also once you move along with your projects, you may discover that shop tools are not required for what you're doing. Anyway while you're in the planning stage, give some thought to the needed tools. At the same time, think about where your workshop will be. The garage is the natural place. No sailor keeps the car in the garage anymore; it's strictly for boat gear, it seems. But in the event you don't have a garage and the living room is out, locate some place to work. Borrow a place if possible or consider renting some space if necessary. Again this is one of those areas where it pays to ask around. The boatyard may be able to help, and at the same time help you make up your mind which yard to use if workshop space is available. My point is, don't wait until the last minute to think about a workshop. Consider it in the planning stage.

When to Get Expert Help

Years ago when I first went to work, I had a boss who told me that sometimes the important thing was not to know what to do, but to know what *not to do*. I think this statement holds true where skilled professional help is concerned with a refurbishing project. Be honest with yourself and don't take on a job that you know is beyond your capability, no matter how keen you are to try it. From experience I can say you will be far ahead of the game to bring in paid help.

The best example of this need for an expert always seems to be in the area of engine work. Unless you really know what you're doing here, let the mechanic do the important work. I'm not talking about ongoing maintenance like changing the oil and spark plugs. That's the sort of thing every boat owner is supposed to know. But when it comes to going inside, don't hesitate to get skilled help.

One idea that may prove useful in the planning stage is when you're checking around for engine work inquire if you'll be able to look over the mechanic's shoulder. For some reason which I have yet to understand, men are expected to be born with an intuitive ability to know what makes the internal combustion engine function. Well, I for one was certainly not blessed with this wonderful knowledge. As a teenager I only did one stint as a fledgling mechanic. A couple of friends and I "rebuilt" a 1937 Chevrolet engine. It never ran very well after we finished. It must have had something to do with the quart jar of nuts, bolts, and assorted "doohickeys" we had left over. Anyway I ended up knowing less when I finished than when I started, so I surmised I had better leave this sort of thing to the ones who were gifted at birth. I've never worried about this blank spot in my education until I bought my first sailboat with an inboard engine, I realized I had better learn something about the engine. The way I solved my problem was to talk to the mechanic who was going to do some engine work I had scheduled. I told him my embarassing lack of information, and asked if I could look over his shoulder. Well, he did me one better; he made me his tool passer. The end result is that although I'm still not a mechanic, I can tell you what goes on inside that engine and why. It's no longer a complete mystery, and I can't begin to tell you how much this has done for my confidence.

See Chapter 11 for much more detail on the engine, but for now I want you to think about any engine work which has to be done ahead of time and plan for it. And if you're anything like me, try and find a mechanic who's willing to give you some basic schooling.

Another area where you may find the services of a professional needed is hull painting. Most older fiberglass boats will need painting. With all the different types of expensive paints on the market, it makes sense to have someone apply it who knows what he's doing.

The sailmaker is one professional I'm sure you'll need to contact, unless you have all new sails on the boat, which is very unlikely. One bit of advice here. Try and use a local sailmaker if at all possible. It just makes getting all the little details looked after much easier.

Along with the sailmaker is the upholsterer. I'm using this term rather loosely to cover those people who make boat covers, dodgers, bimini tops, and cushions. Here is one area where I strongly suggest you use the professional. In my opinion amateur work here really shows up to the detriment of the overall refurbishing project.

You may also feel more comfortable with help when it comes to the wiring on the boat or installing a new radio, so get it. There are several lesser areas where you may want to use skilled help and I'll cover this material in later chapters. For now there's no need to be concerned with these areas.

The important point with these areas requiring professional

expertise is to take them into consideration when organizing the overall project, and at the same time, be honest with yourself about your own capabilities.

Locating Marine Supplies

Although locating marine supplies does not have a direct bearing on planning and organizing your project, this information should prove helpful. At this organizational stage you'll have no difficulty at all locating marine supplies. Every locale has its retail firms which market goods to the marine industry. In addition you also have mail order companies that seem to send out catalogs in a never-ending stream. Of course what we're talking about here is the normal supply line that experienced sailors are familiar with. Having several sources to buy from gives the sailor the opportunity to compare prices and materials in order to get the best deal. All these supply sources are basically retail. Regardless of what their advertising says, they sell to the boat owner and the man on the street, not to other marine firms.

What you want to do is locate the distributor/wholesaler and determine if you can buy direct. Many wholesale companies do sell direct to the public but at a higher price than they sell to a retail store or boatyard. They don't want to be in direct competition with their wholesale customers which can be bad for business. If you can buy at wholesale prices, then great.

Chances are you will save some money buying direct from the middleman, but the real plus I've found is the wide range of items and equipment at a single source, especially if the distributor supplies the commercial maritime trade. If you want a heavy duty bronze sea cock and the ones the marina store has are too light in weight for you, then I'm sure the wholesale outlet will have them in stock because that's what will be used on work boats.

Also be aware of another business segment—the industrial supply firm. Often special items can be purchased here at a saving in cost, or better quality for the same money. A good example of this is water hose for the engine. When it comes to items that could lead to the boat sinking if they fail, you should buy the very best, I believe. Therefore, instead of letting the boatyard furnish the hose for my engine I went to an industrial supply company that specialized in hoses for any use—from heavy equipment hydraulic lines to hose certified for aviation use. I replaced all my engine hoses with aviation grade, paying less than the boatyard price for their hose.

When doing the cosmetic work below, you'll find several non-marine suppliers very useful. For example, formica for counter and table tops will come from a building materials company or cabinet-maker. Contact paper to dress up the interior of a locker or some type of stick-on fabric to use on the hull back of the bunks will come from a paint or decorator supplier. The recreation vehicle supply firms will be able to furnish a number of items so check them out.

I've made it a point to keep this information on locating your supplies rather general. I didn't want to get you bogged down too much now with details. I'll cover more in later chapters as you proceed.

From here on you're through with homework. It's time to get your hands dirty with the nuts and bolts of your upgrading and refurbishing project. So let's go to work!

Three

TOPSIDES, UNDERBODY, RIGGING, AND MAST

The exterior of your boat is the one area that everyone sees all the time. It's the first impression formed about the boat, and, I might add, about you. To me it's important that the first and lasting impression my boat gives is one of *pride of ownership*.

A handsome exterior is a very significant part of your pride of ownership. It's a joy to know your boat has pleasing lines and that it is well cared for. So how a boat looks is important. To take the older fiberglass sailboat, and make her a delight to the eye is very much a part of the upgrading and refurbishing project. But remember also you're dealing with an older boat which has started to show age in many places. Therefore, it's going to take some effort on your part to end up with a truly fine looking sailboat. This chapter will help you obtain this goal as well as cover the structural aspects so that your boat will be as safe as she's pretty.

Topsides

The hull is the basic unit of a boat. Actually, you can say that the hull is a boat if you use the definition that a boat is an object that floats in water. Everything else that goes to make up a boat as we think of it is attached to the hull or fixed to something that's attached to the hull.

It follows then that this is where you should begin your detailed look at upgrading and refurbishing. The area between the waterline and the deck, or to use the correct nautical term, the topsides, is what you'll be covering under this topic.

From a structural standpoint you should have very little to

nothing to do here. The structural places have to do with other items being attached to the hull and as such will be discussed in later chapters. If on the other hand, you do face a structural problem, for example, an area involved in a collision where the patch work is poorly done, I recommend you bring in the professional to make the proper repairs because the topsides is no place for a sloppy job.

Most of the topside repairs will be fixing the many gouges, scratches, and ding marks any boat collects. You'll find some, as I have, that pose a complete mystery about how they got there. The scratches and ding marks will be easy to fix. Lightly sand with a fine grit sandpaper; then touch up with gelcoat or paint. You'll be able to see where you touched up. Seldom if ever will there be an absolutely perfect blending with the nicked area disappearing completely. It should be close, but it will not be perfect; and if you try to get a perfect match, you'll spend a lot of time just getting frustrated.

Allow me to pass on an attitude about this sort of thing which helps bring your work into a proper perspective. The only time the touched-up places will be noticed is when you put your nose within six inches of them. Also what is easily seen when the boat is in the cradle is hardly ever seen when the boat is in the water, so don't worry about a perfect match. If the touched-up places really stand out when the boat is in the water, that's the time to consider a new paint job.

Gouges can be quite another matter. A light touch-up won't do the job because you're dealing with a hole that must be filled. Regardless of whether you plan a complete new paint job or just a touch-up, the gouges will have to be cleaned out and then filled. Small places can be filled with automotive body filler. Of course, you can use a fiberglass compound for these small jobs, but it's not as easy to work with, I've found. Larger gouges will require a fiberglass filler compound. Any good marine store or boatyard will be able to supply your needs. I'll have more to say about filler materials when we cover the repair work on the deck.

In my opinion the place where the handyman doing his own work often falls down is in the final stage of sanding with proper sandpaper. You want to use wet sandpaper starting with 220 grit and ending with 600 grit. This will give you a very smooth finish that should blend in with the surrounding surface. Another handy item when doing small touch-up jobs are small artists' paintbrushes. Buy the cheap ones from your local variety store or art supplies outlet. Buy a handful when you do because you'll find dozens of uses for them.

At this point the topsides repairs are completed, either structural or just filling up some holes. From my experience this older boat probably now looks like it has a good case of the chicken pox. So it's time to look at the cosmetic side. If the exterior of the boat is always on display, the color of the topsides is the main focal point. It really sets the tone for the whole exterior. No matter how beautiful everything else is, the beat up and fading topsides will be the only thing seen. There are three general situations to be considered when you think about refurbishing the topsides. They are dealing with the original gelcoat, touching up painted topsides, or considering a new paint job.

Original Gelcoat. Chances are if the boat still has its original gelcoat, the color will be white or some very light color. The darker gelcoats that were used on the older boats faded after a few years and most have been painted. Anyway, you want to keep the gelcoat color so you're concerned with putting it back in shape. Your first job will be to clean thoroughly the topsides. Start by using a dewaxing cleaner; then go to a fiberglass rubbing compound. If you still have unsightly stains at this point, try a fiberglass stain remover. But be careful not to rub off the gelcoat. Gelcoat is not thick, and since after years of chalking and rubbing it's gotten even thinner, you can easily rub down to the glass underneath. Keep in mind that if this starts happening in too many places, you might be wise to reconsider and think about going ahead and painting. A really tough stain may require a cleaner like Ajax which has a very fine grit material in the powder which acts like sandpaper; again be careful not to go through the gelcoat.

By using any or all of these cleaners, you'll be able to take care of your stain problems because almost all stains are caused by chalking or something bleeding over the topsides—like oil from the water or a rust streak. There is one exception, though, and it's that yellow "dirty teeth" color that's found where water splashes up over the waterline, mainly on the bow. This yellow stain seems to be on a great many older boats which have pushed through miles and miles of water. The mess simply defies removal. Oh, you can get the top layer off, but the slight yellow color is always there.

But don't worry. There is something which will take the yellow away, and you won't find it in the marine store with a big price tag. It's liquid Sani-Flush toilet bowl cleaner that comes from your supermarket and sells for around a dollar for the sixteen-ounce size. The key word here is liquid; it has to be liquid Sani-Flush. It's simple to use in the home but for the side of a boat I recommend rubber gloves. Bad stains will take several applications, but at a dollar a bottle this should present no problem.

Once the topsides are clean, apply touch-up gelcoat to the necessary places, always following the instructions. You'll have no trouble buying gelcoat. The marine store will be able to supply the material, but if for some reason you find gelcoat difficult to locate, I suggest you check with the people in your area that do fiberglass repairs.

When this job is done, you can start on the waxing chore. I say chore because to get a good job requires hand buffing. It's my understanding from people who know that machine buffing does not do a lasting job—it has something to do with too much rubbing at too high a speed.

Let me caution you here not to be disappointed if your topsides do not look like a brand new boat. Chances are they are not going to. You're dealing with old gelcoat, and there's only so much you can do. Do pay attention to how long the gloss seems to last from your wax job. If it's only a short time, say several weeks, then the gelcoat just doesn't have enough left to do its job. So consider painting. Keeping the original gelcoat is a quick way to make the topsides presentable. But in my opinion for the older boat, it's strictly a short-term investment.

Touching Up Painted Topsides. Frankly when you buy an older fiberglass sailboat, you'll probably have two choices to consider: touch up old paint or repaint. Let's say you're interested in touching up, assuming, of course, you've completed the necessary repairs. The actual work associated with touching up is small; just take an artist's brush and stroke it on. Nothing to it as long as the paint matches or even comes very close. But here is where your problem begins. Even if you had a can of paint come with the boat, the paint won't match after the topsides have been exposed to the weather for several years. A recent paint job gives you a fair chance of matching, but don't count on it. Buying a new can of what was used also doesn't offer good odds on matching. Old man weather does the damage, and there's nothing you can do about that.

The solution to this cosmetic problem is to have paint that comes very close to matching when dry, not the color in the can, but the final color in place and dry. Here I have a method to pass on that I've found to work very well with matching paint. It will take a bit of your time, but the end result is well worth it.

First take a good color snapshot of the boat. Have the sun behind you and shining directly on the boat. Second remove a small sample of the paint at lease the size of your thumb nail, larger if possible. If the paint will not come off for a decent sample, go with the picture by itself. Assuming you could get a small sample, take your picture and the sample to a good paint store where there are facilities to mix all kinds of colors. Ask the sales clerk to mix you a quart of paint to match the snapshot and sample. You don't have to have some super-grade marine paint. Any decent enamel base will do. Don't worry about the fact that they're working on only one quart. Everyone has his professional pride and every time I've done this, I've noted the sales clerks looked on it as a challenge to prove they really did know their business. Be sure and ask for a dry-sample match. Once the paint is mixed, small amounts are brushed out and dried with a small hair dryer. Then whatever colors are needed are added, mixed, and again dry sampled. This is not a long drawn-out process. These clerks are used to mixing colors and after you've checked several dry samples, you should have a very good match.

One bit of advice. Try and pick a time when things are slow at the paint store. Don't hesitate to call and ask what would be a good time to come in because you're going to have to have some help matching a color. Don't go in on a Saturday morning when all the amateur house painters are selecting paint. To get the expert help you need, make sure the paint people have the time to work with you. Also, don't drop off your sample. Stay there and look over the shoulder of the clerk. That way you make sure it's done. Otherwise, the job could be easily forgotten after you've left the store.

Okay, now you have the touch-up paint, and it's as close a match as possible. Don't do the entire boat; do only a small place where the sun will dry it. Give the paint at least twenty-four hours to dry and check to see just how close the match is. From my experience it's probably going to be off, and here is where old-fashioned trial and error comes in. Take a good look at the color and try to determine what's needed. Ask someone who's good at colors to determine if a shade more of this or that is needed. Then take the paint back to the store and ask that the little something be added. Return to the boat and paint another small place. Wait twenty-four hours and see what you have. If it matches, then great; if not, then back to the paint store.

Eventually, you'll end up with something you can live with and from three feet away looks terrific. Now I'm sure you understand why I said this paint matching system can take some time, but I feel the end results are well worth the effort. Who knows? You might get lucky and the paint store will hit it right off the bat the first time around.

There's one drawback to doing a match job this way. You'll have two different paints and most likely they will not weather at the same rate. This will cause the touched-up places to begin to stand out after a couple of years. By this time I'm sure the boat has added more ding marks, so just repeat the matching process. Sooner or later, though, you'll have to accept the fact that the boat color is going to weather and you'll be faced with a new paint job, and this leads to our last general topside situation.

New Paint Job. Unless you really know your stuff or have a friend who does, this is one of those special areas where you may want to call in a professional. All the technical advances that have been made in the marine paint industry over the past few years could easily fill a book. At the same time you'll have no trouble obtaining all the necessary information to decide exactly what type of paint you'd prefer to use. Marine paint suppliers or painters will be glad to provide whatever you need. Contacting the paint manufacturer direct is an excellent source of technical information. The point I want to get across here is that once you've decided to paint the topsides, explore several alternatives and pick the paint which suits your particular situation. Most of the time this involves money.

Painting the topsides can be expensive or fairly cheap depending on the cost of the paint, preparation required, and degree of application expertise needed. I hesitate to talk about money because frankly every locale is different and anything I say will have little value except for my particular location, which is the southern end of Chesapeake Bay.

What I want to do is go over your choices, and give you enough information to pull together what you need in order to decide which course to follow. I'll start with the most economical method and work up the scale.

The least expensive way is for you to paint your hull using a good grade of ordinary marine paint. The use of a brush is by far the simplest way, the next is spray painting. Preparation by sanding the existing surface will require time to do. Also, if your boat has been painted previously, try and determine what kind of paint was used so you can make sure your new paint is compatible.

One place to take special note of is the way the old paint adheres to the topside surface. If it's hard to scrape off with a knife blade, you'll probably be okay just sanding lightly and going over the old paint. But if it scrapes off with very little effort or is peeling off in flakes, you'll have to remove all the old paint. In this case a paint remover and sanding will do the job, along with some old-fashioned elbow grease.

Another point to consider is having a professional painter give you a quick economy paint job using a regular over-the-counter marine paint. This is possible if the topsides don't require extensive preparation but only a fast light sanding, protection of the adjacent areas, and spraying the paint.

Either one of these two methods should give you an acceptable looking job. After all, there are some good over-the-counter marine paints on the market and that's what we're talking about.

Now let's look at the expensive paints. Here I'll climb out on a limb and quote some prices. Keep in mind I'll be speaking for my locale only. I'm doing this so you'll have some sort of feel for the expensive end of the paint scale. Awlgrip and Imron are the two brand names widely used to paint both new and older fiberglass boats. I've learned that several boat manufacturers now use these paints in place of gelcoat on new boats. Having seen both products used on boats, I can attest that the results are simply beautiful when put on by a skilled applicator. Since the manufacturers have recognized the fact that these paints require skill, knowledge, and equipment to end up with the expected results, they primarily sell to the

applicator trade and both Awlgrip and Imron are considered trade—
not retail—products. Let's face it: these manufacturers are in business to make money, and every good job is the best advertisement
they can get.

To use either Awlgrip or Imron on your boat will be expensive.
I'm talking about figures like thirty-five to fifty dollars a foot based on
overall length. A thirty-five-foot boat can cost upwards of two thousand dollars. When compared to one hundred dollars worth of over-
the-counter paint, sandpaper, brushes, and other needed items plus a
couple of weekends of work, that's one whale of a difference to think
about.

Of course, there are reasons why Awlgrip and Imron cost so
much. The paint costs more per gallon, and there is a tremendous
amount of time involved in preparing the topsides. Matter of fact, I'm
told ninety percent of the work time involved in using these products
is in preparing the surface. The skilled painter is selling his knowledge, and all of this adds up to big bucks. There is one avenue to check
out that can be used to bring the cost down if the painter is agreeable.
Do your own preparation work; but if you do, then take the time to do
it right. The end result is absolutely dependent on the preparation.

Along with the cost of painting, there're some added costs which
you should be aware of. The boat will have to be hauled. If you don't
let the paint work coincide with your regular haul out, there will be
this additional cost. Furthermore, unless the weather is perfect and
the surrounding conditions are ideal, the boat will have to be moved
into a building which requires dropping the mast. And that's going to
be added to your bill. When shopping around, be sure and include
these added costs to your price so you won't have any unpleasant
surprises after you're committed to the paint contract. You'll have no
trouble obtaining all the information you need to decide if you want
Awlgrip or Imron. Just contact any boatyard which does paint work;
and even if they don't do paint work, they'll be able to refer you to
someone who does. One very important piece of advice here. Before
you contract with any one firm, ask for and expect to get a list of
references for completed work. Then check the people involved and go
look at their boat if convenient. And, always insist on a small can of
touch-up paint; believe me, you'll use it.

I have one last suggestion concerning the painting of your topsides. Since the topsides are the focal point of the exterior, go after the

best job you can afford. And even if the Awlgrip or Imron really strains your pocketbook, this is one of the areas where I feel it's worth the effort because aside from the looks, you're adding positive resale value to the boat.

Boat Name and Numbers. It's as natural as breathing to look at a beautiful sailboat and wonder what the owner has named her. Nothing jars my esthetic sense as much as a fine looking boat with an attractive sounding name and seeing the name put on the boat with ordinary stick-on letters. Here is one place the owner can add his sense of good taste in a world where everything is manufactured to appeal to as wide a range of buyers as possible. (See Figures 9 and 10.) Stick-on letters offer very little variety in style or colors. I recommend you bring in a specialist in boat name painting so you'll be able to get just the right colors and letter style to complement your boat. Of course, the same applies to your state registration numbers if the boat does not have U. S. government documentation. Just a little

Figure 9. Sailboat name illustrating a letter style

Figure 10. An alternate letter style for a sailboat name

something extra like shadow lining the numbers tells everyone your boat is well thought of.

Documentation regulations regarding letters can cause problems, but the painter will still be able to do something with your name that will give it some individual flair. The letters can be no less than four inches high and easy to read. The color has to be one which easily stands out against the topsides. These are the two main requirements that have to be worked around. Figure 11 is a good example of a documented boat with just a touch of individuality added. You could never do this with letters off the shelf.

Locating a painter is easy. Your boatyard may be able to have the work done for you. Or you can ask other boat owners whose boats have nicely painted names. And last, you can turn to the yellow pages and let your fingers do the walking. Boat name painting comes within the sign painting business, so check some sign painters, and go from there. One thing though; ask for a couple of references and then take a look at samples. My experience with sign painters has been that the good ones can be very helpful with ideas on both color and style. It'll

Figure 11. An example of a sailboat name for a documented boat

pay to do some homework. Take snapshots of names that have styles or color combinations that appeal to you. Also save pictures from boating magazines. Having something you like to show the painter is the right way to get exactly what you want. Remember the topsides are the focal point of the boat's exterior, and the boat's name is very much a part of the topsides, so make sure it looks good.

Rub Rails. Our last subject under the general heading of topsides are rub rails. I'm continually amazed at the expensive well-received boats on the market, both new and old, that do not come from the manufacturer with a rub rail. Some builders have made half-hearted attempts to add a rub rail, but very few offer any real protection to the boat's topsides.

Of course, I realize many sailors are not concerned about rub rails. They feel rub rails detract from the appearance and regard the screws used to secure the rub rails to the topsides as potential trouble spots. I offer no argument with this. One thing about sailors—they all have definite ideas about what they like and dislike.

But for those who'd like to consider adding rub rails, I'll go into some details. First, consider a fairly strong wood, one that is able to take abuse. I prefer teak, but it's costly to get it in long sections. You may consider oak or some other hardwood. My preference for teak is that it is resistant to rot and easy to work especially if any repairs have to be made. Second, determine how far the rub rail should project out from the hull in order to give the proper protection. Usually somewhere in the neighborhood of one and a half inches is fine. For ease of handling and working, I suggest that the rub rail be in two sections as depicted in Figure 12. Note the angles on top and bottom. The top angle is to allow water to run off the top of the rub rail; the bottom angle is to allow the rub rail to slide off of any object it is lowered onto. For example, if the tide falls and the rub rail is lowered onto the top of a short piling the angle allows the boat to slide off, preventing severe damage from taking place. Third, add a metal strip to act as the contact area, making sure the strip overhangs the wood as shown in the drawing (Figure 12). This will make water drip off the bottom of the metal strip and not run down the rub rail and onto the topsides.

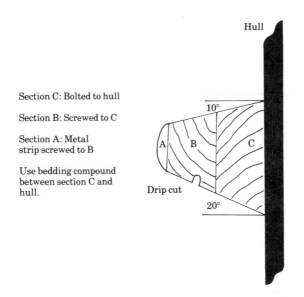

Figure 12. Rub rail

Don't use one screw or bolt to fasten both metal strip and wood to the hull. Secure the wood with bolts going all the way through the hull and the fiberglass over the holding nuts. Put the metal strip on with wood screws that don't go all the way through the rub rail because the metal strip is going to get beat up with use, and repairs are no trouble when the strip can be easily removed. Then you can paint or varnish the rub rail to protect the wood. In the case of teak you may prefer to let it weather naturally with some cleaning from time to time.

If you do decide to add rub rails, take the time to look at other boats and pick up some ideas. Also question the boat owner, if possible, to see how he handled securing the rub rail to the hull. Don't hesitate to ask if you could have a look. Sailors are glad to show off their handiwork.

If you plan to sail your boat with a small crew, say just one couple most of the time, you'll find having rub rails gives you peace of mind both in that you do not have to be overly concerned about banging up your topsides nor worry about trying to hold a twenty-thousand-pound boat off the dock with brute force.

Underbody

Here is where you'll spend hours and hours of work and put the boat back in the water with no one able to see all your accomplishments. But there's no more important area on the boat than the section below the waterline. About the only cosmetic consideration will be the color of your bottom paint while on the other hand, the structural aspects are extremely significant.

Cleaning and Repairs. Your first chore is to clean the bottom so you'll be able to see exactly what you're dealing with. If the boat has been in the water for a while, it's going to have all kinds of growth or scum which should be removed just as soon as it is hauled. I believe now most boatyards clean the bottoms with high pressure water which does a good job on all but the most stubborn growths, like barnacles. In the event you plan to clean your own bottom, be present when the boat is hauled and get right on with the job before the mess dries up because if it does, you'll end up having to sand the junk off. A regular hose with a scrub brush will do the job but you may also need to use a scraper to take care of any barnacles. Try and do this while the boat is in the slings so you can get to the keel area easily. This is a messy job so you may prefer the yard to do it for you if you have a choice, but be there to watch (if possible) so nothing is half-way done, thus creating more work down the road.

Once you've cleaned the underbody lightly sand the entire area. Be sure not to neglect sanding before you paint the bottom, it really makes no difference if you sand after cleaning or before you paint as far as the paint is concerned. I like to sand after the cleaning so the underbody can be inspected and questionable areas uncovered up front. You can do this sanding by hand or with a sander. If you use a sander make sure the paper is not too coarse because this will create deep scratches in the fiberglass. Use as fine a grit as you can that will get the job done. It's going to take more time, but the end result will be a better surface to work with.

Here is where you may encounter blisters that many fiberglass boats have. These blisters are caused by water getting behind the gelcoat. As odd as it sounds, gelcoat has a tendency to allow water to permeate through the outer surface. Anyway you sand off the blisters, dig out any loose material, let dry, apply a filler, sand smooth, and paint.

After cleaning and sanding, check everything thoroughly. Look at the rudder surface to see if there are any damaged places. Take note of any area that looks like it has been subjected to abuse. Give it a good shake and pay attention to the amount of play in the stock that leads from the rudder to the tiller or wheel—especially if you have a spade rudder because it's secured only at the top. There has to be a certain amount of play in the stock, but too much could denote a problem now or maybe in the near future. If your rudder is fixed to the back of the keel, investigate all moving parts for wear.

Next inspect the shaft and prop. Most of the time if it looks okay, it is okay. Smooth out any nicks on the prop, clean up the lock nut, and replace the cotter pin. If you ever have to replace the prop while the boat is in the water, you'll be glad you took the trouble to clean up the nut. Make sure your shaft alignment is correct. You may have to ask for some help here. And last, check your zincs.

There are two schools of thought concerning zincs in my sailing area, which I'll pass along for what they're worth. One is: Use zincs to protect your shaft and prop, but at the same time be prepared to cope with paint that will not stay on the moving parts and present you with a constant battle to keep the metal free of barnacles. The second is: Use no zincs and let your shaft and prop slowly give off particles which will not allow the barnacle to fasten to the metal.

I know what you're thinking right now—better barnacles than no prop, but let me quote from experience. I keep zincs on my shaft, the best I can buy, and I have to clean my prop every three weeks in the summer. Next to me is a 41 footer with a 3-bladed prop and no zincs. There are no barnacles growing on the prop, and the prop looks fine. So who's to say who's right or wrong? My personal preference is zincs; I just have a little better peace of mind knowing they're down there doing their job.

The Centerboard. Take no one's word here on the condition of the board and attachments. When you're hauled, make sure the yard knows you intend to lower the board as much as it will go. Sometimes the yard people will get a little careless, and if the boat is not high enough up off the ground you'll end up having to dig a hole under the boat. You still may have to, but the smaller the better.

If your board is fiberglass, treat it exactly as you would the underbody surface. Most likely though, it will be metal, either iron or bronze. Not much to do here except make sure you get a good coat of antifouling paint and the proper undercoat for the material.

Because centerboards move, they're subject to wear and tear or more accurately, the attachments which make the board move are subject to wear and tear. The parts are simple. You have a wire pendant fastened to the board and leading to a winch. With this arrangement you can lower or raise the board at will; however, the pendant is subject to a great deal of wear so a thorough inspection is called for when the boat is out of the water. The pin also should be checked for wear. I'll have to admit this is hard to do because of the location. Centerboards are notorious for giving problems at the most inopportune times, so replace anything you feel is questionable.

One word of caution. I don't think you would work under your car with just the jack holding it up—you would have some blocks placed to catch the car if the jack fails. So take the same precaution when working around the centerboard if it is in the up position. I have a very good friend who was almost guillotined when the fittings attaching the pendant to the board suddenly gave way. For your own sake, always have a block of wood under the board.

Outside Ballast. If your boat has outside ballast, you'll be able to see the seam between the hull and ballast section. It may look bad at first, but mostly it'll be cosmetic. Outside ballast works as the boat is sailed so do not use fiberglass over this seam. Instead clean out the seam, replace with seam compound, and then cover the area with some material that can be sanded and faired into the hull. When you haul again down the road, the seam will be there. Don't be alarmed; it's supposed to be.

Remember it's very important to thoroughly inspect the holding nuts in the bilge. Check to make sure they're all tight. As a matter of fact, it's a good idea to do this before you do any outside cosmetic work. You may want to clean the nuts and exposed threads at this time so you can see exactly what you have. If you uncover anything that poses a question, don't hesitate to bring in expert help. I really don't expect you to have any major repairs with the outside ballast that you were not aware of before you purchased the boat. Of course, if you have inside ballast, you will have an easier time. Frankly, unless you're doing most of your sailing around rocks and hard bottoms, I would prefer the inside ballast because you have fewer places to leak. One more point concerning outside ballast, certain metals do not do well in salt water. Make sure you know what material the ballast is, and that it has the correct undercoating for protection.

Bottom Paint. If the information on topside paint could fill a book, the same can also be said for bottom paint. You have to tailor the paint to fit the use and location of the boat. If you stay in the water the year round you need one kind of paint, and if the boat is sailed in cold water only five months a year, you can use another kind. It all depends on your preference and pocketbook. You'll have no trouble getting whatever information you need. Just one piece of advice. Find out what works in your area and go from there. You may be faced with sailing in a new locality for whatever the reason, say a transfer, or maybe you're stepping up to a larger boat from one you kept on a trailer and have no personal experience with bottom paint. If you find yourself in this situation, then talk to other sailors and profit from their experience. The final decision will be yours though. Sailors seem to have definite opinions on sailing subjects, and many times no two are alike.

Concerning bottom paint: Buy a good brand which has a proven track record for your locality, and is compatible with what's already on the boat.

Thru-Hull Valves. Although I've been discussing ways to take sections of the older fiberglass sailboat and refurbish them, except for the outside ballast falling off, nothing has been a life-or-death matter. But thru-hull valve fittings are very different, and if you only have the time or inclination to read about one subject in this book, this is the one I would insist on.

Because thru-hull fittings are the places where water is allowed to pass through the hull, each is a potential disaster location. We're dealing with the older boat and chances are very good the sea cocks are original. I'm sure they leak and look like the example in Figure 13, or worse yet, they're gate valves as noted in Figure 14. Figure 15 shows you two bronze sea cocks, which are the only sort of sea cock I

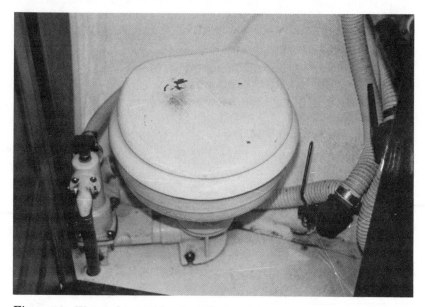

Figure 13. Water closet with sea cocks

Figure 14. Water closet with gate valve

Figure 15. Bronze sea cocks

recommend. It is constructed in such a manner that it's quickly apparent if it's closed, open, or anywhere in between. There are several types on the market, but all have one thing in common. It's easy to see if they're open or closed by the location of the handle or whatever is used to rotate the gate.

If you feel the sea cocks in the boat are not ready to be replaced, I suggest you take them apart and inspect the parts for cracks and wear. Note at the same time if there are pitted areas which will make the gate not seat properly against the housing. See Figure 16. This can cause that constant nagging ugly leak. While you have the sea cock apart (see Figure 17), take a hammer, and give the housing a rap in several places. Climb outside and give the flange a couple of raps. If there has been any metal fatigue, you want to know right now, not later. (Remember the engine cooling water intake snapping off in my hand which I described in Chapter 2!) The problem with keeping the old sea cocks, even if you have confidence in them, is that they tend to leak. Old sea cocks leak, and that's a fact.

I am inclined to buy the best I can and replace each one. You'll have a large size on the discharge side of the head, and a small size on the incoming side of the head, the engine water intake, the sink, and possibly the cockpit drains. The engine water intake should be one of the smallest, something around three-eighths or one-half inch with a strainer on the outside flange. See Figure 18. My advice, if money is a problem, is to let something else go and get new sea cocks for all questionable ones at least.

Let's look at the gate valve in Figure 14. This gate valve is a plumbing item and does not belong on a boat below the waterline. It's not constructed heavily enough to take abuse, and the device that opens the gate can break and you'd have no idea if the valve is open, closed, or somewhere in between. The reason you see so many being used is simple. They're cheap! My recommendation concerning gate valves is to replace them with sea cocks without exception.

Along with replacing older sea cocks you'll want to consider adding some. For example, if you don't have one on your sink drain and the water stands in a clamped-on hose, I would certainly add one. Water standing in a hose makes me nervous. The hose clamp can break, the hose can rot, something can fall against it during a knock-down with no immediate results, but can later show up as a bilge full

Figure 16. Sea cock pitted from age and use

Figure 17. Parts of a sea cock

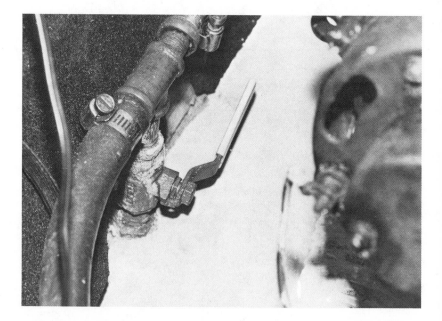

Figure 18. Engine water intake sea cock

of water. Therefore, my rule is never have water standing in a hose unless there's a sea cock.

Now there is one drain system which has to stay open all the time, and these are cockpit drains. If they are closed for any reason, you could end up with water flooding the cockpit. If you review the three cockpit drain options you will have a boat safe from flooding:

1. As shown in Figure 19, make sure that the hose is above the waterline. To check, simply look at what the hose is clamped to and run a thin piece of wood down the inside of the drain until it stops. Bring it up and if it is not wet, the thru-hull the hose is fixed to is above the waterline.

2. If the thru-hull the hose is fixed to is below the waterline, wrap the hose with fiberglass starting at the hull and going above the waterline creating a fiberglass thru-hull with the hose inside. One word of advice. Use 3-inch glass tape. Don't try to cut strips from a large piece. The ends unravel and you

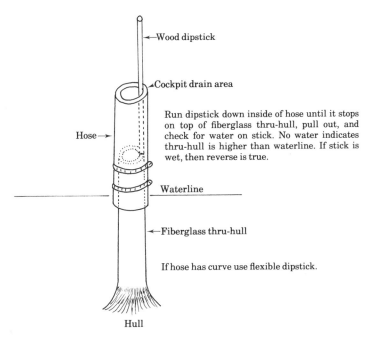

Wood dipstick

Cockpit drain area

Run dipstick down inside of hose until it stops on top of fiberglass thru-hull, pull out, and check for water on stick. No water indicates thru-hull is higher than waterline. If stick is wet, then reverse is true.

Hose→

Waterline

←Fiberglass thru-hull

If hose has curve use flexible dipstick.

Hull

Figure 19. Fiberglass thru-hull

have a mess. The tape costs more, but you get an easier and neater job.

3. Make sure the thru-hulls exit the boat above the waterline.

Another thru-hull is the stuffing box where the prop shaft passes through the hull. The metal parts of the stuffing box may need to be adjusted to allow the proper amount of water to drip so the shaft will not build up damaging friction heat. This fitting should be checked and repacked if necessary. If you get too much water dripping after you've tried to adjust the drip, most likely the packing is well worn.

While you're back in the hardest place to work on the entire boat and wondering if you'll be able to get out, don't forget to take your hammer and give the metal parts a rap. There's one part of the stuffing box arrangement which always seems to be taken for granted, and that is the hose which connects the stuffing box to the fiberglass tube. Give this hose a good inspection, try to twist it and poke around it with a screwdriver to see if the rubber material has deteriorated. At the same time, check the clamps. Clean them up if they need it, and keep them clean so that a quick visual inspection of breaks can be easily made in the future. This is one of those places it's impossible to see under, so if you don't have a mirror on an adjustable handle, I strongly recommend you purchase one. In my part of the country, Sears has the best selection of inspection mirrors for the handyman.

Our last thru-hulls to consider are the sending units necessary for certain instruments. In many of the older boats the thru-hull fittings will be metal, so inspect and rap with your hammer. Remove any sending units or plugs and check the threads so they can be screwed down with no binding. In case you have a sending unit thru-hull that you do not plan to use, remove the fitting and fiberglass over the hole. It is possible you may be in the situation of replacing an instrument with a new model that does not require a thru-hull. In this case, I suggest fiberglass over the hole. I have a good example of this. I bought a depth sounder for my present boat, and, of course, it came with a thru-hull transducer. A sailing friend who hates to cut holes below the waterline, just like I do, did his homework and decided to mount the transducer directly on the hull, using a sealant to hold it in place. The important thing to remember is there can be no air between the transducer and the hull. You apply the sealant to the place where the transducer is to be put, and push the transducer into the sealant until it is seated on the hull. With a putty knife you can push the sealant back against the lip of the transducer making an airtight seal. See Figure 20. There is no need to wait until the sealant is dry to try the instrument, just cut it on, and if you don't get a reading then move the transducer around a bit until you do. Give the sealant a few days to dry to a rubberlike material, and you're in business. This method certainly beats cutting holes in the boat and using water boxes which I've seen as an alternate installation. Remember, the trick is to squeeze the air out so there is airtight contact between hull and transducer. The impulses go through the fiberglass hull with no problem. As a matter of fact, many boats in my area now mount their depth sounder transducers in this fashion.

Before we leave this topic of thru-hulls in general, let me re-emphasize the seriousness of this subject. Don't have it brought home to you as it happened to an acquaintance of mine whose son woke him at three in the morning and asked if the water was supposed to be

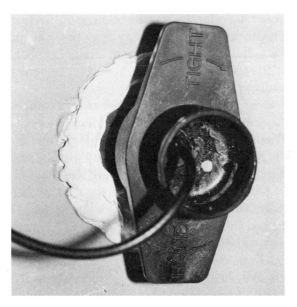

Figure 20. Transducer secured to hull with caulking compound

ankle deep in the boat. To top it off, my friend was at anchor and not snug in a marina. It seems a hose had worked loose and the gate valve that was thought to have been closed was open.

I want to complete this subject of thru-hulls with one more recommendation which will help you rest better. Put double hose clamps on all connections. Clamps can break so have a backup, and then periodically inspect them. Don't hesitate to replace one that may be questionable. After all, since a clamp does not cost much, it's cheap insurance.

Rigging

The subject of rigging, both running and standing, is concerned also with the mast, boom, and everything attached. Also, I'm making the assumption the mast will be aluminum with the boom aluminum or wood. I would think long and hard before I would buy a boat with a wooden mast. The price would really have to be attractive, and then I would replace it as soon as possible. The problem is maintenance since wood does rot. As for the wooden boom, you'll find a great many of the older boats with them, but they don't pose the maintenance problem the wooden mast does. The boom is much smaller and can be worked on with ease, not to mention the fact it's covered most of the time by the sail cover.

Structural inspections and needed repairs are our primary interest here. There's not much cosmetic work except for some painting. Let me emphasize that this is a vitally important area from a safety standpoint. It ranks second only to thru-hull fittings, and should be done as soon as possible if you have just purchased the boat.

The first order of business is to drop the mast so you can get to everything with ease. The only exception to doing this is if the mast has been dropped in the last two years and you have confidence in whatever work was done to the mast and rigging. Even under these circumstances I would still plan to drop the mast as soon as practical. Remember the the old saying, "If you want something done right, do it yourself." Well, I have another to add that's applicable here, "No one is going to look after your interests like you are."

The best time will be, of course, when you haul out to do your hull work. I mention this because often boats are hauled with the mast in place. This also could have some bearing on the yard you use. Just because a yard can haul the boat doesn't automatically mean they can drop the mast, so check this out up front.

Then again you may have bought a boat which is up on land with the mast in the spar shed. If so, take advantage of this opportunity to really give the mast and rigging a complete inspection. The fact you can take home almost everything but the mast itself will provide you with some good winter projects.

Wire Fittings. However and whenever you get the mast down, look at what you have. The first thing is to inspect thoroughly every wire, rope, and fitting attached to the mast or boom. Now how you go about this depends on your plan of action. If you intend to do it all while there in the yard, I suggest you take each individual part in turn and inspect it completely before going on to the next. For example, take the head stay and starting at the deck end, with the turnbuckle removed and using a magnifying glass, inspect the end fitting for any sign of wear, distortion, or cracks. Use a magnifying glass; you may have twenty-twenty vision, but the greater the magnification, the more you can see. Work up the wire rotating as you go; you're looking for broken strands. Mark any you find with tape. When you reach the fitting attached to the mast, remove the clevis pin, and inspect. Go on to the tang attached to the mast. If all seems okay, replace the clevis pin with a new cotter pin making sure the ends of the cotter pin are not exposed which could result in damage to your sails. Next take the wire that you have just looked at with the magnifying glass and run your hand slowly, ever so slowly, down the wire. Often there can be a broken strand that's been missed or almost impossible to see, but you'll be able to feel it with your hand. That's why you must be careful, or you'll come away with a nasty cut.

After the hand inspection of the head stay, check out the turnbuckle. Since the lower threaded jaw is usually left attached to the chain plate, remove it and put the turnbuckle together. Check for wear and cracks with special attention to any distortion. Sight along the turnbuckle to note any bending. Make sure the threads are clean and turn easily. Check the clevis pins for wear, replacing the old cotter pins with new ones.

If everything is to your satisfaction and you're confident about using the stay, then take some tape and tag it "OK." At this point you can attach the wire to the masthead or, depending on what you plan for the mast, you can put it aside. But do tag it, be it noting a problem or if OK. This gives you a ready reference so things will not fall through a crack or be overlooked.

Do every piece of rigging wire on the boat in this manner—stays, shrouds, halyards, and remember the topping lift if it's wire. Pay extra attention to the halyards because the wire will be very flexible with many more strands which mean more breaks. Usually a broken strand or two in a halyard poses no problem as far as strength is concerned, but the "fishhooks" of broken wire ends can play havoc with your hands, not to mention blood stains all over the deck and sails. See Figure 21. The contact point where the shrouds meet the end of the spreader arms should also be given extra attention.

Here I would like to bring up roller furling gear. If you have this gear, it's a recent addition to the boat and probably offers no problems. Do investigate the entire system, paying special attention to the moving parts. At the same time give a good cleaning to the parts so that they'll have less chance of soiling the sail. It's helpful to have the manufacturer's instructions when you check things out. If you

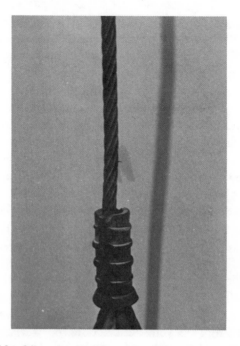

Figure 21. "Fishhook" protruding from wire halyard

don't, get in touch with the manufacturer and have him send you the information.

I'll get ahead of myself for a moment and mention the roller furling sail. Look the sail over for any indication of wear which could be caused by the furling system. If you find anything, match the sail area to the furling system and see what's causing the damage. It could be as simple as a cotter pin not closed properly. My point is to do it now, not when the mast is standing.

The masthead is next, and use your magnifying glass. Record anything questionable; don't depend on your memory. Follow up with the blocks, sheets, and winches. Much of this equipment can be taken home and checked. It makes a good project when you're not able to be at the boat.

When finished with the inspections, you can take inventory of what's to be done. Right off the bat anything that shows an existing or future problem should be replaced. If you're not sure of a particular item, don't hesitate to get a second or even third opinion. Just do yourself a favor, and ask someone who you feel knows what he's talking about. Don't overlook having fittings x-rayed; this is an excellent way to be sure if you would prefer not to replace a particular piece. Your boatyard or rigging shop should be able to have this service done or at least recommend where to start. I understand from rigging people that Mercurochrome painted on a fitting will show up cracks. Also there're now new products on the market to do the same thing.

Probably the biggest replacement you'll be faced with is a new stay or shroud. But first let me quickly remind you we're talking about serious stuff here. I mean safety, and when it comes to this subject there should be no compromise. If you feel a new forestay is in order, have one made up. We're not talking huge sums of money. For example, I replaced the forestay on my thirty-three-foot boat in August, 1983. The wire shop charged me $104 complete and ready to put on the boat. Keep in mind price will vary from location to location, but I wanted to give you some kind of feel for the cost. As I stated in the thru-hull section, if money is a problem, let something else go and do what's necessary to have a safe rig.

Here's some good news. The older fiberglass sailboats when compared to the new boats around will have a shorter mast with heavier riggings which adds up to a built-in safety margin. In other words, the older rigs, like the hulls, were built to last with plenty of extra strength. My point is even though you're dealing with, say, a fifteen-year-old boat, most or maybe all of the rigging could be in good shape. But don't compromise. If in doubt, replace.

Let me add that some fishhooks on a wire halyard don't necessarily mean you should replace the halyard. Even with a couple of broken strands, the wire should be strong enough to handle the sail. So consider cutting the protruding fishhook off just as close as possible, and then push the end back into the wire. When finished, paint with a bright color. The paint will quickly wear off from the outside of the wire, but will stay in the strands allowing you easily to locate the spot. This lets you keep an eye on the loose strand, and I hope that you do not find out the hard way that it jumped out. It will only take a few seconds to inspect the area before you hoist the sail.

Pay close attention to the turnbuckles, making sure they haven't been bent. The obvious one offers no problem; you know where you stand. If slightly bent and on a lower shroud, you may opt to keep it. On the other hand, if it took a good lick, you should at least replace the bent part. What scares me is the turnbuckle that's been smashed really hard, say, for instance, when the boat was rolled into a dock by the wake of a passing boat. If the turnbuckle was clamped in a vise and straightened, I worry about the condition of the metal where it's been bent back and forth. Try to determine as best you can if any of the turnbuckles have been abused. Just think what can happen to the forestay turnbuckle if the boat runs into the dock a few times.

Mast

You've looked at the masthead as part of the rigging. Now inspect the mast itself. Pick an end and start checking every screw and bolt for tightness. You don't want anything loose. The sail track, if you have it, should be checked for alignment and loose screws. If your mast has the groove, make sure the sail slides will run freely.

Examine the spreaders. These may be wood or aluminum. Make sure all fastenings and fittings are in good shape. If the arms are wood, make sure they're in top-notch shape with absolutely no rot. The main problem with wooden spreaders came home to me the hard way. I recall a particular boat with wooden arms that looked perfect from the deck even when using binoculars. I was planning to drop the mast later on in the summer to inspect everything, but while talking with another sailor who casually asked about the condition of the wooden spreaders, I told him they looked fine. "Yes, of course," he responded, "but what you're looking at is the underside and it always looks fine. Have you seen the tops of the arms?" The next day I went up the mast and pushed a blunt-nosed screwdriver through the wood with no trouble at all. See Figure 22. The top area had lost all protection against the weather and the wood was rotten. I had the mast down that afternoon. The point I'm making is whether you do or do not replace the wooden spreaders you need to make sure you provide plenty of protection against the sun and weather on the topside of the spreaders. Of course, if the spreaders are metal, you won't have these problems. As a matter of fact, you may want to consider replacing wood with aluminum.

Inspect the mast step. Keel-mounted masts most of the time give little trouble. Deck-mounted masts sometimes can distort the deck

Figure 22. Deteriorated wooden spreaders

and areas below the deck, so check for this. This is a place that should have been noted in the planning stage, but with the mast out you'll get a much better idea about any corrections. Unless the boat has been raced hard or abused, you'll probably not have to worry here. By today's standards the older boats were overbuilt, but to me that's a plus.

The last area to check are the chain plates. Make sure they are bolted tightly and that what they are bolted to is solidly attached to the hull. Again you shouldn't have too much to be concerned with here because of the way the older boats were put together. I'd like to emphasize that when I talk about well-constructed older boats, I don't mean every older sailboat. I'm talking about the reputable builders, many of whom are still in business. As I stated in Chapter 1, it pays to consider boats that had a good reputation with the sailing fraternity.

Lights and Electronic Gear. Lights first: each fixture should be taken apart to check for corrosion. If the light only needs to be cleaned, fine; but always replace the bulb with a new one. This can save you a trip up the mast later. If you find the fixture shot or even questionable, replace it. These lights have only one purpose: to be seen. What's not seen can be hit, so don't take any chances on a light not working when needed. While on the subject of lights, let me suggest that if your mast doesn't have spreader lights, add them. You're not talking about much money (say fifty dollars for everything), but they are convenient. And I don't mean just for walking on deck at night. You can find yourself in a sticky situation either at anchor or underway where you may wonder if that tugboat, ship, or another sailboat that's moving its anchorage really does see you. Snap on the spreader lights and you'll stand out for the whole world to see. I snap on the lights before guests step off or on the boat from a dock, not to mention when everyone is getting back to their particular boat during a rafting party. Not having spreader lights is like not having a front porch light at home.

Your mast may or may not have electronic gear on it. If it does, I recommend you take care of obvious problems like a loose mounting bracket. But unless you know what you're doing, get an expert to check out the electronic side if this is necessary. The same goes for installing any new equipment. And while on new gear—if possible, go ahead and install the masthead equipment even if you don't plan to install the deck part right away. I know in some cases this will be hard to do because the item most likely will come complete in a package. One exception that comes to mind is the radio. You can buy the aerial and wire separately; so if you plan in the future to add a radio, I suggest you go ahead and add the aerial while the mast is down. I sailed my present boat for four months with the aerial and no radio, but when I installed the radio there was nothing to it. The hard work had already been done.

All this masthead electronic gear requires wires. If you're like me and don't care for the rattling and slapping of wires inside an aluminum mast, I think I have a suggestion you may find helpful: Tape twelve-inch strips of soft cushion foam to the wires every four or five feet of wire. See Figure 23. The strips are flexible enough to get by any partial obstruction, like bolts through the mast to secure the spreader sockets. The foam never allows the wire to touch the inside of the mast, which is a built-in safety feature, since all sorts of things, like screws, project into the mast. The foam will do a good job of keeping the wire from banging against these sharp edges and eating

Figure 23. Foam to keep wire quiet inside mast

into the insulation. And believe me, it's quiet. Keep in mind that if you have internal halyards, they will have to be taken into account.

As far as the boom is concerned, follow the general procedures just discussed where applicable. Check all fittings, paying attention to the gooseneck and roller furling gear. Since the aluminum boom may have some internal wires and fittings for the outhaul, make sure all this is in good working order.

This is as good a place as any to mention internal halyards in the mast. Not many older boats will have them but if your boat does, make sure you remove everything that's usually not seen, and inspect for wear. One bit of advice: When you take out a halyard, you'll have to tie on a leader line so you can pull the halyard back in place. Don't use some cheap string here; use something that won't break easily. Then after you've tied the knot, tape the ends down. A lot of this small line is very slick and knots seem to untie at will and at the worst possible time.

Painting the Mast. The last segment on our subject of mast, rigging, and booms is strictly cosmetic. If you don't intend to paint your mast and boom, you can skip this section. But if you do or aren't sure, I hope I can help you.

My personal preference is a painted mast and boom. It looks better and you, your crew, the halyards, and most importantly the sails will stay cleaner. Unpainted aluminum masts and booms, especially the older ones that you're dealing with, seem to get black streaks everywhere.

The main objection to painting is, of course, the maintenance. Sailors will say never paint your mast because once the paint starts flaking off, you're faced with a lot of work to keep the mast and boom looking good. I agree. The trick is to keep the paint from coming off the aluminum. Now here you have two choices. Have a professional paint your mast and boom with one of the new superb paints which will stay on the metal. The problem here is it will cost you a bundle. I've found a better way which will do the job, and the cost will be around $30 (for a 45-foot aluminum mast) and will include the paint brushes. The Rust-Oleum products include an undercoat material for use on aluminum and other metals, called Galvinoleum Undercoat Clear Blue Tint. This is no highly technical space-age stuff that takes all kinds of experience to use. You simply follow the directions which tell you how to clean the aluminum. Then with a new paint brush, paint on the undercoat which is clear with a slight blue tint. I recommend a new brush because a used, but cleaned brush may still have a chemical residue left that could react with the undercoat. A cheap throw-away brush is perfect.

When the undercoat is first applied, it does not seem to flow in an even thickness which gives the impression it will keep the paint from lying flat. Don't worry about this. The end result will be fine. After brushing on, follow the directions for drying time which, by the way, isn't long. The drying time will vary (depending on the weather and temperature), but my point here is to make you aware you'll be able to put your first coat of paint on the same day you apply the undercoat. After you apply this undercoat, you use Rust-Oleum paint. The color is up to you, but frankly I prefer white. It just looks right on a sailboat. After reading the directions, apply the first coat, using a good quality brush. Be careful not to put the paint on too thick. What you want is a thin coat with no runs or high build up. Don't be disappointed with how the paint looks. It will look thin and the blue tint will show through in many places. Let it dry for twenty-four hours, no matter how dry the paint feels after a few hours have passed. Then add the second coat which does a better job of covering, and let it dry 24 hours. Then apply the third coat and maybe a fourth and even a fifth, always allowing the paint to dry twenty-four hours between coats. What you're doing is slowly building up the thickness with many thin layers. As the layers add up, you'll notice the paint lying smoother with the last couple of applications giving you a smooth surface. The end result is a top-notch paint job, and the paint will not start to flake off after a year or two. Certainly it will chip, but touching up is a simple matter.

You may find it interesting that Rusto-Oleum paint is primarily a hardware store item, and easy to buy. Note Figure 24, a Rust-Oleum-painted mast, which is four years old on a boat that stays in the water all year.

The process I've just outlined applies both for the aluminum boom as well as for the mast. Here I'd like to say that the brush lends

Figure 24. Painted mast

itself very well to painting around all those fittings you may not want to remove before you paint. Of course, you're going to find there'll be fittings that seem to have welded themselves to the mast and are impossible to take off unless you drill out the holding screws. So for whatever the reason you leave fittings on the mast, don't worry about painting around them.

How about the wooden boom? Well there's nothing special here to do. Matter of fact, I use the same Rust-Oleum paint that I used on the aluminum mast, leaving off the undercoat. And let me quickly add the same many thin layers of paint apply here as well as in the metal paint job.

Do make it a point to remove all the fittings from the wooden boom. There will be no trouble backing the screws out of the wood, and you want to make sure the wood is not rotten. Pay attention to rot in and around screw holes. You don't want a fitting pulling loose. A small amount of rot that can easily be repaired is okay. But if it looks like a major job to put the wooden boom in good shape, I suggest it be replaced.

If you chose to keep the wooden boom, you have the opportunity here to keep alive an old, traditional yachting look by varnishing the wood. Before you discard this idea because you may think that's the very reason you have a fiberglass boat with an aluminum mast—so you won't have to varnish—hear me out. First, the boom is easy to work on either on the boat or off, and second, sun is what destroys varnish, and since most of the time the boom is protected by the sail cover, once it's varnished there's no reason why it should become a maintenance burden. Frankly, I like the look a little varnish gives to a boat. Remember you can always paint later if you need to.

By now you're probably thinking all this material on topsides, underbody, mast, and riggings is somewhat overwhelming. It does read like there is a tremendous amount of work to do and perhaps you're wondering just what you've let yourself in for. I want you to sit back and relax. Believe me it's nowhere near as bad as it reads. To check everything on your mast and boom once it's down should take no more than a Saturday morning. To paint one layer of paint on a fifty-foot mast will take somewhere around an hour. Replacing a thru-hull for the head is no more than a two-hour job under the worst of conditions.

For the most part all you'll be doing is inspecting, and each place or thing that's checked doesn't mean work has to be done. As a matter of fact, I suggest you look on the material covered so far as simply a checklist to follow so that nothing is overlooked. And as a checklist, it won't take a great deal of time.

Unless you bought a complete wreck, which I would advise against, you have a usable boat. Oh, sure, there are a lot of little things wrong which need fixing, but the bottom line is you have a boat that can be used and enjoyed. Therefore, the amount of work that you choose to do will be determined by what you decide is necessary to make the boat safe and then by the extent of upgrading and refurbishing you plan to do. The key here is that you're in charge—not the boat or this book. So again sit back, relax, and let's move along to the next chapter.

Four

DECK AND COCKPIT

The deck area is where you're going to spend most of your time when using the boat. The deck, cabin top, and cockpit are what you'll be sitting, walking, sliding, leaning, lying, and stumbling on. So the very first thing you want to do is clean them up. I'm talking about plain old soap and water with a little Ajax thrown in when needed. This goes for any unvarnished teak trim that's turned gray. It's dirty also; so scrub it clean.

Structural inspections are the next order of business. The two areas we're interested in directly affect you and everyone on the boat. Lifelines, pulpits, and handrails are on the boat for one reason and one reason only: to keep people from falling overboard. I strongly recommend you give these items the same attention you would thru-hulls and riggings. If anything is even remotely questionable, replace it. I'm sure everyone with sailing experience has had the occasion when the only thing which kept someone from going overboard was something substantial to grab.

Make sure all pulpits and stanchions are securely fixed to a plate that's bolted through the deck with a back-up plate. Check all nuts and tighten if necessary. Inspect lifeline wire and fittings with emphasis on where the wire passes through the stanchions. See Figure 25. There's a lot of wear and tear at this point. If you find everything okay, then give things a few good jerks. Don't worry about breaking anything. Let it break now, not when the wind is gusting to 30 knots with heavy seas running.

One more thing about pulpits and lifelines. If your boat doesn't have both bow and stern pulpits with lifelines along the deck, I strongly recommend you add them, as a matter of top priority.

Figure 25. Lifeline showing wear

Chances are the handrails on the top of the cabin are wood—and teak at that. On the older boat this can present a problem. As a teak handrail is scrubbed and cleaned over the years, it becomes smaller due to the surface wood being removed. See Figure 26. This causes you to end up with a thin handrail that can break when a load is applied. If your handrails look unsafe, replace them.

And, while on the subject of replacing handrails, I think it's a good idea to always use a handrail that you can wrap your hand around. There are some in use where you hook your fingers in a groove on the back side of the handrail. This type of handrail is nowhere near as safe as the one you can lock your hand on.

Next see how the handrail is secured to the cabin top. It should be bolted through; if it is not, I suggest that you secure it properly.

The last structural area to check includes the Genoa track, main sheet traveller if you have one, pad eyes, blocks attached to the deck, and last, but certainly not least, the winches. The most important thing you can do here is make sure all of this equipment is properly secured by through bolting. I don't think you'll have a problem on most of the better built older boats, but check anyway.

Figure 26. Handrails, old and new

Next give everything, including your sheets, a good visual inspection for any wear. Make sure the blocks and fairleads don't have bent or twisted parts that may have caused metal fatigue. Replace where you feel necessary. Again I don't think you'll find much here to bother you unless something has really been abused, but it pays to check.

The internal workings of older winches, when compared with what's on the market now, are rather simple. Though not made of many parts, what's there is spring loaded. Be very careful when dismantling the winch. Let me pass on a tip that can save you the grief of seeing a pawl fly overboard when you lift the drum. After removing the drum holding screw or screws, wrap the winch with a cloth. Then slowly lift the drum and push the ends of the cloth under the drum. Feel through the cloth with your fingers and get the small parts under the drum into the folds of the cloth. Then lift the whole thing to untangle and sort out the parts.

I suggest you use the cloth method no matter how familiar you are with a particular winch; you never know which way a pawl will jump. Use it even when the boat is on land as it's easy to lose something small on the boatyard ground.

You're now at the end of the deck structural items which should be inspected. From here on you'll be looking at the cosmetic side of the deck and cockpit. Until now, you've been mainly concerned with safety and hull integrity while the cosmetic areas discussed had to do with the topside color and painting the mast. But now we're getting into the area of personal preference where you can do something because you want to, not because you should, or have to. The questions that determine what you do are: is it functional? and does it look good?

Let's start with the deck in general. On the older fiberglass sailboat the deck most likely will be in need of some repairs. See Figure 27. Minor work is the rule, but you can also have a serious repair job as indicated in Figure 28. Or the deck can be generally unsightly as Figure 29 shows.

The first order of business is to make the needed repairs. The small ding marks can be easily taken care of by sanding. Knock down

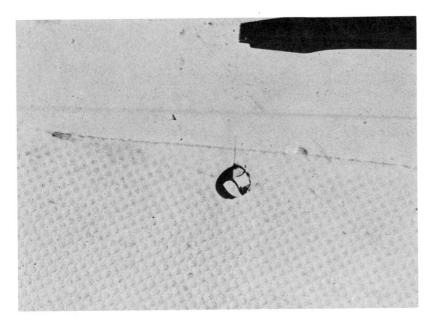

Figure 27. Void in deck gelcoat

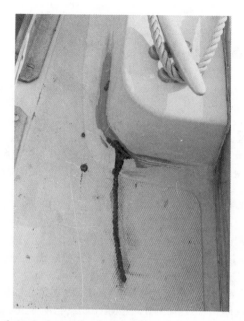

Figure 28. Crack in deck repaired with filler

Figure 29. Dinged up bridge deck

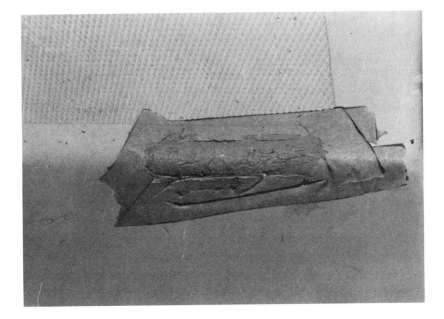

Figure 30. Deck repair filler

the edges with a coarse grit and follow with 400 grit wet and dry sandpaper. You can find wet and dry paper at your local hardware or auto parts store. Make sure you use it wet when smoothing out the dings. Sometimes a small amount of filler is necessary to make the ding fair into the deck surface properly, a subject to be covered shortly.

The larger cracks and holes are all going to require a filler before they can be sanded. Before the filler can be used, the holes and cracks must be cleaned. Use whatever works, be it sandpaper, knife scraper, or mabe a chisel, to remove loose material and rough up the fiberglass. Then clean thoroughly with acetone, which is a solvent associated with fiberglass. There are several filler materials you can use, but the one that is the easiest to use when the area is to be painted is body putty from the auto parts store. It's made to do exactly what you're using it for—to fill a void, then be sanded and painted. This material will dry hard enough to sand in a few minutes, so you don't have to lose time waiting. Note Figure 30.

You can use a fiberglass filler material if you so desire which has the added advantage of allowing a gelcoat to be used to match color if you don't plan to paint. Since fiberglass filler will require more sanding, don't expect to give it a couple of passes and get good results. There are also good epoxy fillers on the market.

A particular special-use filler that I like is Marine-Tex. When dry, it's very strong and can be sanded with ease. I recommend this when you have a situation where extra strength is necessary and yet you want the final result to look good. And this thought leads us to our last repair problem which is the badly damaged deck area (see Figure 28.).

While the large surface split does look bad, it nevertheless can be repaired. The really serious trouble is caused when water is allowed to penetrate the core material directly under the deck. For good visual evidence of this note Figures 31 and 32 which show deteriorated balsa wood core removed from under area shown in Figure 28.

In this case you would have to cut away the bottom layer of glass and remove all the rotten wood, and then allow the area to dry out. It's also a good idea to cover the openings in the deck with tape or plastic to keep out rainwater because it can sometimes take weeks to get this kind of area dry. Once it is dry, scrape off all the old wood until you're down to good fiberglass and clean with acetone.

Next, using fiberglass cloth and resin, build up the area under the deck surface allowing the fiberglass to overlap the exposed good core material. This will add strength to the deck area that will feel spongy without the core material and bottom layer of fiberglass while at the same time sealing off the balsa core from any further penetration of moisture.

This type of repair can be messy because you're working on an underneath surface. The trick to keeping the fiberglass in place is to have it set up very quickly. My answer to this is to use a hair dryer to warm up the area before work starts, and then use the dryer to speed up the process as you proceed. Even with quick set up time, it's still a messy job, so I suggest you use cloth tape and not strips cut from a larger piece of fiberglass material. The tape will cost a little more but is much easier to use, and the end result looks better. The cut pieces unravel along the edges and in short order you have long strands all over the work area. The tape gives you a finished edge which does not

Figure 31. Deteriorated balsa deck core

Figure 32. Deteriorated balsa deck core shown from a different angle

unravel. After the underneath has been repaired, the surface damage is fixed with Marine-Tex and sanded for painting.

One bit of advice here on using any type of filler. Read the directions and then follow exactly what they tell you. Also here's a tip you should find useful. When using something for the first time, make a trial run with the material and familiarize yourself with it. Don't learn as you go along; there's too much room for costly errors.

Once all the deck repairs are completed, you're back where you were with the topsides—the kind of paint to use and who's going to do the work. You may have already opted to have the deck painted by a professional when the topsides are painted. Along with the painting you may have decided to contract out the repairs and preparation. But let me remind you it won't be cheap. This type of work is almost all labor so I recommend you have an estimate before you proceed.

A good compromise is to work out a deal where you do all the repairs and preparation and then the painter comes in to apply the paint. This is an excellent way to get a professional job at a reasonable cost, although you'll have to be willing to put out the elbow grease.

If you intend to do your own painting or at least the preparation, it's very important to know exactly what kind of paint is to be applied. Many of the new coatings can require something special during the preparation so it will pay to do your homework ahead of time. I might add this applies for the topsides as well as the deck area.

Now when it comes down to what paint to use, you'll have plenty to choose from. Just as with the topsides, your decision should be based on your ability, time, and available money. But I'd like to add one thought. Painting the deck for the most part is working on a flat surface. The exception, of course, are the cabin sides, whereas the topsides are a vertical surface and much harder to work with because of the need to control runs and sags. The deck's flat surface lends itself to the weekend painter.

My point is, don't let this idea of painting the deck overwhelm you. Give it some thought and if you feel you want to do it, go ahead. Also I'd like to add if you do opt to paint the deck yourself, pick a paint that's easy to use and doesn't force you to maintain a certain pace. You set the speed of application with any good grade of regular marine paint which lets you do a neat job, whereas with some of the new two-part paints you may be pushed with the application because of the drying rate.

If you decide to do the work, I have one last suggestion. Use a good paint brush, and make sure it's designed to be used with the particular paint in question. If your marine or hardware store doesn't offer you a decent selection, I suggest you visit a paint store. You want a straight edge brush and one with an angled edge which gives you a pointed end for tight places. While at the store, also pick up some good brush cleaner that will do a proper job of cleaning. Under no conditions try to use a cheap throw-away brush. These have their place, but not for this type of painting.

Painting does create one drawback that has to be taken into account. Fiberglass decks have moulded in nonskid surfaces, and the paint will have a tendency to fill and level out these surfaces with the result being loss of good traction while walking on deck. You may want to paint a small area of your nonskid and check the results when dry. If you still have enough nonskid after painting to give good footing, then you're okay. But if not, then I strongly advise you add nonskid sand to the paint. This will give you excellent traction, though it's hard on the seat of your pants sometimes. Your boatyard will be able to furnish you with the proper type of sand.

Another nonskid surface you can look into is a mattelike material that is stuck right to the deck where needed. I know you've seen nonskid strips in showers before and this is the same thing, only for boats. It comes in strips and larger sections, and again your boatyard or marine supply firm can help you here.

On-Deck Wood. The older, more traditional sailboat will have more wood than the newer boats. When that wood becomes unsightly and shows neglect, it badly detracts from the general appearance. The older boat will have wood cockpit coamings, toe rails, handrails, tiller, and companionway crib boards. It may also have assorted hatches, dorade boxes, cockpit grates, and so on. With all this wood I'm sure work will be required. Your main guidelines concerning the on-deck wood should be two questions: what will the end product look like? Will I be satisfied with the end result?

I'm making the assumption the on-deck wood is teak except for the tiller. Teak is widely used, durable, easy to work, takes a beautiful finish, and is the accepted on-deck wood of sailors and the yachting industry. Teak, in general, even after being allowed to weather to a dirty gray-black color, can be brought back with cleaning, sanding, and refinishing.

Your first step to refurbishing the wood is to remove all the trim from the boat. The only exception is the toe rail. Most of the time you can get along without removing toe rails except for a damaged section. It's a major job to remove the entire toe rail and if the toe rail does not leak and is not too badly damaged, I suggest you refinish it in place. However, everything else should come off.

I'd like to make you aware of a basic rule of refurbishing. *What goes on will come off,* and this applies especially for wood trim. Most of the trim fasteners will be obvious, but there's always that puzzle that makes you scratch your head. My experience has been that often the fasteners will come from the inside and enter the wood from the back. Another place that presents a problem is where screws are covered with wood plugs, and weathered to the point the plugs blend right in with the trim and disappear. Most of the time cleaning where you think the screws should be will be enough to show up the plug.

After you've taken out all of the fasteners and before removing the particular piece of trim, I want you to always think about a second basic rule of refurbishing. *Never force anything.* When you run out that last screw, and the trim pops right off in your hand, that is great. But if it doesn't and after a gentle tug it's still in place, don't grab your largest screwdriver, pound it between the wood and deck, and start prying. Go back over the screws and check thoroughly. Most of the time you'll find where you've missed one. However, you can have the case where the wood is held by bedding compound, and you may have to apply force. Fine. All I'm saying is know that you have removed all fasteners before you start.

It's very important for the trim to be removed in order to do a good refurbishing job. And along with this, it's just as vital to remove the wood in the best condition possible, even the pieces since it's obvious they must be replaced. See Figure 33. The damaged trim becomes the template when cutting and shaping the replacement. If it is possible, work with a belt sander on a workbench when you refinish the pieces of trim you plan to place back on the boat. Doing so will make the difference between a passable job and a first-rate one. I also believe you should plan on doing the trim as a single project.

Figure 33. Split cockpit coaming

Once you're geared up to do the refinishing, your job will go faster when you belt sand everything at one time, go on to the hand work, and then finish with your protective coating. When you piecemeal the work, half your time is spent getting ready to work and cleaning up afterwards.

Let's see just what you have. Any split or cracked teak should be replaced; that's quite obvious. The next step is to consider the not so obvious. With teak that has seen years of service, the grain may be noticeably standing out and after sanding smooth, the wood will be too thin either to look in proportion to its size, or strong enough to do its job. Take the cockpit coaming, for example. After sanding, it may look razor thin once it is in place because of its length. At the same time the coaming has a job to do. People use it for comfort and since all kinds of equipment are attached to it, its strength is important. In this situation I'd replace the coaming. Now the cockpit coaming will be your most difficult case because one bad side will dictate replacing both sides in order to have the cockpit look right. The coamings will be your two largest sections to work with, therefore costing more. One word of advice. If you do anticipate replacing the coaming, select the new teak yourself and try to get the two sides from the same board. Teak boards can come in large sizes too. If you take the time to shop around, I'm sure you'll find what you need. Along with this advice, decide what is to be replaced and purchase all the teak you need at one time so you can make sure all the trim will match in color and texture.

When you start to cut out the new pieces, use a saber saw, and for best results with the cut, use a blade with small teeth. I prefer a metal-cutting blade with fourteen teeth to the inch. The teeth of a regular wood-cutting blade have a tendency to splinter the edge of the cut on the up stroke. The wood blade allows you to cut faster which increases the splintering and makes it possible to make mistakes. The metal blade gives you a clean cut and moves slower through the teak. It'll take longer to make a cut, but after all it's only minutes, and the end result is well worth the extra few minutes.

When outlining the old trim on the new wood, make sure your pencil doesn't become too blunt. You don't want it so sharp the line cannot be seen, but at the same time you don't want a line that's an eighth of an inch wide either. This can throw off the cut just enough to make a joint not have a clean neat fit.

Always cut on the outside edge of the line; that way you're adding just a touch more wood to the piece you're working on all the way around. Remember you can sand off any extra, but it is impossible to add. For the flat surfaces use a belt sander, being careful not to dig into the surface. For this reason I suggest the final sanding be with a small vibrating sander or hand sand with a wood block. Fit the sandpaper grit to the job you're doing. Number 50 or 80 is okay to knock down high spots and level out the surface with a belt sander, but end up with 120 grit for the last sanding to get a smooth surface. For vibrating or hand sanding to finish with, I recommend 150 and 220 grit. Never, never use a disk sander for this kind of woodwork. A disk sander has its place, but not here.

A wood rasp or shaper is the best tool to round off edges, for example, the rounded edge on the top of the cockpit coaming. Once you have the general shape, finish off with hand sanding. It's easy to do in this case because all you do is cup your hand over the shaped wood holding the sandpaper and go to it. One bit of advice here; use a pair of heavy work gloves so you won't ram a splinter in your hand as you sand back and forth along the rounded edge. Even if you find gloves hard to work in, which I do, you'll have no trouble using them here because all you're doing is using your hand to hold the sandpaper around the edge as you sand.

After the new trim is sanded, take it to the boat and check for fit. Don't be surprised if some minor adjustments are necessary. Take your tools along and do what's needed to make a good fit. Most of the time it will involve just a little sanding. When the fit suits you, drill what holes are needed for the fasteners.

Now, you have two choices: finish the trim before you install it, or install the trim and finish it on the boat. My suggestion is to finish the wood while it is off the boat. Believe me, you can do a much better job whether you use varnish or teak oil. You are, of course, eager after all this work to start putting things back together. You want to see what that new coaming is going to look like, and the idea of taking it back home and waiting until next Saturday is too much to ask. Do it anyway: the end result will make you glad you did. Let me add also to seal the areas that won't be seen. This will help keep moisture from penetrating the wood.

So far we've talked about new teak. Now we'll tackle the old teak that you plan to refinish and use. The first thing you'll notice is how the grain is standing out. This will have to be sanded smooth. Again the belt sander is the best tool with say number 50 grit. Start out sanding at right angles to the grain. This allows you to quickly knock the grain down to a level surface. Care must be taken though because once the grain is smoothed over you don't want to sand at right angles and mark the entire area with deep scratches.

Now change over to a 100 grit paper and sand with the grain and finish up with 150 and 220 grit using the vibrator or hand block. The beautiful thing about teak is no matter how bad it looks, with a little work it can be made to look like a million. Next, sand the edges by hand, using the same sandpaper sequence. Remember to use your work gloves here. Then since you'll have no trouble installing the trim, go ahead and finish with what you prefer.

I think here's a good place to look at the type of finishes to use on teak that's exposed to the elements. Your first choice is to use nothing and periodically clean the wood with a teak cleaner. I personally don't care for this and to my way of thinking you're slowly scrubbing the wood away. Your second choice is to use a teak oil and keep the wood oiled as needed. The oiled teak does look good, but it requires attention. Your third choice is to use that old accepted standby—varnish. To me varnish gives teak an absolutely beautiful finish but it does require attention; and if it ever gets away from you, it can be a bear of a job sanding. Your fourth choice is a product called Deks Olje. It's a type of teak oil which doesn't require sanding between coats. You clean the teak and apply the Deks Olje and just keep adding coats. The trick is to get a good buildup; and when it needs some freshing up, just brush on with no sanding. I've used this product and like it. But there are some drawbacks. Deks Olje will stain your deck, and it takes a strong solvent to get it up. It also turns the teak a dark varnishlike color which some people don't like. And it takes many coats to get a good buildup which requires some labor on your part. None of these objections are all that bad to me; after all, the other products have drawbacks as well.

I guess I like Deks Olje for the simple reason that it works for me. My toe rail has no less than twenty coats, and all I do in the spring is give it a couple more coats with no sanding, and it looks good. It is tedious to apply because it's like an oily stain and runs easily. But once you have a good buildup, it'll give good service. I might add a good buildup is ten or more coats!

The real problem with all these wood treatments is the sun causes them to deteriorate. Keep the sun off the wood when the boat is not being used, and the coatings will last much longer and look better. This leads us to our next subject: protecting the wood trim from the sun.

Sun Covers. I'm envious of one thing in particular our powerboat friends have over sailors. They can keep their boats under cover when not in use during the summer. Of course this isn't practical for a sailboat so the next best thing is sun covers for your wood trim. See Figures 34 and 35.

I keep my handrails, cockpit coamings, and lazaret hatch under cover when the boat is not in use. The teak thus shows no damage from exposure to the elements and the only maintenance required for the past three years has been a couple of coats of Deks Olje to freshen up the appearance. It makes absolutely no difference what finish is on the wood. Keep the sun off, and the finish will last for years. There will be some pieces of trim that are not really worth the trouble to

Figure 34. Sun covers

Figure 35. Larger sun covers for wood trim

cover up. I suggest you concentrate on the larger areas like cockpit coamings, handrails, crib boards, and tiller.

You have two choices when it comes down to getting the covers made. You do it, or have them made by a professional. Let's look at the easy way out first. You want to contact a sailmaker or a specialist in boat tops. Meet with who will be doing the work at the boat so the extent of the job can be determined and the necessary measurements taken. That's all there is to it, except of course reaching for your checkbook.

Now for your second option, which is making the covers yourself. Let me quickly add that these covers are simple to construct because for the most part you're dealing with flat surfaces which only need sewing around the edges.

The sun covers should be made of the same cloth that sail covers are made from because the sail cover is designed to do exactly what you want the sun cover to do protect from the sun's rays. Try to match the color of your sail cover if possible; it'll look better. You should have no trouble buying the material. The sailmaker or boat top specialist can supply you. A good marine store can get what is needed if it's not already in stock, and there are a number of mail-order firms which supply cloth goods. Your main effort will be to check around for the best deal. I'd recommend you buy locally if you can for the convenience.

As for materials, all you need is the cloth, thread, and snaps. A few minutes on your boat with a tape will give you the amount of cloth needed. Some thought should be given to the thread though because of the type of sewing machine you plan to use. I assume we're talking about the everyday home variety of sewing machine. This will be different from the heavy-duty machines the professionals use, hence chances are the home type machine may have trouble handling the heavier threads. From personal experience I've found the home sewing machine gives no trouble with the sail cover cloth. As for thread, I have used regular polyester that the machine is designed to use. There is some argument the polyester thread won't hold up as long as the commercial grade, but I feel this is no serious drawback. If the thread starts to give way after a few years, just take the covers home and run them through the sewing machine again.

There's one thing you can do here that gives you the best of both worlds. After you have sewed everything together, take the covers to a professional and pay him to resew the covers using the heavy-duty thread.

As far as snaps are concerned, what you want are button snaps and the tool to install them. The tool can be a small grommet setter or a set of pliers. While the professional will have the snaps, I don't think they'll have the setting tool for sale. Your best bet here is a well-stocked marine store or mail-order firm. This tool is not expensive, and the snaps are very reasonable, something in the neighborhood of 20 cents apiece.

The snaps are very easy to add to the covers, and the snaps that are fixed to the deck are simply screwed in. As a matter of fact, I'm sure you'll find many uses for these snaps once you buy the tool and get a little experience using it.

Listed below are four types of sun covers you may want to consider. (Two of them, the tiller and handrails, have drawings with instructions.)

Tiller: (Figure 36)

Handrails: (Figure 37)

Crib boards and companionway: (Figure 38)

Cockpit coamings: (Figure 39)

Note Figures 38, 39, and 40. As you can see, there's nothing very complicated here. Once you learn how to turn down and hem the edge and sew together two pieces you can make any sort of sun cover. I think it's a good idea to practice if you intend to do your own sewing, and learning to use a sewing machine is simple.

There is a difference between the homemade variety of sun covers and those made by someone skilled in the trade. The most obvious difference is the finishing details and to a lesser degree, the fit. I know you want the finished product to look good, but you can only expect so much.

I'll tell you the same thing an old construction superintendent told me years ago when I was helping him with a building foundation. "That's as good as you're gonna get it. We ain't building a Swiss watch." So if the covers do the job and look all right generally speaking, then don't worry about the small mistakes in detail. After all, they're put away when the boat is being used and no one sees them.

Hatches. On the older boat there's no telling what kind of hatches you'll have. They might be original, brand-new, or anywhere in

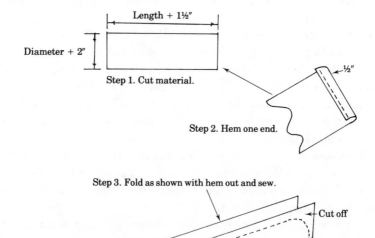

Length + 1½"

Diameter + 2"

Step 1. Cut material.

½"

Step 2. Hem one end.

Step 3. Fold as shown with hem out and sew.

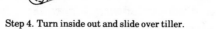

Cut off

Step 4. Turn inside out and slide over tiller.

Figure 36. Tiller cover

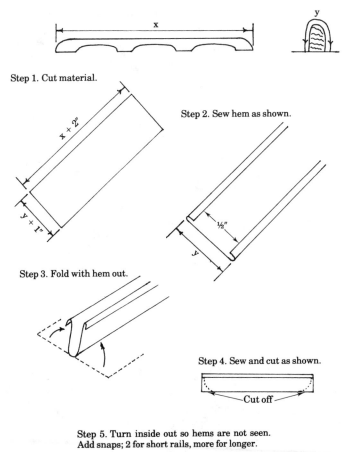

Step 1. Cut material.

Step 2. Sew hem as shown.

Step 3. Fold with hem out.

Step 4. Sew and cut as shown.

Cut off

Step 5. Turn inside out so hems are not seen.
Add snaps; 2 for short rails, more for longer.

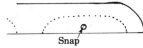

Snap

Figure 37. Handrail cover

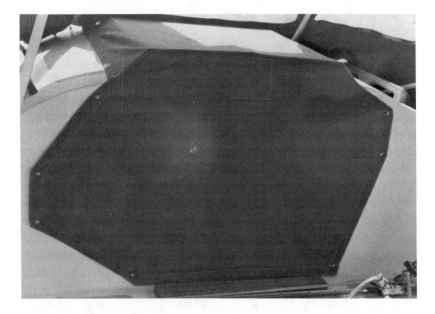

Figure 38. Companionway cover

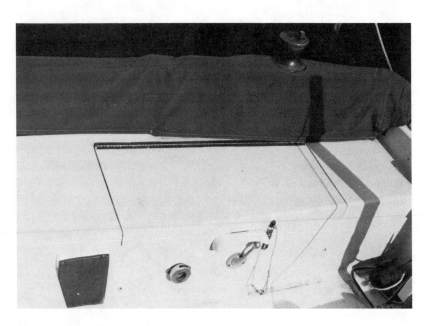

Figure 39. Coaming cover

Figure 40. Instrument covers

between. Replacing hatches will be covered in Ventilation, Chapter 10, and I recommend you read this chapter before you do anything about your hatches.

If you intend to use what you have, inspect your hatches for leaks and broken hardware. Make sure the latches and hinges are in good working order; if they are not, then I suggest you replace them.

As for the leaks, they can range from simple, which a little sealant can fix up, to major, which means tearing out and replacing all the wood trim. The only advice I can offer here is to do what must be done to meet your needs.

However, I do have one suggestion that may help as far as the cosmetic side is concerned. If you have a usable hatch which doesn't look very good, consider covering it with a sun cover. The sun cover will hide the unsightly hatch and at the same time dress up the boat in general.

The Cockpit Area. The cockpit is the most used area of the entire boat. It's where most of the on-deck action takes place whether you're sailing or just watching a beautiful sunset. And because of this, you want the cockpit to be safe, comfortable, and pleasing to the eye.

The very first thing to do in the cockpit is to empty all the lockers. Get all the gear and sails out so all you have is bare fiberglass and partitions. If possible, try to get all this equipment away from the boat so you don't spend your time always moving things that are in your way. Once the lockers are empty, your next chore is to clean the space thoroughly. Start with removing any bits and pieces that may clog a vacuum cleaner now or bilge pump later. Use whatever does the job, including your bare hands. After this, give all the spaces a good going-over with the vacuum cleaner. Then give the areas a good scrubbing with warm water and a strong grease-cutting household detergent, using a scrub brush. Make it a point to try to use warm water. It simply does a much better cleaning job and it's easier on your hands. If there's hot water nearby, fine; but in the case there's not, I can pass on several tips for getting warm water.

You know about solar shower bags I'm sure. Well, just put one in the sun and in a while you'll have your warm water. Another method to get warm water is to bring it with you from home. Fill some jugs with hot water and then wrap with an old blanket for insulation. This will work fine unless you have to drive a long distance or the day is extremely cold. And last, don't forget you can use your galley stove to heat water.

When you're scrubbing the lockers, remember the bottom side of the deck and seats. Use plenty of detergent with several scrubbings and rinsings. As for rinsings, a hose is best because the water is under pressure and can be sprayed over the entire area. All this cleaning water is going to end up in the bilge, but don't worry. The soapy water will help clean your bilge. Just keep an eye on the water level and pump when necessary.

Once the lockers are clean, you can concentrate on getting them organized. The first thing to consider is adding items which will have to be painted. This way when you do paint, everything is covered at one time.

One addition I especially like is installing a floor in the bottom of the cockpit lockers. Now I don't mean something that's going to rob you of space. Cockpit lockers all slope inboard and all loose or small gear will gravitate to the bottom. This means all these various items end up wedged in the space where the vertical partition meets the bottom of the locker. I don't think the new wide body sailboats quite have this problem to the same extent as the older boats do. Generally speaking, the older boats will have less beam making the slope in the bottom of the lockers steeper. The end result is no matter what you want from the locker, it's always down in this low area; and as you push something aside, something else slides down to frustrate you.

The way to eliminate this problem is to add the floor I mentioned. Just a few inches wide is all you need and the small amount of space you lose is not a bad trade-off. See Figure 41.

The next thing to think about after the floor is doing everything possible to keep the gear off the floor. Hammock nets are very handy storage items and you can see at a glance what they hold. Try to hang your sheets and dock lines in some manner. Usually the vertical partition in the locker lends itself to hooks or pegs for this job. Also you can attach a strip of wood to the underside of the seat locker cover and tie your lines to this. There's no denying the lines are convenient when the locker top is lifted, but there's one small drawback. Most seat locker tops only open around ninety degrees so the weight of the lines will always be trying to close the top. You can take care of this by adding a loop of shock cord to the underside of the cover and simply loop the cord over a winch or cleat. Matter of fact, add this loop of shock cord even if you don't hang your lines from the bottom of the cover. It's no fun getting banged on the head while looking for something.

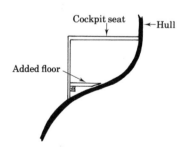

Figure 41. Cockpit locker floor

While we're talking about locker covers, I have another thought to add. One thing you'll notice about the older sailboat if you haven't already done so is the better grade of hardware. Locker latches are real yacht grade and designed not only to secure but to do so tightly to eliminate rattles. In the case of a seat locker with a hinged cover, the designer may have done too good a job. Why, you ask? If the top slams down, the upper part of the latch comes down with enough force to engage the bottom part and lock. And you may find yourself as a friend did—locked in a seat locker. It happened in the middle of the week when the marina was deserted, and he waited three hours before help came.

At the same time this tendency to lock means you always have to open the cover by lifting the latch. This can also be inconvenient. The solution is easy. Turn the latch over so the moving part is on the bottom and hanging down out of the way. Then it can easily be engaged by lifting in place.

Boxes make handy storage places for all those small items of gear and are easy to install when you have a flat surface to work with, like a floor area. Now I mean a box that you can make with some thin plywood and screws, nothing really fancy, but design it to fit the space it will occupy. Chances are the floor in the seat lockers will only be three or four inches wide, so make the box narrow but long. And don't forget to add some strips of wood to the floor so the box won't slide around and yet will be easy to remove. A couple of holes with line run through to make handles is nice when you want to lift the box out. Don't make this box too deep: two or three inches is fine.

Older sailboats have lazarets which you can compare to your garage at home. It's a catch-all area and always seems to be in need of straightening. A small floor area here with a couple of boxes is extremely useful. See Figure 42. There are always those messy items which can be difficult to store. I use a box for all cleaning items and another for stove fuel, engine oil, and the like. When the box gets a little messy, I take it out and clean it. The real advantage is that all these cans and bottles aren't rolling around in the lazaret. Just imagine what a can of oil is capable of doing if it develops a leak while you're sailing in heavy air.

Sometimes it's difficult to plan ahead and organize all your cockpit storage. Don't let this worry you. Nothing we're talking about is a large project. Even if you're not a hundred percent sold on an idea,

Figure 42. Storage boxes

don't hesitate to try it. You'll never be sure until you do. At the same time ideas that should work great in theory may not when actually tried. There'll be a certain amount of trial and error, but your main guideline should be everything in as convenient a place as possible.

After you have made your additions, the next step is to sand in preparation to painting. Here again we're not building a watch; the painted area won't be on display. You just want the surface sanded enough so the new paint will adhere. Now you can use a disk sander to speed the job up, because it works well on a curved surface. One word of caution. Most of the time the hull area of a locker will have a waffle texture created by the heavy glass fabric used in constructing the hull. Don't sand this smooth when trying to remove the old paint. You'll be removing a lot of glass and weakening the hull.

If you're using a disk sander, lightly sand the tops of the waffle texture first and then come back and hand sand, using just your hand and 80 grit paper. The idea is your hand will press the paper into the waffle low places and rough up, not remove, the old paint.

Chances are you'll not have to sand the entire locker area if you did a good job of cleaning. Any loose paint will have to be removed, bare spots feathered in, and large areas sanded to take the new paint. You will still have the hard-to-get-at places and you'll just have to make a decision about them.

The paint can be any good grade of marine enamel. From experience I've found that a quart will give you a one-coat cover in the seat lockers and lazaret of a thirty-five-foot boat. I would suggest you plan on at least two coats.

As for color, I'd recommend something that is less apt to show scuff marks and stains. The darker, the better, but this is a personal choice on your part. A good middle-of-the-road color is a light to medium beige or blue. You may want to contrast this color with your deck color for eye appeal. I suggest you stay away from white paint in the cockpit lockers. It gives me the impression I'm opening a refrigerator every time I lift the seat cover; but more to the point, it shows stains and scuff marks too easily.

You have two ways to go when applying the paint. You can spray it on or use a brush. The paint sprayer will allow you to get into every little nook and cranny, but at the same time you have to be careful about getting paint where you don't want it. There's nothing wrong with using a brush. It's more work with rather awkward positions at times. Frankly, there's no easy way to paint lockers and be comfortable. It's just a chore that has to be done.

If you're going to use a brush, I recommend using a brush no less than three inches wide. It's surprising how quickly you can cover area with a wide brush where you would work yourself to a frazzle with a smaller one.

While you're painting the seat lockers, don't overlook the underneath of the deck. I know it's difficult and half the paint will run down your arm, but the main idea of cleaning and painting the seat lockers and lazaret is to have a clean place to keep gear. And what good is it to have a neat bottom and sides if the top is like a coal mine?

I do have one suggestion for combining brushing and spraying. Use a brush for everything except the underneath of the deck, and here use several cans of spray paint to do the underneath area. You don't even have to look at what you're doing; just put your arm in the locker and spray by feel. You won't get a perfect job, but it will serve. I do, however, advise you to spray the underneath first so your brush work will cover the paint that settles out of the air. Speaking of air, you may want to use a fan to ventilate the locker while you're working.

There is one place that should always be painted—underneath the seat cover. Nothing will ruin the looks of a clean and neat cockpit like opening a seat locker and showing old flaking paint covered with black mold. No excuses here because it's easy to paint.

A good paint job will also allow you to freshen up the lockers in the spring with little trouble, or you may want to touch up a few places during the season. But the real plus is the clean condition of your equipment by being kept in a painted locker.

The older fiberglass sailboat will offer good storage under the seats and in the lazaret. The one place they do not offer some convenient storage is in the cockpit proper. There are always several items that need to be out of the way and yet handy, the winch handle for example. Many older sailboats will have teak cockpit coamings with no storage box built into the coaming or winch base, so I have a suggestion to remedy this. See Figure 43. This storage box is simple

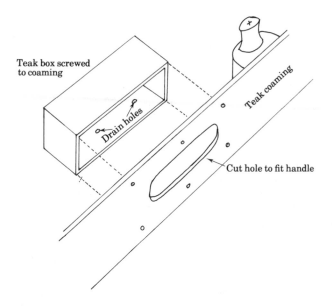

Figure 43. Cockpit coaming winch handle and stowage box

to construct and install. It also gives you a good place to sit when you wish to be higher than the cockpit seat. When you buy the teak for the box, note the color and texture of the coamings and try to come as close as possible to a match. Some teak has a lighter color, so don't use this on dark teak. You want it to blend in so the box doesn't stand out. In the case your boat has a fiberglass winch base, but no storage box there are fiberglass boxes available that can be inserted into the winch base.

The mainsheet arrangement should be given some thought. You may have something similar to that shown in Figure 44 which can be awkward since you have to tie the sheet to a cleat every time the mainsail is trimmed. I'd suggest you consider adding a traveler with a cam cleat assembly. See Figure 45. This type of mainsheet control is much more convenient when sailing shorthanded or racing, and, just as important, allows you to have better control of the sail trim. Another advantage of the traveler system is you can move the main- sheet to the side and not have it in the way of getting to the lazaret. This is really nice when relaxing in the cockpit after a sail.

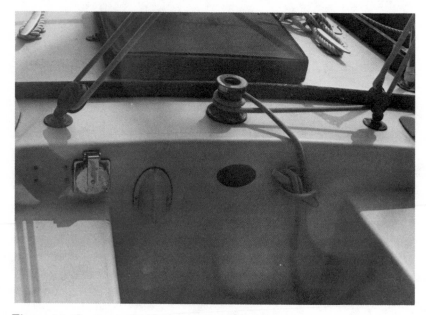

Figure 44. One type of mainsheet arrangement

Figure 45. Mainsheet arrangement using cam cleat and traveler

Nothing will dress up the cockpit like a teak grate, and at the same time it's very practical. If you do any sailing at all, you'll have water on the cockpit sole from time to time, and with the grate you won't be standing in the water. Unless you're a whiz with woodworking or know someone who is and who's willing to help you, you'll be better off having it made. Don't be surprised if the cost is more than you anticipated; this type of woodwork is expensive, a good-looking grate will cost. There're a number of ads in the classified sections of boating publications about teak grates, so you should have no trouble getting all the information you need.

Cockpit cushions are another item which add comfort to the cockpit. If the boat came with cushions and they're beginning to show their age, then consider having them recovered. Use a material that can easily be cleaned with soap and water, and keep the color light or white to cut down on heat. One suggestion to save money is if you plan to replace the bunk cushions below with new foam as well as material, consider using the old bunk foam for the cockpit cushions thereby eliminating the cost of new foam.

No matter how you go about obtaining the cockpit cushions, make sure they're thick enough to be comfortable even when sleeping on them. I've seen many cockpit cushions that were so thin that after a short period of time it was like sitting on the bare fiberglass, and sleeping on them was out of the question. I recommend no less than three inches, but four is better.

Our next two subjects of discussion for the cockpit are from the standpoint of safety. First the fire extinguisher. Make sure you have one mounted just inside a cockpit seat locker. It should be located where it's always visible and can be brought out at a moment's notice. Never store it under something else; make all other gear secondary to the fire extinguisher. In the case of a fire on a boat, seconds are vital and can quite possibly mean life or death.

My reason for locating the fire extinguisher in a seat locker is convenience. Most of the time there's someone near or at the helm, and this person can lift the seat cover and quickly have the fire extinguisher in hand. By comparison it can be time consuming if this same person has to move aft to the lazaret. Now this should not be the only fire extinguisher on the boat. My main point here is to impress on you the importance of having a handy fire extinguisher in the cockpit.

Our second safety subject is the manual bilge pump. I'm the first to recognize the convenience of the electric bilge pump. And when all's working well, it's great; but you still need a dependable backup. I suggest a gusher type of bilge pump because these types are capable of moving large volumes of water quickly. Next mount the pump where it can be worked without having to stand on your head. I've seen some installed in seat lockers in very awkward places. They present no problem when you have to pump only a few strokes; but faced with having to keep the boat afloat, the pumper would be exhausted in a very short time. Mount the pump where it can be pumped from a comfortable position by the helmsman. See Figure 46. This allows the helmsman to do double duty if a crisis happens, and it becomes vitally important if you're single handing.

If your boat has an older model of manual bilge pump, I would suggest you consider changing to a gusher type. I think the proper place for pump location is the top of a cockpit seat. You don't want to

Figure 46. Cockpit seat mounted bilge pump

have to worry about a seat cover and/or an open locker if you're taking water over the bow. There are flush mounted access fittings available that go right in the top of the cockpit seat and look nice at the same time.

No discussion of the cockpit would be complete without looking at the wheel versus the tiller. Your boat may have a tiller, and as part of the upgrading process you're thinking of adding a wheel. The choice will be yours to make. What I want to do is help by giving you the pros and cons. The tiller is simple and cheap. You can see at a glance the position of the rudder. You have a better feel for how the boat is performing and you can push the tiller up, and clear the cockpit at party time. The other side of the coin is that sometimes you can get tremendous weather helm that makes steering hard work. Every time the boat is tacked, the tiller sweeps over the cockpit, and using the engine controls can be very clumsy.

As for the wheel, it's very easy to hold—just like driving a car. Tacking is no fire drill; with pedestal mounted engine controls maneuvering under power is a pleasure. And having the compass as well as other instruments mounted on the pedestal is also very convenient. The other side of this coin is that the wheel is not simple; there are a lot of moving parts and this makes it expensive. Because the wheel is not directly attached to the rudder, you don't have that fingertip feel of how the boat is doing, and you have a permanent fixture in the cockpit that sometimes can get in the way when you have a cockpit full of people.

If your boat already has a wheel, you're not concerned with making a choice. But do think about adding a compass and instruments to the pedestal if you don't now have them.

The only advice I would like to give concerns replacing the tiller with a wheel. If you don't have any hands-on experience with a wheel, take the time to sail on some boats equipped with them. When you do decide to spend the money for a wheel, make sure it's because you know you want it and not because you think you'd like to have one.

Every boat needs a compass, and I'm sure you'll want several instruments mounted in the cockpit area. What you decide on is, of course, again your personal choice. My recommendation is to make sure the equipment is mounted where it can be easily seen and yet out of the way. Many of the older boats have the compass mounted below when not in use, and then placed in the cockpit for sailing. This would be the first thing to upgrade because when the compass is below it takes up space and when placed in the cockpit, seems always to be in the way of someone's big foot.

I suggest a bulkheadtype compass mounted on one side or the other of the companionway going below from the cockpit. Make sure it also has a light for night use. This same area is fine for your other instruments since they will be out of harm's way and yet easily read. The only exceptions to this are the pedestal-mounted compass and instruments.

Engine gauges are properly a part of the chapter on the engine, but since they're located in the cockpit I feel they should be touched on here. You'll be concerned with how the gauges are installed in the cockpit area, not mechanical information. Because it's cheaper to mount all the engine gauges and controls flush in a vertical section of the cockpit well, a great many boats will have flush-mounted engine panels. The problem comes from the fact everything is out where it can be kicked, banged with a winch handle, or have a jib sheet foul the starter key. Even boats with throttle and gear levers on the wheel pedestal have the key and choke (or in the case of a diesel, a cutoff handle) located in the gauge panel, and all are in the way when the boat is being sailed.

If you're going to replace any engine panel parts, look into replacing the panel itself with a recessed-type panel at the same time. Matter of fact, even if all the panel equipment works fine, you might consider a new recessed panel and just transfer the gauges and controls. No matter how the engine panel is installed, I think it's a good idea to protect the gauges and controls from the elements. Gauges in particular start looking weathered in no time at all when exposed to the sun.

A sun cover for the panel is easy to make. Using sun cover material hem a cover which will finish up one inch larger than the panel on all four sides. Then add button snaps to the corners of the cover with the other part of the snap screwed to the fiberglass just outside the panel. It only takes a couple of seconds to pop the cover on or off, and your engine panel will look good for years. It's a good idea to cover your wheel, compass, and winches with sun covers as well.

One final thought about the cockpit. You want it to be comfortable and pleasing to the eye. But at the same time, the cockpit is there for a reason—it is the control station when the boat is under way. Any time comfort and eye appeal conflict with safety and the efficient working of the boat, always give priority to the main reasons you have a cockpit.

Metal Gear and Fittings. On the older fiberglass sailboat metal gear and fittings found on deck, the boom, and on the lower part of the mast will show wear, so I'll go over the choices you have to upgrade this gear and fittings. Your four choices are:

1. *Do nothing*—You can leave what you have as it is.
2. *Clean*—Using a good cleaner and polish to match the metal, thoroughly clean the fitting. Items made of bronze or brass, like lights, cleats, pad eyes, or boom and mast gear should clean up nicely, or at least to the point of being acceptable; 400 grit wet and dry sandpaper will do a first-rate job. See Figure 47 and Figure 48. A good cleaner will usually take care of

Figure 47. Pad eye before cleaning

Figure 48. Pad eye after cleaning

stains on stainless steel: for example, lifeline stanchions and pulpits. But nothing will help very much those chrome-plated items from which the chrome has started to peel, which leads us to option number 3.

3. *Rechrome*—You'll have a number of chrome-plated fittings that show their age: for example, cleats, pad eyes, hinges, latches, gooseneck, and, in some cases, winches. The answer to this problem is to remove the fittings and have them re-chromed. Your boatyard may be able to have this done for you. If not, I don't think you'll have too much trouble locating a firm to do the work. Ask around your marina and use the yellow pages.

4. *Replace*—This is by far the most costly way to go. In some cases you may have no choice but to replace because of a structural problem. On the other hand, you may prefer the looks of the newer gear: but remember, none of these items will be cheap.

From experience I would say that you'll end up following all four suggestions. No one of the four is the total solution for the metal fittings on deck, but a combination of what works best to give you the end result you want is the preferred course to follow. Additional upgrading suggestions are:

1. Self-tailing winches.
2. One or more pelican hooks to be able to drop lifelines, making it easier to step on board.
3. A boarding gate with special stanchions for even better access.
4. Plastic winch handle holders.

While the topside color sets the tone for the general overall appearance, it nevertheless is not seen when you're on the boat. What you see when on board is the cockpit and deck area. Even though the condition of the deck is not readily apparent to anyone not on board, it's in front of the people on board all the time. Hence it's just as important as good looking topsides. Therefore, take the trouble to do all you can to make the deck and cockpit safe, comfortable places, while at the same time pleasing to the eye, from which to enjoy sailing your boat.

Five

SAILS AND AWNINGS

Sails have only one purpose on a boat, and that is to catch the energy in moving air and use that energy to move the boat through the water. The mast, boom, rigging, winches, halyards, and sheets are there solely to hang out sails and control them.

Sails are what makes "going sailing" the pleasant experience it is, and at the same time, a part of this pleasing pastime is how your sailboat looks and performs. Therefore, the condition of your sails is just as important as the deck, topsides, and underbody. By "condition" I'm talking about new or old, proper shape or blown out, still usable after minor repairs, or if what you have will do until you can spend the money for new ones—and last but no means least, how the sails look.

When a boat is tied up, the topside is the first thing that catches the eye; but when that same boat is under sail, it's the sails that are noticed first and set the tone for the viewer's reaction. No matter how beautiful the topsides are, ratty looking sails overwhelm everything and that's the impression the entire boat gives. Now, I'm not talking about the occasional small rust spot or smudge where the spreader has rubbed. I'm talking about the sail that should only be used for a paint drop cloth; and when you start to refurbish the older sailboat, there's more than a good chance you'll have a drop cloth or two.

The place to start is to know how you plan to use the boat. Then take an inventory of the sails. Fit your sail needs to what is required for the way you intend to use the boat. The next step is to see what you already have on the boat, taking note of the condition of the sails. The final step is determining if any new sails will or should be purchased. Let's take a look at each of these steps in detail:

How You Plan to Use the Boat

This topic should be approached from the general overall picture of how you intend to use the boat. The first point to consider is who will make up the crew for the majority of the time. Chances are the answer to this question will be a couple with occasional guests. This being the case, then you'll have to think about shorthanded sail handling. Of course, if you plan to take your teenage son and some of his friends, you can load the boat with all the sails it can carry.

Now along with who will sail the boat, it's important to know how and where the boat will be sailed. Are you going to do blue water sailing out of sight of land for days on end? Or, are you going to weekend with the annual two-week cruise and anchor or tie up each night? How about day sailing mainly with just a few nights spent on the boat? Let's not forget about racing. The PHRF (Performance Handicap Racing Fleet) rating system will allow the older fiberglass sailboat to be competitive.

Along with the above, where the boat will be sailed has to be considered. Will you be in an area known for very light air in the summer? Or maybe you sail where there's a good stiff breeze most of the time. My point is think about the wind conditions when looking at how you plan to use your boat.

The three areas I have just mentioned are all part of how you plan to enjoy your boat. The number of crew, what you intend to do with the boat, and the wind conditions in your sailing location all dictate what sails to use. I feel it's very important to have this information before you can proceed to take stock of what sails you have and what you need.

Inventory

In this case inventory means cleaning as well as assessing the sails. When you were looking at the boat before buying, you checked all the sails, I'm sure; so you have some idea of the condition. But you're really not going to be sure of what you have until you look at them objectively. Your first step is to wash the sails. The older ones will all need cleaning; at the same time the newer ones also will look better if washed. The only exception you may consider is a brand-new sail that has had very little use. The cleaning-up process is as follows:

1. Obtain a washing receptacle—washtub, dinghy, inflatable raft, kid's wading pool.
2. Use warm water to do a better job of loosening the grime. The rule to follow is the water should be warm enough to allow you to keep your hands in without discomfort.
3. Use Arm & Hammer detergent, and add to warm water just like you're washing clothes.
4. Place sail in the soapy water and move around until entire surface is wet. Every so often swirl the sail around in the water and then allow to soak overnight.
5. Rinse thoroughly first with at least a two-hour rinse soak, and follow with two more rinses with no soaking time. Cold water is fine for this.
6. Repeat the above process using a nonchlorine bleach like Clorox 2. Don't use a *chlorine bleach* under any conditions; it will cause the sail material to turn yellow and harm the fabric. Also don't use detergent and bleach together.
7. Hang to dry when all the soaking and rinsing are completed. If you have to spread the sail out on the ground, be careful of adding a grass stain and note any birds that may add a "spot of trouble." Dacron dries in a hurry, so stay close if the sail is on the ground and don't leave it any longer than necessary.
8. Do not use a washing machine to clean sails, neither the one at home nor the corner laundromat. The washing action is too fast and harms the fabric.
9. Start to remove stains with the detergent and the bleach but for specific ones the following are to be recommended:
   a. Rust—oxalic acid from the drugstore will do a good job on these stains. Mix one ounce to a pint of water. When using the oxalic acid, leave the spot in the sun for about fifteen minutes. This will speed up the spot removing process, then rinse. Zud powder does a good job, also.

b. Mildew—this is extremely difficult to get out and usually what's left after the detergent and bleach wash won't come out. A soft scrub brush and detergent paste may help some. Be very careful about the mildew solutions on the market. They are not made for sails and can badly damage the fibers.

c. Blood—usually the washing will take care of this. If not, then a scrubbing with detergent paste should help.

d. Metal smudges—for example, the foot of the Genoa rubbing on the bow pulpit is actually bits and particles of metal that transfer to the fabric. Usually what stains remain after washing and scrubbing will not come out.

e. Creosote and oil—these, in my opinion, are the two worst stains you can have because the chemicals that remove the stains are so bad for the sail cloth. Not much you can do here except scrape off any buildup and try mineral spirits.

10. Patch as the final answer to a bad stain if practical. Here, I think you should have a sailmaker to do the work.

Tips while cleaning the sails are to use more than one "washtub" if you can get it. This helps to speed up the washing and soaking process because it will take some time to clean an average sail inventory. Use a toothbrush on small spots that may require some extra scrubbing. Always keep rinse water at hand when using any type of stain remover so you can flood the area with water at once. Don't wash white and colored sails together. The end result should give you clean sails that have been whitened by the bleach. You won't have improved their performance, but they'll certainly look better and be more pleasant to handle. This is important if you plan to sit in your den at home, and make repairs.

Sail bags and sail covers should receive the same cleaning process as the sails. It may be convenient simply to include the bag and cover when the sail is cleaned, but only if they are *white*. Colored bags and covers should be washed separately so as not to take the chance of color transfer. Also when involved with all this laundry work, I suggest you wash and soak your rope halyards and sheets. It's amazing how dirty they can become.

While you're in the process of cleaning your sails, take note of exactly what you have. Make a list of all the sails and then determine the condition of each. For example, how's the stitching? Do the jib hanks work freely? Are there any thin places from rubbing on a spreader that may tear? Are there any tears or rips? Are there any places that have been patched with tape? In other words, record everything you can about a particular sail, no matter how insignificant. Knowing the age of the sail is helpful. Many older sailboats were rated to race, and the date the sail was measured will be recorded in some corner of the sail. There could be some old bills of sale in the paper work which may give you the date. Another source is the sailmaker; his name should be on the sail, so an inquiry with the boat data may prove fruitful.

I would like to say that I'm not advocating you wash every sail on the boat. Put your effort in the sails you plan to use or at least the questionable ones. Don't waste your time on the sails that are obviously shot. However, if you plan to use an old sail for say an awning, it certainly should be washed and the same goes for any sails you intend to sell. Selling old sails will be covered later.

Sails Needed for Boat Use

I'm not going to give you pages and pages of definitions about all the various sails found on sailboats. My main concern is how the sails fit into the upgrading and refurbishing guidelines. The basic sails needed will depend on the intended use of the boat, so let's look at the options.

Let's take cruising first. You'll need a mainsail, working jib, 150 percent Genoa or maybe a 170 percent Genoa for lighter air, and a spinnaker for downwind sailing. If your boat is a cutter, you'll have to consider a staysail. If a yawl or ketch, you'll have to add a mizzen. In the case of a schooner, there'll be the foresail.

If you plan to cruise with only a couple for crew, with the occasional guest, I suggest you forego the regular spinnaker which needs a pole. Also, use soft sails that are easy to handle. Sail cloth comes in all grades of finish with some the consistency of cardboard. Believe me, once out of the bag this stiff material is impossible to bag unless the sail is folded—and quite frankly this is difficult to do while on the boat. You want soft sails that can easily be furled or bagged, and pushed into a sail locker.

Your cruising sails should be in the proper condition to drive the boat. They should not be old blown out rags that only push the boat downwind. If they have no shape or life left, don't consider using them unless you enjoy everyone else sailing by.

Last but not least, the sails should look good. From a distance the sails are the only thing seen and I personally want anyone looking at my boat to think—what beautiful sails.

If crew is no problem, don't worry about spinnaker poles and extra Genoas. But always keep in mind extra sails have to be stowed away, and on a cruising boat space is precious. A sail that has a very limited range of use may be a space-gobbling luxury you can ill afford.

Our next category of use is a mixture of cruising and racing. The basic sail inventory is the same. However, while a sail may be perfectly fine for cruising, it still may not deliver the speed needed for head-to-head racing. In this case, you'll want to consider adding to the sail inventory new sails to fit the racing needs, and this leads us to our next area to consider—racing.

Thanks to the PHRF rating system, the older fiberglass sailboat can once again race. If this is where you intend to use the boat, I recommend you have fast sails. Fast sails make for fast boats and fast boats win races, so there's not much to consider here except, of course, the cost of racing sails.

Blue water sailing is our last category and may interest only a small percentage of readers, but nevertheless, it's an important part of the boat-use guidelines and should be included. It can be summed up in two words: sturdy and tough. Blue water sails should be well built of durable materials and be able to take punishment. A sailmaker in my area who makes many blue water sails states an interesting fact: several weeks of ocean sailing equals several years of weekend sailing insofar as wear and tear on the sails are concerned. My point here is don't take sails that have been used for normal sailing activities and automatically assume they will stand up at sea. A torn main on a Saturday afternoon is an inconvenience; at sea it can be disastrous. If you plan to do any blue water sailing, I strongly recommend you have sails that you know will take the punishment as well as a storm jib and trysail, for real heavy weather.

Matching Sail Inventory to Needs. By now you have an idea of how you intend to use the boat and what sails are necessary. You have also washed and checked over your sails. Now you're going to take a look at what you have. First, it goes without question that any new or almost new sails will be used. The only exception is if you're going offshore in which case they may not be heavy enough to take the beating.

Next, discard the sails that are obviously no good. You'll have no trouble recognizing the signs: the cloth tears easily, the stitching pulls out with little effort, the fabric has little bulges and pouched-out areas when hoisted and sheeted home. These are signs of a blown out sail. In my opinion, you should also consider not using a sail if after washing and bleaching it still looks unsightly, even if you feel it has a year or two of use remaining.

Worn-out and new sails present no problems. It's the ones in between that will make you scratch your head. From experience the large majority of the sails which came with the boat will fall in this category.

Any new or almost new (and by almost new I mean a sail used for only one to two seasons) sails that come with the boat will be the exception, not the norm. Most people don't buy a new Genoa in May and sell the boat in October. With some exceptions, deciding to sell a boat is not a spur-of-the-moment undertaking. It's something that's thought of for a while, and during this stage not many new sails will be added. So take any new sail the boat has as a bonus, but don't expect it.

Most of the sails you'll have in your inventory will be anywhere from four to fifteen years old. To just go out and purchase a complete new sail inventory would require a large outlay of money; therefore, I suggest you take upgrading your sail inventory in stages. For example, if the mainsail is old, but it cleaned up nicely and the general condition of the sail is acceptable, start out with this particular sail. The working jib is in the same shape as the main. Since your area has mostly light air in the summer, you won't be using the jib that much, so you can keep this sail as well. On the other hand, the 150 percent Genoa is a real loss, and you decide to buy a new one. The spinnaker is not in such good shape either, but the sailmaker says the fabric has some life left in it; so with restitching the seams and not trying to carry it when the wind is honking, you'll get several seasons out of it.

The bottom line is that your basic sail inventory will be a usable main and working jib with a restitched spinnaker and a new 150 percent Genoa. Added to this inventory you could have several special sails that are in pretty good condition which you plan to keep on the boat, for example, a spinnaker staysail, a light air drifter, or a storm jib. With these special-use sails added to the basic sails, you have an inventory which will allow you to fly the proper sails whatever the weather conditions.

When you checked the condition of the sails, I'm sure you noted some repairs that should be made. These repairs, as well as expert help concerning the fabric, are reasons enough to bag the sail and visit your local sailmaker. Even if you can make the repairs to the sail yourself, don't waste your time if you intend to get an opinion from a sailmaker about using the sail, and I definitely recommend your getting the expert advice here. The sail may be useless and your work all for nothing.

Depending on the expert's opinion, there're several options open as to what you can do with the sail. You have no problem when the sail has good fabric, and can be put into usable condition with minor repairs and maybe some restitching. But how about the Genoa that's not all that bad and yet at the same time you don't feel like it will do the job? I suggest you recycle the sail and have it cut down. The trick here is not to have a lot of money tied up in a recut sail which has a limited use. I'm afraid this will have to be a judgment call on your part.

Your last option concerning a questionable sail is to keep it, make what repairs are needed yourself, and then add it to your sail inventory, but not as a regular sail. You intend to fly it only under certain conditions. For example, you're on a cruise and you have a forty-mile downwind run to make in heavy air. There's a bumpy sea starting to build up so it's going to be a full-time job at the helm. You would like not to use the main as you want all the pull up on the bow to make steering easier. The spinnaker is out of the question, so that leaves the Genoa to do the work. This is a perfect time to drag out the old 150 percent Genoa and fly two Genoas downwind. You have balance, pull from the bow, positive steering control, and what can be at times, exhilarating speeds.

Keep in mind there's no reason at all for you not to make what repairs you can to the sails. Every boat should have a sail repair kit consisting of: palm, needles, several types of threads, beeswax, awl, and a rigging knife that has a sharp blade and a fid. Add to this some spare hardware and you're in business. There is literature available on sail repairs that should prove very helpful. Just look in the classified section of sailing magazines for the names.

New Sails

If your sail inventory is really showing its age, I'd suggest you order new sails. This is one of the most positive ways you can upgrade the older fiberglass sailboat. The boat will sail better and faster with the added plus of looking like a million dollars. I know we're talking about a lot of money; matter of fact, it's probably one of the largest outlays you will have if you bought a new complete suit of sails. But I ask you, where else better to spend the money on a sailboat?

If you plan on doing any racing at all, you'll need new or almost new sails. Keep in mind the new sails that came with the boat may be strictly designed for cruising and won't give you the speed needed for racing. The bottom line is that in order to race, you'll have to spend some money.

These new sails give you one advantage you didn't have before, *choice*. Use the new sails for racing and the older cruising sails for your other sailing activities.

When it comes to picking a sailmaker, I have only two pieces of advice. First, he should enjoy a reputation for good work and *service after the sale*; and second, he should be close enough so you can visit his loft and conduct your business in person, if possible.

Used Sails

Now, I'm the first to agree new sails or having a sailmaker rework what you have to upgrade your sail inventory is the ideal way. It's also the way to spend a lot of money and sometimes you're not in a position to do this. This leads us to take a look at used sails. This is a very good way to solve a sail problem when money is a consideration. But let me add that it's the same when buying anything used. Let the *buyer beware!* Used sails are simple to locate, so let's take a look at your sources:

1. Sail brokers—these are the people who make selling used sails a business. Look in the classified sections of the boating publications for their names.
2. Sailmakers—contact the sailmakers in your area. Sometimes they have used sails for sale.
3. Word of mouth—just start asking around your sailing friends if they know of a used so-and-so for sale. Talk with marina operators and people at your marina. One of the best sources for used sails is the racing crowd. They're buying new sails all the time and after a while they collect a number of sails which I'm sure they'd like to sell. If you don't know any racers personally, ask any sailmaker for some names. And speaking of the sailmaker, don't hesitate to take a used sail to a sailmaker for a professional opinion if you're not sure what you're buying.

So far all I've talked about is how to spend your money. Now I'm going to give you some good news. Used sails are a two-way street; you sell as well as buy. From experience you'll probably have a sail or two that will just be in the way. So why not convert them to cash? Here's a personal example. My boat came with two mainsails, a working jib, a 150 percent Genoa, a light air drifter (to take the place of the Genoa in light air), a spinnaker, and a small spinnaker staysail which is the brightest orange color I've ever seen. I intended to use the boat to cruise most of the time and do some racing in the spring and fall. As much as I would have liked a complete new suit of sails, the cost was simply too much so I mixed and matched to get the best for my planned use. I kept the better of the two mains, the working jib, the spinnaker, and the spinnaker staysail. The 150 percent Genoa was a basket case, and I ordered a new one. After all this, I ended up with a main, a drifter, and a beat-up Genoa that I sent to a sail broker to sell. They sold the Genoa and drifter but sent the main back with a nice letter that really said, "You have to be kidding. I doubt we can give this mainsail away." So I put the main in the garage for the time being. (There's a very good use for this old sail which I'll get to shortly.) The spinnaker did not work out with just me and my wife sailing the boat, so I decided to buy a cruising spinnaker which doesn't require a pole. This by the way didn't affect my racing because I prefer to race in the nonspinnaker class of PHRF. But, before I had a chance to send the old spinnaker to the sail broker, a neighbor came over and asked me if I would consider selling it to him since he understood I had purchased a new cruising spinnaker. Needless to say, he carried the sail home with him, and I ended up, when all this buying and selling was over, with enough money to pay for the new cruising spinnaker. The point of my story is to make you aware that you should at least try and salvage what you can from unwanted sails. Give them to a broker, use a sailmaker if he brokers sails, and talk it up in the sailing community. If you make the effort, you may be pleasantly surprised.

Sail covers should be considered when you're upgrading the sail inventory. If the one you have shows its age after being cleaned up, I suggest you purchase a new one. Mainsail covers are what we're talking about here. When compared to the cost of sails, they're not very expensive. As well as protecting the main when the boat is not in use, the sail cover looks good. It's another indicator of just how the boat is cared for. I happen to like a sail cover which has the boat's name along the side; it just adds a personal touch. The sail cover can be white which goes with any color of topsides. If you prefer a colored mainsail cover, use a color that goes well with the hull color or the intended color if you plan to paint in the near future.

Roller Furling

In my opinion roller furling is one of the best improvements to come along in the past few years for the larger sailboat with a small crew. Roller furling makes handling the Genoa convenient, comfortable, and safe. When the foredeck is like a roller coaster and spray is hitting the numbers on the main, it's a good feeling to know you can take care of the Genoa without leaving the security of the cockpit.

Just a word here about mainsail roller furling. There are now systems on the market to furl the main, either inside the mast or directly behind the mast. To my way of thinking, from a cruising standpoint it would be nice to have roller furling both on the headsail as well as the mainsail. But this becomes very expensive. Practically speaking, while the roller-furling main is convenient, it's more important to have the roller furling for the headsail. My reason is the main is secured on two sides by the mast and boom, and the crew stays aft of the mast when furling the sail which makes the mainsail much easier and safer to control than the Genoa. While on the other hand, the Genoa can be a bear with heavy air and choppy seas.

I'm the first to admit that roller furling is not for everyone. The biggest objection seems to be the shape of the Genoa when reefed down. Many sailors prefer to change headsails to meet the required needs, instead of using one sail to try and meet all situations. Then again, the cost may dictate whether you add roller furling. When it comes down to the bottom line, only you will be able to determine if you'll have this gear on the boat. You'll have no trouble obtaining all the information you need. There are many makers of roller-furling gear, and each is quick to point out why his particular one is the very best you can buy. Just look in the sailing magazines for the advertisements. Of course, you may hit it lucky and purchase a boat already equipped with roller furling. If your boat did come with headsail roller furling, as I suggested earlier when the mast is dropped you give it a good inspection for worn parts. It's to your advantage to have the directions and diagrams; so if the information didn't come with the boat, make it a point to contact the manufacturer.

In order to save money and time it's important to include in your sail-inventory guidelines the fact that you intend to add roller furling. The sailmaker should know when he's given the order for a new Genoa if it is to be used with roller furling. This also applies to older sails that are to be reworked. Believe me, it is expensive to change over from hanked-on headsails to roller-furling luff tape, so have this done right up front if it can be arranged.

If you have no actual experience with roller furling, make a point of sailing on a boat equipped with it, regardless of the fact you're sure, not sure, or undecided. Make up your mind from personal experience before you spend any money, because roller-furling gear is not cheap.

Awnings, Biminis, and Dodgers

The last subject for this chapter deals with comfort and convenience. Awnings, biminis, and dodgers won't help you go faster, but they sure let you enjoy the trip and your being on the boat when you arrive at your destination.

Take awnings first. Chances are your boat came equipped with a rectangle-shaped awning that rests on the boom, whereas biminis and dodgers have their own frame. The purpose of the rectangle-shaped awning is to protect the cabin and cockpit from sun and rain. It should be made of sail cloth material. So clean it following the same procedures used for cleaning sails. After cleaning, inspect the seams, the pockets that hold the poles, and the grommets used to tie the edges. Most of the repairs that may be needed can usually be performed by using the sail-repair kit. The one place the sailmaker may be required is to resew the seams if the old thread is starting to let go.

Your awning may be in good condition after cleaning with plenty of service remaining, or you may have hit it lucky with a new one on the boat. In any case, you don't have to worry about the awning. In spite of this, I'd like to suggest you read on. You might just pick up an idea or two about awnings for future reference.

My pet peeve concerning awnings is that most of the awnings I see being used are really too small to do a good job. The best awnings I've observed have been on cruising boats where the crew lives aboard for long periods of time. When you're on a boat for months at a time, it doesn't take long to know where the priorities are. And a large awning is one of them. If you intend to order a new awning, I recommend you take the measurements and order as large an awning as practical. Also a 12-inch turndown on each side parallel with the toe rail is an added advantage.

Even though you have a perfectly good awning you may want to consider increasing the area, or at least adding the side flaps. One word of advice here; make sure the end result will look good because the awning is very much on display when in use. The awning is really simple to make so you may consider doing so. Buy your material, sew it together, hem the edges, add the pole pockets, and bang in the grommets along the edges. There: nothing to it. After all, it's flat and can easily be cut out on the den floor. As a matter of fact, making an awning is a good off-season project.

And, I can make it even easier with another idea. Remember that old mainsail I mentioned, the one the sail broker returned saying it was not worth the effort? Well, it may not be much of a mainsail but it sure did make a great awning. The beauty of using an old sail is the fact you're working with a large piece of material. All you have to do is lay it flat and cut the shape you want. As far as the mechanics of sewing are concerned, they're no different than what is illustrated for sewing sun covers. If you can sew a hem along the edge, you can make an awning. All this is predicated, of course, on the cleaning up of the sail being okay.

There's a bonus when you use an old sail for an awning. After the main awning rectangle is cut, you end up with a large triangle that will make a perfect awning for the foredeck. This foredeck awning will be smaller than your regular awning and have no poles which means it will fold into a small shape and be easily stowed. It will be a blessing on those hot summer days at anchor when you're able to put the foredeck in the shade as well as the rest of the deck. See Figure 49.

The bimini is a special type of awning that is most convenient on a sailboat when sailing. It's designed to shade only a small area, but at the same time to be extremely easy to put up and down. If your boat came with a bimini and if you can remove the cloth, wash as you would a sail. If the material cannot be removed, lay the bimini on the dock and do the best wash job you can.

If you don't have a bimini and plan on adding one, I don't recommend trying to make it yourself. The problem is the frame. It takes some experience here so I'd suggest you go to a professional.

Figure 49. Foredeck awning

Sailmakers sometimes do biminis, but from my experience the people who specialize in boat covers are the ones to contact. You should have no trouble locating a bimini maker; just ask around the boat crowd or check the yellow pages.

One bit of advice on biminis: don't consider any type of metal frame except stainless steel; you not only want it maintenance free, but strong enough to take abuse. Everything on a sailboat gets bumped into sooner or later, and some of the nonstainless steel frames may fold up on you when you stumble against them.

Biminis, like everything else on a sailboat, are not cheap. Even though the custom-made bimini looks great, the cost may be a little steep so take a look at the marine mail order catalogs. You'll be able to save some money here, but remember it's not going to look like the custom job.

The dodger is one of the most useful items on a sailboat. Its main purpose is to protect the companionway and the people sitting behind it from wind and rain. It does offer some shade, but its area is small. The dodger is made to be used while under way so plastic windows are necessary. But, they are nice on a chilly day and make life a little more bearable when the rain starts to come down. I've even seen some boats that have a bimini and a dodger made in such a way that the bimini is attached to the back edge of the dodger thereby protecting the cockpit area. See Figure 50.

If your boat came with a dodger and it needs some cleaning, do so in place, being careful of the plastic windows. On the other hand, if you plan to add a dodger, use a professional to custom fit it to your boat and make sure you get stainless steel framing. A dodger would be tough for the amateur to tackle because it's nothing but curves. This is another item that will either add or detract from your boat, so make sure it looks good.

Awnings, biminis, and dodgers are not crucial. You don't need any of them from a sailing point of view. The boat will sail just fine without them. The determining factors are you and your crew. These items are for your use and what you add and how much you spend for them is for you to determine. If you have to establish a priority on these items, I would recommend the large awning because it will have more uses, simply because of its larger size. It may not be as convenient while sailing, but you get more protection for people for your money.

Figure 50. Bimini attached to dodger

Six

MAIN CABIN

With work on the exterior of the boat pretty well taken care of, you can turn to the problems concerned with upgrading and refurbishing the interior. While it is true that you will spend a great deal of time on deck, you will also use the accommodations below almost as much. While the cockpit is the center of action on deck, the main cabin is its counterpart below. Therefore, it's very important that this area be comfortable, convenient, and attractive. To me, being able to enjoy the quieter moments below in pleasant surroundings is as much a part of sailing as a good thrash to windward in heavy air.

A great many subjects and ideas on upgrading and refurbishing projects will be detailed, none of which are absolutely necessary. It will be up to you to determine exactly which you wish to pursue. Since I cover a lot of ground, there will be plenty of information which I hope you'll find helpful.

Comfort, convenience, and pleasant surroundings are desirable for the entire below-deck area, and although the forward cabin and head will be used, it is the main cabin which you will live in so we'll be concerned with it first and cover the other areas later. Note also that the galley will be detailed in Chapter 8.

Subjects discussed here will be applicable to the entire below-deck area, for example, the cabin sole. Therefore, I intend to cover these topics in this chapter and simply refer back to this chapter later on. Matter of fact, my first step falls into this category.

Cleaning

Remove everything possible from below decks, and I mean everything: the bunk cushions, all those little bottles and things from the head, pots, pans, dishes, and rusty cans with no labels from the galley, and that lump in the bottom of the hanging locker you have been avoiding. Remove all the drawers if you have the storage room. You can clean them just as well no matter where they are, and the drawer openings will enable you to get into many places with no trouble.

Now unless the boat was completely stripped before you took possession, there's a good chance you'll be in for a surprise or two. For example, when I removed all the gear from the forepeak of my boat, I found a wind chute for the forward hatch that was practically brand-new. Then later in the back of the tool drawer I came across a set of socket wrenches still in the plastic wrapping. I'm the first to admit that surprises of this type are not the norm, but in my case the owner was getting out of boating and really had no use for any type of boat gear. Therefore, I bought the boat "as is," and everything except personal items stayed with the boat.

On the other hand, under the port bunk in the main cabin, I found a black substance over an inch thick and covering about a square foot. It reminded me of the kind of "thing" some luckless soul stumbles across at the beginning of a horror movie. It took an entire Saturday morning to clean up the mess, and to this day I have no idea what it was.

After the boat is unloaded, give it a good going-over with a vacuum cleaner. Make sure you remove all the bits and pieces of whatever even if you have to resort to using your hands. One item I've found most useful on a boat is a new three-inch paint brush. It will allow you to sweep out all those impossible places that even the vacuum cleaner has trouble reaching. Frankly, what really works is to use the brush and the vacuum at the same time. Dig out the mess with the brush and pick it up with the vacuum. By the way, this's a good combination to keep the boat clean while working.

My next suggestion you may or may not want to follow. It is to completely wash the interior with warm water and strong liquid soap. What I did was to put on my swim trunks and with a 5-gallon pail of soapy water, scrub brush, and hose I went at it; the overhead, in lockers, around the head itself, under the bunks—in short, every-where and this includes the engine area if you have room to work. Not the engine, but some soapy water in the area next to the engine won't hurt. Just be careful with the brush and hose. Don't be overly concerned with cleaning this particular place spick-and-span, because when you get into the engine proper you'll have the opportunity to really clean the area. All I'm saying is while you're there with soap and water, do what's feasible.

A word about the scrub brush will be helpful—it should be the kind that has a handle about ten inches long and long soft bristles so it can hold enough water to do a proper job of cleaning. This also allows you not to have to keep dipping your hand in the wash pail. Not that this will make much difference after a short while. Believe me, you'll be the wettest thing on the boat. The handle does, however, give you more reach which enables you to cover more area faster and get into the out-of-the-way places.

An added benefit is that all this soapy water will end up in the bilge and help clean this part of the boat. Of course, it's the rinsing that really adds the water. Since what goes in must come out, make sure your bilge pump is in good working order. Now, you're going to be glad you vacuumed the boat so all these little stray things are not being washed down to be sucked up by the bilge pump.

A word of caution—I'm not saying to flood the entire below decks. For the most part you'll be cleaning surfaces of fiberglass, formica, or painted wood, and the water will easily drain. But you'll find the odd place that common sense tells you not to get soaking wet; for example, the drawers if left on the boat may have insides made of unsealed wood that should not get wet. And speaking of drawers, if you don't take them home at least get them out of the below area while cleaning because as I previously said, it makes the work easier.

Another place that should receive special attention is any area where food or drinks were kept. Usually spills will accumulate back in the corners over the years and while I don't think you'll catch the black plague, I do think these spills add to the musty smell boats can have. But to me the most important problem is to take care of bugs. A mess in food lockers not only draws bugs, but worse yet, supports them. There's nothing quite as creepy as being in your bunk and feeling something on your arm. Do all you can to eliminate a nesting place for them.

One more point concerning this interior wash down. It requires warm weather, both for you and for the boat. It's vital to get the boat dry as quickly as possible, so when you leave for the day make arrangements for some ventilation; don't close up all that moisture, even for one night.

What you end up with at this point is an empty but clean interior which is the real starting point for your refurbishing project. Let me add that it's impossible not to make a mess as you work along, but there is a big difference between sawdust and what can accumulate over a decade or more in all the hard-to-get-at places.

From here on we're involved with positive upgrading and refurbishing projects. That is everything will, for the most part, have a direct visual impact on how the below area looks. The following subjects are roughly listed in the order they should be pursued to lessen the chance of damage to an already completed project. But feel free to rearrange anything to meet your own particular guidelines.

Companionway Plastic, Ports, and Overhead

One of the first things I suggest is to replace the wood crib boards in the companionway with a solid sheet of clear plastic. The reasons are simple. In cold or inclement weather, you can close up the companionway and still have natural light to work by. At the same time on those cold sunny days direct sunlight will give you solar heat. Remember (Chapter 2) about my recommending placing your boat to the best advantage in the boatyard? Well, add to that idea the thought about placing it so you can get direct sunlight if you're working in the colder months. At the same time don't forget about this when the boat is in the slip. It may be something as easy as reversing the boat.

You should have no trouble buying the plastic. With the part plastic plays in our lives today, I imagine almost every locality has its plastic supply firm. Buy a sheet slightly larger than the companionway opening with the thickness between one-eighth and one-quarter inch depending on how large an area you are dealing with. Make sure it's clear; you're after light and sun coming through. Make sure the plastic has stick-on paper on both sides for protection while cutting to fit.

With the paper protection still in place, arrange your crib boards on the plastic utilizing one existing edge at least, and two if possible of the plastic sheet. Then draw the outline of the boards on the paper and cut along the line. But before you reach for the saber saw, one bit of advice. The saber saw will turn up such a fast rate of speed the friction heat melts the plastic back together after the blade has passed, so the best method is to slowly hand cut the plastic. A regular hacksaw blade works fine. There's a tool now that acts as a blade holder in place of the standard hacksaw frame. It only costs a couple of dollars and certainly beats using your hand with a rag around the blade. It's also extremely handy to have in your tool drawer. The next time you have to cut off a bolt next to a nut in a close space, you'll be glad you did.

Once cut, peel off the paper and sand the cut edges with fine grit paper to knock down any sharp places. Another idea you may find convenient is to cut a small U-shaped notch on the bottom of the plastic near a corner so a power cord can be passed under the plastic when in place.

As to the size of the plastic, I suggest you keep it in one piece because it's very handy to remove when you're coming and going. If your boat has a bridge deck, the companionway area should not be too large and the single piece works well. However, many boats have no bridge deck and a large opening for a companionway, making it impractical for the one sheet of plastic. In this case, try and get by with just two sections and remember to make the cut where they join on an angle so water won't run in.

I'm sure you'll find, as I have, that the clear plastic is great for cruising when it's raining and you don't want that closed-in feeling. The thinness also allows the plastic to be stowed under a bunk cushion with absolutely no problem.

Ports. Most of the large fixed ports will have plastic for safety reasons, but the chances are they're beginning to show their age. See Figure 51. The solution to this is to replace the plastic, and here you do exactly what was done for the companionway plastic but with two exceptions. First, the thickness will have to match what's being replaced, and second, you have a choice of color. Of course, you can always use clear plastic; however, let me make a suggestion for you to think about.

Sailboats, because of where they happen to be at a particular time, sometimes offer very little privacy. I like a description my wife made one time while we were tied up at a busy marina: "being on the boat was like living in a shopping center mall." People seem to enjoy peering in sailboats so your alternative is to keep the curtains closed.

Figure 51. Plastic port that needs replacing

But this can give you that closed-in feeling. In my opinion, the answer to this problem is to use colored or "smoked" plastic that lets you see out while outsiders cannot see in. Now, I know there's stick-on material that offers this advantage and is fine if you don't intend to replace your ports. If you do replace them, though, consider a dark plastic that gives you privacy and at the same time improves the appearance of your boat.

Another word of advice—if the ports are mostly curves, you may want the plastic supplier to cut it to fit. He will have the proper tools and the cost should be minimal. Just carry along an old one for a pattern.

At the same time you're replacing the plastic, don't forget to clean up the metal frames. Here is one place you may consider rechroming if the frames are chrome and showing their age. If not, then a good metal polish should dress them up.

The opening ports will be smaller than the fixed ports, and they come in many designs. From my experience the ports on older boats will have metal frames with either a glass or plastic vision panel.

Depending on the condition of the port, you have several choices on how to go about refurbishing. You can clean up what you have and use as is. You can clean up and replace the vision panel. A word of advice—replacing panels in opening ports is not the same as with fixed ports. There's a little more to it so if you're not sure, have it done for you. Or you can simply rechrome and use the existing vision panel.

Frankly, I don't think you'll have many problems in the area of opening ports. Here's another place where it pays to have an older fiberglass sailboat built by a reputable firm which used good hardware. But no matter how well built an item is, if it has moving parts there'll be wear and tear. A port must keep the water out when closed, so pay attention to the seals; if they're even questionable, replace them.

You do have one last option when it comes to opening ports and when everything is considered, you may decide to replace the port itself. If so, you'll have plenty to choose from. Ventilation is another reason to replace an opening port, but in this case the idea is to add a larger port for better flow of air, a topic which will be discussed again in Ventilation, Chapter 10. However, at this point, I want you to keep the exterior appearance in mind when replacing a port with a larger one. It's possible the new port or ports will be completely out of proportion and could detract from the looks.

Opening ports should have screens. If yours don't, I suggest you make or order screens because insects can ruin a cruise faster than anything I know except maybe running out of ice for drinks.

Overhead. For the most part as far as the overhead is concerned you'll be stuck with what you have, which will be either painted, unfinished-looking fiberglass, or a smooth fiberglass headliner. Let's take the easy one first. The headliner should give you no problems. It's easy to clean and looks good. The only real problem I've experienced is the headliner will sometimes pull away near the edges. This is easy to fix with a good adhesive. The trick is how to apply force during the curing process; after all, you cannot use a C clamp. In answer to this, I refer you to Figure 52. As you can see, the idea is simple, but you may have to use your imagination to put the idea to use.

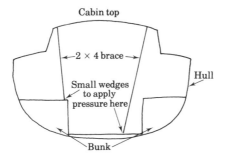

Figure 52. Headliner brace

As for the painted unfinished overhead, you have two choices—paint or cover up. From the practical viewpoint with upgrading in mind, I'd suggest repainting. On the other hand, if you are planning a complete refurbishing job below decks and you can't stand to see that painted fiberglass pattern, you have no option but to cover. You can use some form of stick-on fabric. However, your best bet is to glue and screw strips of wood to the overhead and then fasten to these strips whatever surface you choose. There is teak plywood, or wood planking, painted or varnished.

There's another area that needs to be addressed while we're looking at the overhead: all those exposed nuts, bolts, and screws that penetrate the cabin top. And most of the time it makes no difference if the boat has a headliner or not, the fasteners still show.

With the headliner there's not much you can do except make sure they are clean and replace any that are discolored and unsightly. However, without the headliner you have the option to paint and make the nuts, bolts, and screws less obtrusive. See Figure 53. If you choose to cover the unfinished overhead, the fasteners will be hidden. As a matter of fact, a large number of them may be the deciding factor in covering the overhead.

One final word—two of the three subjects covered here apply to the entire below area and not just the main cabin. So when you're planning and working with the overhead and ports, think in terms of the whole interior of the boat.

Figure 53. Painted exposed fasteners in overhead

Making Major Changes

My purpose here is not to give you specific details on how to do this or that particular project, but rather to give you general ideas and suggestions on considering making major changes below decks. Let's look at some examples of major changes, keeping in mind how you intend to use your boat. First, I'll give you the benefit of my personal experience. My boat had the standard main cabin layout of a settee bunk on each side with a pilot berth behind each settee. This arrangement allowed the main cabin to sleep four. The starboard side had a pipe and canvas pilot berth that folded back against the hull (see Figure 54) and became a catchall for just about anything you would care to name. The port side (see Figure 55) had a pilot berth projecting over the settee bunk. This port pilot berth also seemed to collect all kinds of stuff as well as creating two problems with the use of the settee bunk. One, the bunk had to be pulled out and locked in place in order to sleep. Although this was really not a problem to me, the second situation was. When the settee bunk was pushed back in place

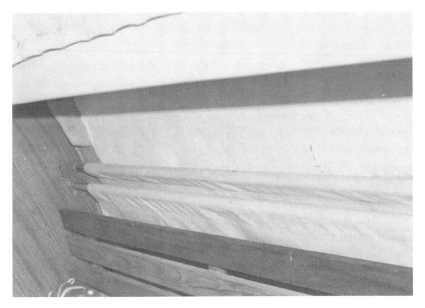

Figure 54. Pipe and canvas berth

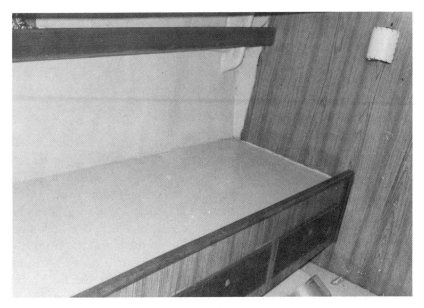

Figure 55. Pilot berth

creating a settee for sitting, you ended up with hardly enough room to get your backside on. In short it was downright uncomfortable. But what was I to do?

Well, the first thing my wife and I did was analyze how we intended to use the boat in general and how we wanted to use the accommodations below in particular. Not much trouble with the general use. We reviewed our original guidelines which were mostly cruising with a little racing. In any case, we didn't plan on spending days at sea so sleeping in a safe comfortable bunk underway was not necessary. When cruising we were going to be either tied up or at anchor for the night so comfortable conditions were of prime importance.

Next we gave careful thought to our personal preference for the use of the below area. The boat would sleep six, four in the main cabin and two in the forward cabin, but we never intended to have six on the boat overnight. Four yes, but never six. We asked ourselves if we only need four bunks, why do we have six?

As a result we did away with two berths. The pipe and canvas berth to starboard was replaced with storage bins. See Figure 56. I then pushed the backrest of the port settee outboard until there was room on the settee to sit comfortably. What remained of the pilot berth was a long shelf that was perfect for storage lockers. See Figure 57.

When all the work was completed we had a main cabin that slept two, was comfortable to sit in, and had plenty of storage. The cost besides money and time, of course, was the loss of two berths, but for our particular needs and intended use of the boat the loss of the two berths presented no problem.

Let me add here that most of the major changes which you'll contemplate will involve sleeping areas. For some unknown reason many sailboats are built with only one real requirement, and that is to sleep as many people as possible. It seems boat builders think sailors travel with a huge entourage and it's important they can all be bedded down on the boat. If you've recently bought a boat, I'm sure people who are not boaters have asked you the two standard questions: how long is your boat? and how many can it sleep? I always chuckle when I recall an old gentleman sailor I've known for a good many years who when asked how many his boat slept replied, "Well, that depends on if they are standing, sitting, or lying down."

Figure 56. Storage bins

Figure 57. Storage lockers

Anyway, if you don't plan on having a host of visitors all the time, consider converting some of that sleepng space to better use with regard to your particular requirements. Granted sleeping areas are involved in a large part of the major changes, but the other side of the coin is storage. Therefore, almost all major changes will mean converting sleeping areas to some form of storage. A good example is the quarterberth, which is one of those compromises you learn to live with on a boat. I like the quarterberth under certain conditions, for instance under way through the night; but on the other hand, the quarterberth uses space that can be put to much better use. It's the older sailboats that have the space problems. The new generation of wide body sailboats have the beam to allow for a U-shaped galley on one side with the navigation station and quarterberth opposite.

The traditional sailboat will have less volume below than a new boat of the same overall length; therefore, you'll have to utilize what you have to the fullest. An older boat forty feet or less that has a quarterberth can have a small galley area with very little countertop space. Chances are the icebox will be jammed in next to the stove and sink making it inconvenient at the least and dangerous at the worst when the stove is in use. At the same time, the quarterberth projects back into the cockpit storage area and takes up space you may prefer to use for sailing gear.

The solution to this space problem, assuming you don't need the quarterberth to sleep in, is a major change. I recently had the pleasure of going aboard an older fiberglass sailboat classic, the Rhodes 41. The owner had done away with the quarterberth and extended the countertop over the quarterberth area. The end result was a countertop that ran the full extent of the beam. There were plenty of storage places under and at the back of the new countertop. The area next to the hull was used for the radio, tape deck, and navigation instruments with the countertop serving as a chart table when needed. When the galley was used and during the cocktail hour, the expanded service area really came into its own as there was plenty of room for everything. Along with these advantages the extra space in the cockpit locker was put to good use by allowing more cruising gear to be stowed with less trouble. The Rhodes 41 still slept five after the major change which was more than enough bunks.

Another major change that may give you something to think about is changing the sleeping arrangements in the forward cabin.

For example, your wife likes to read in bed and sleep late on the boat. You, however, get up early and her reading lights keep you awake so it makes sense to sleep in different parts of the boat. Your wife would prefer the forward cabin which will give her quiet time in the morning, but the V berths are kind of narrow. She wants more comfort. What to do, you ask? Well consider taking out one V berth and enlarging the remaining one with the extra space going to storage for your wife's personal things. The only real drawback to this idea is if you need bunks for four or more, you'll have all the bunks except the forward one in the main cabin. If this major change has some merit, think your entire bunk arrangement through before proceeding. If you plan to have only four overnight, then you'll have no trouble sleeping three in the main cabin. On the other hand, you may have a couple of kids to provide for so maybe that quarterberth you were thinking about doing away with should stay, at least for a while anyway.

Another good example of a major change is to convert a U-shaped dinette to an L-shaped dinette. See Figures 58, 59, 60, and 61 for a step-by-step illustration. The reason for this change was that the U-shaped dinette made the area around the companionway very close and even awkward and created inconvenience in this high-traffic section of the main cabin. Although making the change meant the loss of one sleeping accommodation (the U-shaped dinette could sleep two and the L-shaped dinette could only accommodate one in addition to the fact some storage was lost by this major change), this caused no problems with the owner because he could still sleep five. Although no one usually wants to give up storage space, adding room in the main cabin had priority. There are, of course, other changes to be considered but none so large an undertaking as my examples, so they can wait until we cover the particular topic they're associated with.

My point in using these examples is to make you think about considering a major change as a part of your refurbishing project. I'll be the first to admit these projects may seem like a tremendous job on the surface but they're really not. All you are doing is cutting some plywood, screwing it together, and running the trim.

The truly difficult part of a major change is making up your mind to do it. There is always a certain amount of reluctance to be overcome before you feel comfortable with a project. Perhaps, the biggest objection is wondering how the change will affect the resale value of the

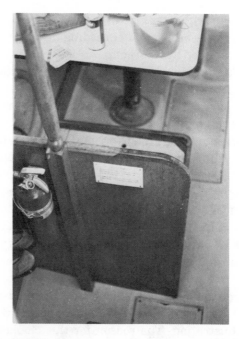

Figure 58. U-shaped dinette

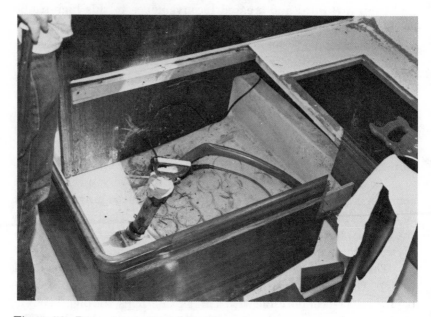

Figure 59. Removing section of dinette

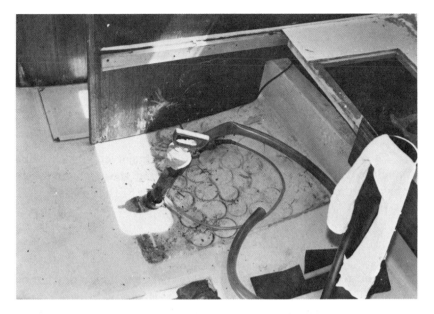

Figure 60. Cabin sole under removed section (Note bilge pump that should be located in cockpit)

Figure 61. Berth ready for trim after dinette section removed

boat. My personal opinion is not to worry about this objection. The examples I've given you enhance the use of the below deck areas, not detract from it. If anything, a major change could add value to the boat. Bear in mind I'm not talking about some outlandish radical change. Just remember a major change should not violate good old-fashioned common sense. If you feel the change will improve your use of the boat and other people will also see the merit of the project, then by all means do it!

One last word on the subject. If any major change is being considered, this is the time. The refurbishing goes smoother with better results if the large projects are done first with the lesser work following.

Navigation Station and Wet Locker

On the larger boat you may be fortunate enough to have a navigation station. The new boats all seem to have this very worthwhile work place—even on the boats under thirty feet. But most of the older fiberglass boats under thirty-five feet will not, and there's really no way to add one without chopping up the entire main cabin. Therefore, if you don't have a navigation station and can't add one, you'll just have to make do with the general use table. But on the other hand if you have a navigation station there are several ways to upgrade this space.

First, make sure that if the desk top shows its age, you replace it. This is a good place for new formica or maybe adding formica over a scratched or scarred wooden top. Remember to take into account your colors. You may want the navigation desk to match the galley and main cabin table, or at least be compatible.

As for the wood, it's treated just as all the wood below deck. If you have drawers, then I refer you to a later section of this chapter on drawers. There'll be a good number of ideas for small projects that I'll discuss in this chapter which can be applied to the navigation space, and you'll be aware of these topics when you get to them. At that point this space is treated exactly like the main cabin in general.

For now I want to highlight two refurbishing ideas concerning the navigation station for you to think about. One is if the desk top is slanted, consider making it flat. Slanted tops are only good for working with papers and books, but a flat top can be used for paperwork and then become a countertop when necessary, making this space much more versatile. Two is raising the desk top so it can be used while standing instead of sitting. What this does is allow the normal space needed for sitting and leg room to be used for many other uses. After all, navigation today does not require one to spend long periods of time at paperwork—it is more like a quick dash below to check the chart, then back on deck. I personally like the flat top stand-up navigation desk because it's a good use of space, and very convenient.

Next, let's look at the wet locker. If you have one, then fine. They're extremely handy when the rains come down. Make sure the drain works properly and the space has normal ventilation. The inside should be painted with a good enamel that will take the water with no problem. If you don't have one, consider how you can add a wet locker. Do keep in mind one very important fact. We're not talking about a hanging locker with all kinds of clothes. A wet locker need only have room for several suits of foul weather gear, say eight to ten inches wide. In case there's no way to add the wet locker then at least think about adding a hook where you can hang a wet jacket and have it out of the way until needed. On the smaller boat, thirty-two feet and under, the wet locker will be a luxury so you may have to accept the fact it's something that would be nice to have but not practical because of space limitations.

Drawers, Lockers, Stowage Bins, and Shelves

The one thing a sailboat can always use more of is storage areas. Let's take a look at ways to improve what you have and also how you can convert wasted space to stowage areas.

Drawers. The first thing to be aware of concerning drawers is they're expensive for the boat builder, so there'll probably be only what was necessary to make the boat marketable. That's why as you look around the cabin it's easy to spot some places drawers would be handy and you wonder why the builder didn't add them. The answer is simple; why add the drawers when the boat will sell without them?

For now you're interested in the drawers already on the boat. Chances are your boat is a production boat from a manufacturer that has a line of boats of various sizes so it's possible the drawers in your boat are the same style and size as drawers used in other models.

What this means is a particular drawer may do a good job of using the available space on a thirty-foot boat but that same drawer used on a 40 footer may do a poor job of using the available space.

You want to check all your drawers for distance from front to back and then measure the available space behind the drawer. You may be in for a pleasant surprise. For example, you can have a fourteen-inch drawer in a twenty-four-inch space which means you'll be able to extend the length of the drawer at least six to eight inches. See Figure 62.

All the drawers in my boat, with the exception of one, had the space to be expanded. The net result was about a 40 percent increase in volume which was well worth the work involved.

Enlarging a drawer is a relatively simple matter. First you take the drawer apart, being careful not to damage the front or back because these are the only two sections that will be reused; bottom and sides are the sections that will have to be replaced. Use a good grade of cabinetmaking quality plywood for your new bottom and sides. Using the original bottom and sides as templets but adding the necessary new length, cut out the new bottom and sides. Next, assemble the parts, and here I would suggest you consider sealing the interior of the drawer. I happen to like the interiors of my drawers varnished. It gives you a smooth easy-to-clean surface that will not let splinters pick and snag clothes. Also, the varnished interior gives a pleasing appearance.

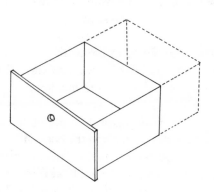

Figure 62. Expanded drawer

I might add, you can carry this lengthening of a drawer one step further. Often the back of the drawer will stop on a curved surface like the hull; and if you take the trouble to put an odd shape on the back of the drawer, you can pick up a little more space. See Figure 63.

I wish to add one last suggestion about your existing drawers. If the drawer fronts have a small finger hole that's used to pull the drawer out, I have an idea you might like to consider. Personally, I find the finger hole a very poor method to open a drawer; it's excellent, however, if you want to break a finger. My suggestion is to enlarge the finger hole. See Figure 64. This allows two or three fingers to be used to lift up and pull out the drawer. At the same time, it gives the drawer front a smooth surface with no protrusion. This is important if the drawer front is behind a sitting area and leaned against. The enlarged finger hole has another plus: air can circulate through the opening.

Lockers and Storage Bins. For the sake of clarity let me say that lockers have doors or sliding partitions while bins are storage places

Figure 63. Odd-shaped drawer

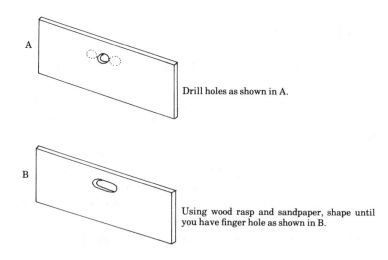

Drill holes as shown in A.

Using wood rasp and sandpaper, shape until you have finger hole as shown in B.

Figure 64. Enlarging finger holes

with no front. You'll probably have a good number of lockers and bins because they cost less than drawers. The biggest fault I find with them is the space inside isn't used very well. For example, behind a locker door will be a large area, but for practical reasons only the bottom third of the space is ever used. In a case like this adding one or more interior shelves and hooks will allow almost all of the space to be used. The finger hole seems to be used often with the locker door so you might consider enlarging this hole to accommodate more than one finger as was done with the drawer fronts.

While we're on locker fronts, take a good look at the hinges if the door is hinged. Consider replacing them if their age is showing, but remember to coordinate this new hardware with whatever else you're replacing so everything matches.

Many bins will have large areas that waste a portion of the space, just as lockers, and the solution is the same as with the locker; i.e., add shelves and hooks. There's nothing else to be done to a storage bin to improve it. After all, it's only a hole in a partition where you stuff things.

Shelves. Existing shelves are even simpler than bins, but there are two improvements which can be easily added. The first is to install a higher front piece. Most shelves have an edge that's only a couple of inches high which allows items to fall out when the boat heels. The solution is to add a higher edge. The second is to put dividers running from front to back so items will not slide fore and aft as the boat sails.

Our last storage area is the hard-to-get-at places under the bunks. These spaces are similar to lockers in that they're very simple arrangements but with access from the top. A useful suggestion here is to designate certain lockers for a particular type of gear. For example, place all the large or bulky items in one locker and then store smaller gear in one or more lockers that have been partitioned. The dividers will keep everything neat, secure, and convenient to locate.

Options for Additional Storage. You've been involved in improving your existing storage, now you may want to consider your options for additional space. On the stock production boat there'll be a number of places that can be converted to storage. Also, you may want to give attention to making under-bunk space more convenient to use. Chances are, you'll have a choice of drawers, lockers, bins, or shelves when working out the details of exactly how to utilize the extra space. The decision on what form of storage to add will depend on the intended use and how much work you're willing to do. More about this will follow shortly, but for now I wish to discuss where storage can be added. Remember you're dealing with the main cabin and that the galley area is a separate chapter in which galley storage will be covered. The most obvious space to be put to work is what's made available when you make a major change.

Take a good look at vertical surfaces. For example, bulkheads, partitions, areas that already have drawers; in short every surface that may be able to receive a storage unit. Next, you determine what's behind these surfaces. And here again, you may be in for a pleasant surprise, because the odd dead space that can be used pops up. It can be any size, but most likely on the small side from my experience. Don't let the fact that the area behind a vertical surface is utilized stop you from thinking about adding storage. Just because the hanging locker is behind the bulkhead is no reason not to think about doing something with the bulkhead. Since I may have confused you here, I'll give you an example.

The bulkhead would be a perfect place to install a shallow bin with shelves which could be used for books. Of necessity the storage unit would project into the hanging locker about eight inches. Because of this you decide against adding the bookshelves even though it would be convenient and attractive. But, do you actually need the eight inches in the hanging locker? If after losing the eight inches there's still enough space for what hanging clothes you plan to have on the boat, by all means add the bookshelves. If not, then which would you rather have? I would like to suggest that when you find yourself in a dilemma like this, you take some time to find out just how the hanging locker will be used and then make your decision.

Suppose you're on the tall side and would like to extend a bunk six inches. It's easily done by adding a foot hole in the bulkhead. Just because the head is behind a bulkhead is no reason not to think about adding storage. It's possible to have some wasted or hard-to-use space in the head which could be reached with no trouble at all if you came through the bulkhead.

I not only want to give you some ideas, but more importantly I want you to think about where to add storage in a flexible manner. Once you've decided where to add storage you're faced with how, and that's our next subject.

The first thing to decide is how the new space will be used. If you have a specific idea in mind, you'll have to decide if a drawer, locker, bin, or shelf is the best type of unit. On the other hand, you can be planning on the area being put to general use and you'll have to decide what type of unit will work the best.

There's one important fact about all these storage units that I want to impress on you. No matter what you add, ask yourself this question. What happens when I put the lee rail under water? Storage areas above all have to do their job when the going gets rough. If they don't, they are not only worthless they may even be dangerous.

Other possible storage places are the compartments under the bunks. This area is not wasted space as such; however, it's most inconvenient to get at when the bunk and all on it must be pushed aside to open the cover. There are ways to make this area more accessible.

The same idea we applied to the bulkhead with the hanging locker can be considered here. Think about having a drawer, for example, projecting into this space. Granted the drawer will take up a lot of room, but for your particular use it may be worth the compromise. Figure 65 is a tool drawer added under the port bunk. The tools are very convenient when you are working on the engine and all those other times when you need a certain tool and you don't want to stand on your head to drag out a tool box—just open the drawer and help yourself.

Another method is to cut an access hole and add a locker door. See Figure 66. This provides quick entry and looks good. You can always fall back on just an access opening and consider the under bunk compartment a large bin. If you do add the simple access opening, locate it as high as practical so items will not easily fall out. This's why the drawer or locker door is best, I feel, with the access hole my third choice.

There can be an obstacle in your way when it comes to under bunk space—the water or fuel tank. If you have one or both, then you'll have to either move the tank or live with it. I'll discuss tanks later.

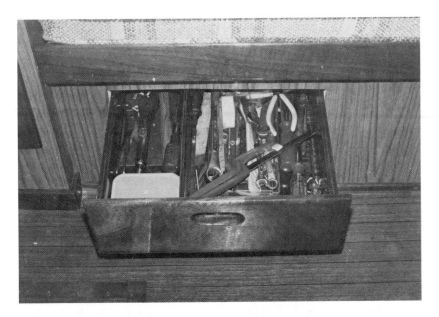

Figure 65. Tool drawer (Note hacksaw blade holder)

Figure 66. Under berth access with locker door

From my experience most of the added storage units will be lockers and bins. Along with this, the location for the added storage units will be behind the bunks using the hull as the back of the storage unit. It makes no difference if the space is available because of a major change consisting of doing away with a pilot berth or simply poor utilization of the space on the part of the builder. The end result will be the same—more storage.

As you can see from Figures 67 and 68, you have some options on exactly what you can add and how to go about putting it all together. The more ambitious work is not very difficult. I refer you to Figure 69 which details the building of lockers with an added open space for general storage. At the same time this open space keeps the lockers from closing in the main cabin.

Until now, I've said nothing about the type of closure to use on lockers. The two choices are the hinged door and sliding panel. The actual material used is your preference, but I will pass on some suggestions. Hinged doors should be made of wood. The wood looks

Figure 67. Added strip to hold in larger items

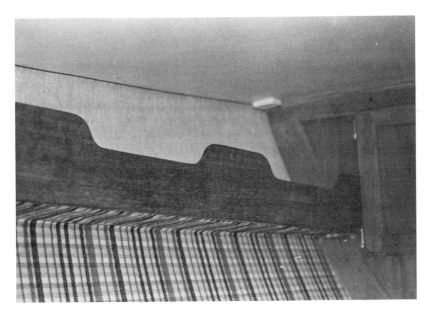

Figure 68. Enlarged trim on front of shelves in forward cabin

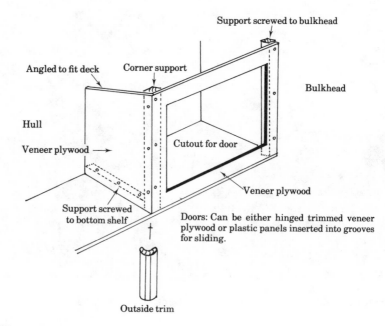

Support screwed to bulkhead

Angled to fit deck   Corner support

Bulkhead

Hull

Veneer plywood →   Cutout for door

Veneer plywood

Support screwed
to bottom shelf

Doors: Can be either hinged trimmed veneer
plywood or plastic panels inserted into grooves
for sliding.

Outside trim

Figure 69. Locker construction

good in an area most probably dominated by fiberglass and formica. At the same time wood is easy to work, especially teak. The door can be solid or have an insert, whichever suits your fancy. However, the solid door can be made with simple woodworking tools or turned out quickly by a woodworking shop at a reasonable price. On the other hand, doors with inserts require more work on your part or more money if you have them made.

You may consider the end result well worth the expense. My favorite insert is the basketweave material that looks very yachtlike and also allows the locker to be ventilated. You can also have the wood panel the same wood as the frame, or you can paint the panel to contrast with the frame. An added touch is some sort of design cut in the panel to allow air to pass through.

The size and shape of the door should be given some thought. Have it large enough only to do the job that's intended and no more. You don't want a barn door swinging around in the cabin. There's no reason that doors have to be the standard rectangle everyone envisions when a locker door is mentioned. As a matter of fact, a locker door that looks like a drawer and is hinged on the bottom can be very functional. This allows the door to swing down instead of in an arc that can be in the way. See Figure 66. This idea will work well with any type of narrow horizontal door regardless of what it looks like.

Our next form of closure is the sliding panel. This panel can be wood, formica, either on wood backing or by itself, or plain plastic. As for the wood panel, it's similar to the wood door. It can be a wood panel by itself or have a frame with some type of insert exactly like the door insert. The formica panel offers the choice of colors and when tastefully done can be used to enhance the appearance of the cabin. Also the colors can be useful in the galley. Both the wood and formica sliding panels can also have decorative designs cut for ventilation. By far the simplest sliding panel is solid plastic. It's inexpensive, very easy to keep clean, and offers a choice of colors. You'll find the material at the same place your plastic companionway board and port lights came from. If you want to cut the panels yourself, I refer you to that section in Chapter 3.

As far as I'm concerned, the plastic sliding panel in a dark color gives an excellent up-to-date appearance. Along with this, I'd suggest, if your boat already has sliding panels of formica or plastic and they show their age, that the panels be replaced with new dark plastic. See Figures 70 and 71. (I'm sorry these before-and-after photographs are not in color. The black-and-white picture just does not do justice to how the dark panels upgrade the looks of these lockers.)

The bilge area under the cabin sole is the last storage area to investigate. Most older sailboats will have some room under the cabin sole that can be utilized. This is an excellent place for those messy items that are kept in containers and will not be affected by a little bilge water slopping around. Your main interest here is to consider adding partitions so the stored items are not continually rolling about. If the area under the cabin sole is large enough to handle other pieces of gear, you may want to take the necessary steps to stow this equipment there, for example, extra anchor line, or one of those collapsible anchors. This is a good place for the little used but important tools as long as they're in a waterproof box. It's also a great place to carry cans of drinks.

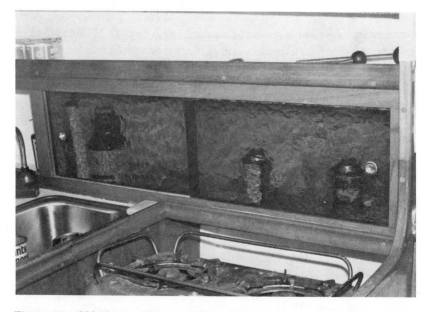

Figure 70. Old plastic sliding panels

Figure 71. New dark plastic sliding panels

After all, we're dealing with a sailboat and the more weight that can be carried under the cabin sole instead of some other place on the boat, the better off you are. So, give this area your serious attention and don't hesitate to put it to work. Just make sure everything is secured.

Premade Units. On the market there are a large number of premade racks and shelves to stow just about anything that's used on a boat. These units are very handy because they allow you to use the odd space. The example that comes to mind is a rack to hold the binoculars. I also particularly like the rack which can be added to a bulkhead to hold folded charts. It's practical and looks nautical as well. You'll be able to find what you want at the better marine stores or the mail order catalogs.

The Liquor Locker. I have a suggestion concerning the use of one of your lockers, be it one already in place or one added. If you enjoy a toddy when the sun gets over the yardarm, there should be a secure place to store the bottles. The only sure way to do this is have each bottle in its own slot. See Figure 72. Your liquor locker can be something simple with holders for a couple of bottles inside a multipurpose locker, or it can be elaborate and hold all manner of refreshments. Your guidelines here are your personal preference and the space you're working with, so give this idea some thought if your boat did not come equipped with a liquor locker. At the same time if it did, you may want to look into improving what you have to suit a particular need. Two good examples come to mind. Slots in liquor lockers for the most part are round, but your choice may come in a square bottle so you're going to have to alter one or more slots to fit. Or how about that certain after dinner liqueur that comes in a squatty bottle and requires a larger round hole? The old saying, a place for everything and everything in its place, applies very well to the liquor locker.

Construction Tips

The first thing you already know or will know once you start to work on your boat is that everything is a curve or angle with precious few ninety-degree angles. Stock production boats are run out just like anything else on an assembly line, and mistakes are made. These

Figure 72. Bottle slots in liquor locker

mistakes seldom create a problem or are even visible to the eye until you add something. When you add a locker, bin, or shelf, expect to have to do a little fudging to make things work out. That's the bad news; now for the good. It's not very difficult to fit wood to these curves and angles. The installation is simple; the shelf rests on a support at each end which in turn is screwed to the upright sections. The skill here is cutting the back edge of the shelf so it has the same curve as the hull. This is easily done without using cardboard and the trial and error method to make a templet. I refer you to Figure 73 which shows you a simple and foolproof way to duplicate the curve of the hull.

This method works for any type of curve, large or small. You'll find it just as handy and accurate for a vertical panel as for a horizontal one, or for any type of surface in between.

If you'll recall in Chapter 2 I talked about tools and the belt sander. Well, along with the regular standbys like drill motors and hand tools, the belt sander is practically indispensable when doing woodwork on a boat. A great deal of the pieces will require an angled or beveled edge, and this can be easily done with the belt sander. You

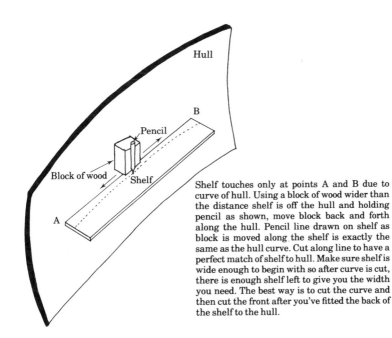

Shelf touches only at points A and B due to curve of hull. Using a block of wood wider than the distance shelf is off the hull and holding pencil as shown, move block back and forth along the hull. Pencil line drawn on shelf as block is moved along the shelf is exactly the same as the hull curve. Cut along line to have a perfect match of shelf to hull. Make sure shelf is wide enough to begin with so after curve is cut, there is enough shelf left to give you the width you need. The best way is to cut the curve and then cut the front after you've fitted the back of the shelf to the hull.

Figure 73. Matching hull curve to back of shelf

have two choices: you can clamp the wood and move the sander or reverse the process and clamp the sander and run the edge along the belt. If you have places where a panel or shelf meets another surface at what appears to be ninety degrees, but the angle is off just a little bit, the belt sander is the perfect tool because it allows you to shave a little off against the grain until the joining angle fits. Many times wood trim seems to meet at all sorts of weird angles, and the belt sander with some persistence will let you put the trim together like a professional. However, the belt sander does have one drawback when being used below deck. It will create a cloud of dust that will cover everything, including you, not to mention breathing the stuff. I suggest you do your sanding out on deck or better yet, on the dock. It means a bit more walking, but you'll have better working conditions.

Refurbishing Older Wood Surfaces

For the most part the wood below deck will be plywood with a veneer of mahogany or teak usually with some type of finish. From my experience this wood will have begun to show its age, with the added problem of black or dark areas showing. See Figure 74. To bring this wood back to life and put it in first-class condition requires only one thing on your part—elbow grease.

The first step is to remove every fitting possible, for example, light fixtures, clocks, racks, and any other item screwed to the surface. What you're after is a clear surface to work on. It's almost impossible to work around, for example, a light and have the wood look one hundred percent finished.

Once the surface is clear, start sanding. If the area is large enough for a power tool, consider using a vibrator sander with a belt sander as second choice. It's hard to damage the wood veneer with a vibrator sander, but the belt sander is another matter. It turns at such a high rate that even with fine sandpaper, the veneer can be damaged in short order if close attention is not paid. Under no conditions use a disk sander. This tool will chew through the veneer in the wink of an eye and at the same time cut ugly whirls in the wood.

There'll be some places where you'll be able to use a sander, but for the most part it's going to take hand work, especially in the smaller, hard-to-get-to places. The sanding is the really hard part, but it has to be done, and done well. All the old finish has to be removed and then the wood has to be sanded smooth with fine sandpaper, say, 120 grit. This final sanding to get the surface smooth is important because the smoother the surface, the better finish you'll have. I'll have more to say on this shortly.

Let's get back to the preparation process and consider how to handle those unsightly dark spots. You can, of course, remove them by sanding, but often the dark color goes so deep you'll have to go through the veneer which will look about as bad as the dark area. What you do here is treat the dark spots with oxalic acid which is a bleach which returns the wood to its natural color or very close to it.

Oxalic acid can be found at your local drugstore. Mix about a five percent solution with lukewarm water, and using a clean paint brush, apply to the stained area. Let dry, and there should be a residue left on the wood. Sand the area to remove the residue and help lighten the dark spot.

Most likely one application won't do it, so be prepared to brush on the oxalic acid as many times as necessary to lighten the dark area.

Figure 74. Deteriorated wood

Note Figures 75 and 76 which are before-and-after pictures. It took four applications to blend in the dark wood with the end result turning out very well. Be sure to wear rubber gloves when using oxalic acid as it is caustic.

If you don't get very good results, you might try increasing the oxalic percentage. Don't use hot water as it can give off rather unpleasant fumes.

After preparation comes what I consider the enjoyable part, applying the finish. My choice by far is varnish. It's easy to keep clean, and the high gloss adds a real nautical touch to the cabin. However, with varnish you get exactly what you give, so to obtain a smooth mirror finish requires work on your part. The wood must be sanded smooth; varnish will not fill voids, so don't depend on it to smooth out the finished product. The wood has to be smooth, and the varnish applied according to instructions with light sanding between coats. To get a professional looking job, expect to give the wood at

171

Figure 75. Stained wood before treatment with oxalic acid

Figure 76. Stained wood after treatment with oxalic acid

least five to six coats, not the usual two layers you may feel are sufficient, since the sun won't be able to attack the varnish below deck.

Of course, you may prefer another type of finish, teak oil, for example. You can even use paint, and the preparation would certainly be easier, but I'd recommend this course only if the trim is in such bad shape that it's almost impossible to prepare it for varnish or oil.

In any case and no matter what you use, do use something. If the wood and especially trim wood are left natural, they will quickly pick up body oil from hands and even suntan oil from the occasional shoulder. This oil will start to turn the wood dark and in short order you'll have unsightly stains. This is really why I think varnish is the best finish. Its hard surface allows these types of oils to be wiped away with ease.

Cosmetic Treatment of Exposed Hull Sections

Fiberglass sailboats have a great deal of the hull exposed below deck. Since fiberglass by itself has all the warmth and personality of a refrigerator, you need to add a pleasing atmosphere below deck, and these exposed areas should have cosmetic treatment.

Let's take the most obvious first—painting. This will be your fastest and cheapest way to dress up exposed hull areas. I'm sure for the most part the areas in question are already painted. However, what you're interested in is not only covering the fiberglass but making it a pleasing color that complements the other colors, for example, the formica on the counter tops and the fabric on the cushions.

My choice is an enamel in a light-to-medium cream or beige. This color goes well with the darker woods like teak and mahogany, and at the same time is compatible with most countertop and cushion colors. The color is, of course, your preference, and the only color I suggest you stay away from is white for both the main cabin and the forward cabin as well, as it's simply too stark and cold. Let me quickly add the head is another matter, and white paint has its place there. This topic will be discussed later.

While on the subject of painting, a word about the hull areas that form the back of lockers and bins. Use the same color paint which is used for the other hull areas. This ties everything together and looks good when the locker door is open. Along with the back of lockers and bins I recommend the areas under the bunks receive the same treatment. Attention to these details will give the main cabin that finished appearance. Even if paint is not used on exposed hull places, use paint for the inside of lockers and bins, and make sure the color is compatible with the rest of your color scheme.

Your next choice to hide the exposed hull sections is using some form of fabric or vinyl wall covering material. A trip to a store which specializes in home decoration items will supply you with plenty of ideas. There's a stick-on burlap material that really looks good and is easy to apply. You can even use carpet if you prefer. This is a good choice if you need something between you and the cold hull say, for example, behind a bunk. One word of caution; make sure the fabric is not natural. Natural fibers will absorb moisture and this can lead to all kinds of problems from rank odors to rotting material. There's one more source of supply you may try when it comes to decorator items; and that's the recreation vehicle and camper dealers. Often these firms will have something you can use.

The last method to cover the exposed hull is, in my opinion, the nicest looking and at the same time the most nautical. I'm talking about strips of wood an inch or so wide. Figure 77 is a perfect example of what I'm talking about. You don't necessarily have to use a dark wood like teak or mahogany; a light wood like ash gives a very pleasing appearance when varnished. The application of the strips is simple. See Figure 78 for details. Granted the wood strips will cost more both in money and time, but here is another good example of the end result being worth the effort.

Before leaving this subject of cosmetic treatment, I wish to say something about formica-covered bulkheads and panels. This finishing technique was, and still is to a certain degree, very popular with the builders. Chances are your boat may have formica-covered bulkheads in some woodlike color. Unless you intend to get into a major replacement project, I'd suggest you live with the formica. Once everything else is completed the formica will tend to blend into the background and not be too noticeable. At the same time, the formica is very easy to keep clean, and there's something to be said for this, especially on a boat.

Figure 77. Wood battens used to cover exposed hull

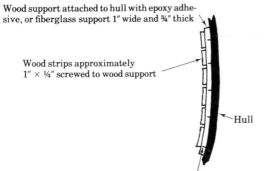

Wood support attached to hull with epoxy adhesive, or fiberglass support 1″ wide and ¾″ thick

Wood strips approximately 1″ × ¼″ screwed to wood support

Hull

Saw cuts every 3″ to 4″ to allow support to conform to hull curve.

Figure 78. Wood battens attached to hull

Tables

You have two basic types of tables, bulkhead-mounted and deck-mounted. The older sailboat will have less area below deck than the new boats of the same overall length. For this reason, when you have the more traditional layout of a bunk on each side of the main cabin, the bulkhead-mounted table is the best arrangement. It's out of the way until needed and easily folded down in seconds. On the other hand, the deck-mounted table associated with the older boat usually is a part of the side galley with a dinette-opposite layout. The dinette table can be made so it can be lowered to allow it to be converted to a double bunk. I'll admit the dinette table is handy when you don't have a navigation table and at the same time adds to the usable counterspace.

There's a third type of table that's being used on the new boats, and you may want to consider the same idea for your boat. It's the deck-mounted table that has each side folded down so you have a long skinny table permanently in place. The two side sections are raised in place when the full tabletop is needed. This table works well for the traditional bunk-on-each-side layout and can be used in the full dinette or a modified dinette to make access to the seats more convenient. I would like to point out that older sailboats thirty feet and under will have a space problem with this table even in the folded down position, so make sure you're not jamming things together below decks if you're considering this type of table.

Advice concerning tables was passed on to me some years ago and I'll pass it on to you. Tables on a sailboat are used very little. Much of what's eaten is done so in the cockpit, or when below from a plate held in your lap. I personally know of several boats in the thirty-foot range that have removed the table altogether. It was too much trouble for what the owners got out of it. The bottom line here is keep your table simple and easy to use, and make sure it's out of the way when not in use. Also make sure it's secure when the boat starts bouncing around in rough weather.

For now though, you're concerned with upgrading the table that came with the boat. Most likely the surface will be covered with formica in either a color or wood tone design. If the color is acceptable and the formica can be cleaned up, then everything else is easy.

But suppose the formica looks like a workbench and the color has to go. Then you have no choice but to replace the formica, and this is really no big deal. The convenient part of a table is it can be taken off the boat with no trouble so this allows you to carry it to a cabinet shop to have the formica replaced. At the same time, replacing formica is not difficult so you may consider giving it a go yourself. For the details of removing old formica and adding new, see Chapter 8.

If you do replace the table formica, give some thought to the galley countertops, at the same time. Both the galley and the table are part of the main cabin and will be seen together. If the colors are not the same, they should at least be compatible. There will be more on this topic in Chapter 8 on the galley.

Next is the wood used on the table, and here you follow the same outline that was covered a few pages back on preparing and finishing interior wood. Take special care if your tabletop is wood because when it's put to use it's the focal point of the main cabin. Be sure you can be proud to show off your handiwork.

I mentioned that the table can be taken off the boat. Because of this convenience I suggest you do all your work on the table in your garage. It keeps the mess off the boat, and will give you a home project to work on.

There's one sure way to upgrade your existing table. Chances are your table has formica and the edge was finished off with a plastic strip. Consider adding wood trim to the table edge. This not only looks good but serves the very useful purpose of acting as a fiddle board to keep items from sliding off. The trim comes from the same suppliers who furnish the racks and shelves (which were covered earlier). However, this trim may present a problem with the bulkhead-mounted table. You may have to move the hinge point away from the bulkhead to accommodate the added thickness of the table when the table is in the up position.

The last thing to look at on upgrading the table are the fittings. The bulkhead table will have a hinge arrangement and several latches to make all secure. The deck-mounted table will most likely have some sort of pipe affair for support. So both types do have some kind of hardware that should be upgraded for the sake of appearance. In the case of the bulkhead table you'll not be spending much money to simply replace all the fittings. Use yacht quality items, not something from the local hardware store, because the bulkhead table is always on display.

As for the floor-mounted table, you can replace the support if it does not work as well as it should. But in any case, paint what you have and keep it clean. When the table is in use, the support is constantly being brushed against; and when the ladies get their white slacks dirty, you'll wish you had painted that pipe support.

Hardware Fittings

I'm talking about hinges, latches, and the like that will be found on doors and locker fronts. If these items were on the boat originally, I'm sure they have begun to show their age. You have two choices here. First you can clean them up; and if they don't improve very much, you can consider having them rechromed. While this means your fittings will look first-rate, you still have the problem of adding fittings for new doors and locker fronts that most likely will not match the existing ones. Then there's your second choice: you can replace the old fittings, and frankly this is what I would recommend. The new fittings will all match and sparkle, and believe me, this goes a long way to help create that pleasant atmosphere you want below. The new fittings will also allow you to add lockers and doors and still be able to make sure everything will match.

Lights

No items show their age on the older fiberglass sailboat more than do the light fixtures. I think every older sailboat I've been on which hadn't been upgraded had the same kind of light fixtures. See Figure 79. These lights are not very attractive and seemed to get worse with age. The shades get dirty, and the frames rust to a dingy brown material. Also, if you have to read by one more than a few minutes, you are in real trouble. I guess the reason so many of these fixtures were used was the fact that they were cheap. Anyway I suggest you replace them with new ones. See Figures 80 and 81. The new lights come in several styles and at the same time are much more practical because they can be moved about. This really comes in handy when reading in your bunk. You'll have no trouble locating the new fixtures. A good marine store or mail order firm can fix you up. As for the

Figure 79. Old unsightly light fixture

Figure 80. A swiveltype light fixture matching the wall covering

Figure 81. Another swiveltype light fixture

actual work, it's simple. It's just a matter of hooking up two wires and screwing in the fixture.

There's another type of light you'll find on your boat and most likely in the galley area, the dome light. Chances are, this light will show it's age so plan on replacing it. Compare Figure 82 with 83 to see the difference.

Installing new light fixtures throughout the boat is one of the most positive upgrading projects you can do below decks. And just don't put the same fixture everywhere. Add some variety. Maybe one type in the main cabin with something different for the head and forward cabin. Be sure not to throw away the old fixtures. You can make good use of some of them later on.

Cabin Sole

With the older stock boats you'll usually have two types of cabin soles—teak veneer on plywood and fiberglass liner probably covered with carpet.

Figure 82. Old unsightly dome light

Figure 83. New dome light

Take the teak veneer sole first. If yours is in fairly good condition and all you have to do is sand and varnish, count yourself extremely lucky. Or better yet if it's good enough to use as is, don't read any further and just skip over to the next topic.

Chances are, though, your cabin sole is showing its age, and you can count each year with no trouble. No matter how much work you put into the sole, it's probably not going to look as good as you would like. Figure 84 is a good example of a teak veneer cabin sole which has been allowed to go too far to be put back in first-class shape.

You're faced with two choices at this point: replace or cover. To replace requires new veneer which can be supplied by your boatyard and a lot of work on your part. If you're not that comfortable with carpentry tools, consider having the work done for you. This is one place where you certainly want the end result to look good.

As for covering the old sole, carpet comes immediately to mind. Granted this is the quickest, easiest, and cheapest way to get the job done. You even have a choice of colors. But I personally don't care for rugs on a boat. They catch everything and when they get wet, they can create problems. I think the cabin sole on a boat should be able to take water and be easily wiped dry; at the same time, housekeeping is easier when the deck can be wiped clean with a damp cloth or swept with a small broom.

Let me tell you about a good inexpensive compromise; i.e., a deck covering which doesn't look like a rug, gives the same service as teak, and looks like teak decking—it is called Nautolex. It comes in several colors, feels like plastic covered cloth, and can be cut with shears or a razor blade. Also, since it's made to be used on outside deck areas it's durable. The teak color is very attractive below decks. See Figure 85.

Installation is not difficult. The receiving surface has to be clean and the best way to do this is by sanding. First you cut the Nautolex roughly to size and leave it in place on the deck. Next fold back a section and apply the contact cement, paying attention to the directions. Then place the folded section on the cement, being careful to work from the "hinged" point outward, smoothing the material as you go so there are no air pockets trapped creating a bubble. Stand on the newly cemented section and fold back another section and work yourself along.

Now for some tips. Don't worry about the edges; you can come back and cut them off with a razor blade and cover with trim. Bilge-

Figure 84. Stained cabin sole

Figure 85. Nautolex over stained cabin sole

access hatches present no problem. Remove all fittings and trim, if any, and replace the hatch. Run the Nautolex over the hatch cover exactly like the rest of the deck. When this is done, you can come back and find with your finger the edge of the cover; then cut out the cover with a razor blade. Add the trim and fittings and it's ready to go back in its opening. The advantage to doing the hatch covers this way is that the lines in the Nautolex are all lined up.

The best trim to use is flat stainless steel which hides the rough edge of the fabric and outlines the cover in the deck. See Figure 86. When pressing the material into the contact cement, use a balled-up rag in your hand. The areas you're working with are not large and you'll be able to press down what's needed in short order. The rag allows your hand to slide easily over the surface as you work.

You will get some air bubbles, not many if you're careful, but nevertheless, you will have some. Keep a razor blade handy or, better yet, a utility knife that has a sharp point. Cut a small slit in the bubble and press down. The slit will disappear with no trouble after the air is pushed out. If the bubble area doesn't want to stay stuck to

Figure 86. Cabin sole hatch trim

the deck, buy a hypodermic needle from the drugstore and inject some glue into the bubble. You should also buy glue that will work with the needle at the same time. The contact cement used under the Nautolex is too thick to use with a needle. This method works well on the odd bubble that may appear later on.

The Nautolex has an added advantage for the older boats. Many have the turn of the bilge showing between the cabin sole and interior panels. These curved areas were difficult to cover with the teak veneer and so they were left exposed. If you prefer these areas to be covered, the Nautolex is ideal. It can be run from a flat to a curved surface with no trouble as shown in Figure 87.

The other type of cabin sole is the fiberglass liner, usually with a carpet. This arrangement is pretty simple and foolproof. Although the carpet will probably need replacing, this is easily done. The liner itself can be cleaned up if necessary, and can even be painted if you prefer not to have the carpet. All in all this type of cabin sole is very little trouble and easy to keep. There is one drawback, however; it

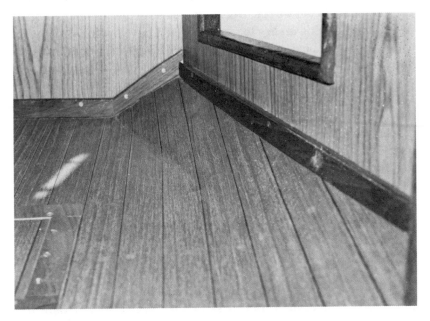

Figure 87. Nautolex on curved surface

doesn't have that yachting look that decking does, whether real or imitation.

One suggestion you may want to consider is installing Nautolex directly on the fiberglass cabin sole if you don't care for the exposed fiberglass or carpet. Too much fiberglass can give you that stark plastic look and using Nautolex is a good way to "warm up" the boat. The bottom line with the cabin sole is to make it as attractive as possible. It's another one of those high visibility areas that helps set the tone for the boat's interior.

Bunk Cushions

The last cosmetic topic you should consider is perhaps the most visible item below deck. Bunk cushions can set the tone you desire on the boat because the eye is constantly drawn to their color. If the color and pattern are pleasing to the eye, then all is well; but if the bunk cushions look as if they came from the drunk tank at the local jail, no matter how beautiful everything else is you've missed the opportunity to create a pleasant atmosphere. See Figure 88.

From my experience the older fiberglass sailboat in a somewhat run-down condition will be in desperate need of new cushions. Fortunately for you, this is easy to remedy. You'll have no trouble locating someone in the boat cushion business. Asking fellow boaters, boatyard people, or looking in the yellow pages will give you plenty to choose from.

Let me pass on now some suggestions to consider when thinking about new cushions. It goes without saying the covers will be replaced, but at the same time look into the condition of the foam. Is it on the thin side? Does it still have the ability to rebound? Is it holding together? Does it smell a little funny? In short, do you want to sleep on this foam? What I'm leading up to is for you to think about new foam as well as covers. Completely new bunk cushions will certainly enhance the boat's interior and at the same time be more inviting to use. See Figure 89.

I'm not going to get into the different types of foam on the market today. You can easily acquire all the necessary information you need. I am, however, going to suggest you look at five-inch thick cushions in place of the old standard of three to four inches thick. I went five inches thick on the suggestion of the cushion man, and the results

Figure 88. Old vinyl bunk cushions

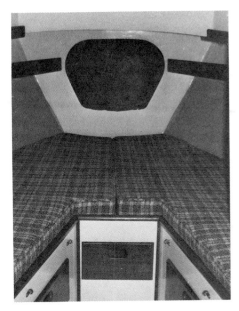

Figure 89. New bunk cushions

were outstanding. The bunks on my boat are as comfortable as my bed at home. As a matter of fact, when my back was acting up, they were more comfortable.

As for the covering I suggest you choose one of the new fabrics which are treated for moisture in place of the old standby vinyl. My reasons are the fabrics come in a variety of colors and patterns, and even more important, they allow air to pass through making this material far better to sleep on than vinyl.

I have a few more suggestions. There are all kinds of foam and fabrics. You want foam that will be comfortable for years and a fabric that has "memory" which is the ability to return to the original shape after someone gets up from sitting. So make sure you get these qualities but don't expect them for the cheapest price. A consideration involving comfort is to think about a seat that is slightly higher in front under the knees. The problem with boat cushions is that they lie on a flat surface, and when you're sitting you don't have that little bit of support in front. See Figure 90 for how to solve the problem. This riser makes sleeping more comfortable as well as sitting because the edge doesn't give you the feeling you are about to fall off the bunk. They are simple to make.

Safety

Foremost, a sailboat must be safe, and this is no less important below deck. Make sure you have or plan to add handrails where they're

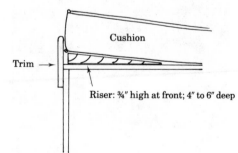

Figure 90. Riser for front of bunk cushions

needed. They should look good as well as be handy, but the important thing is to have them.

Most boats will have overhead handrails in the main cabin, but often these are not enough especially for the folks not considered tall. Figures 91 and 92 are good examples of bulkhead-mounted handrails that I have found indispensable for getting around when the boat is underway.

To conclude, keep in mind the main cabin is where you'll live when on the boat. You can make it comfortable, convenient, pleasant, and safe with good planning, hard work, and last, but by no means least, a little money.

Figure 91. Handrail in companion-way

Figure 92. Handrail in head area

Seven

FORWARD CABIN

The forward cabin is used mainly for sleeping, dressing, and storage. While many projects discussed in the preceding chapter will apply to the forward cabin, this area has enough special features to be treated separately here.

Forepeak

The older sailboats have access to the forepeak through the forward cabin so we're going to consider this section as part of the forward cabin. The forepeak is nothing but a big hole in which you stuff all manner of gear. It is hard to get to when you have to crawl over the V berths; therefore, the forepeak usually tends to collect the items that are not used on a regular basis.

If the forepeak was emptied and cleaned along with the rest of the below deck area, start by looking at ways to improve the storage convenience. I say convenience because the forepeak has the oddest shape of any storage place on the boat. Everything is continuously sliding toward the access opening which means that short of climbing in the forepeak itself, you probably have to take out half of what's inside just to get a particular piece of equipment.

My first idea is a repeat of the locker floor section discussed in the section on cockpit storage. Make a triangular-shaped floor for the place toward which everything is always moving. Screw it in place if possible, but don't hesitate to use fiberglass to secure the floor if necessary. Next consider adding one or more partitions running from side to side to create storage bins. Again screw or use fiberglass to get the partitions in place. Another suggestion I like is the adding of hooks. The forepeak section is separated from the forward cabin by a bulkhead. Just inside the access opening and on the inside of this bulkhead, you can attach whatever number of hooks you want. This enables you to hang up all sorts of gear which are much handier when needed.

After you have your storage sorted out, your next step is to paint. Make sure you use an enamel that can be cleaned easily, and use a light color because the lighting is none too good in the forepeak.

While on the subject of poor light in the forepeak, let's consider putting one of your old light fixtures to good use. Remember in the last chapter I suggested you hold on to them. Well, an old dome light from the galley makes a great forepeak light when mounted on the bulkhead just inside the access opening. The other type of fixtures can be used as well, but the dome light offers protection to the bulb where the other style has the bulb exposed to damage from moving objects in rough weather.

I've said nothing about keeping the anchor line in the forepeak, but I know there are sailors who prefer this. The newer boats have solved this problem nicely by providing a well in the foredeck. This gives you the best of both worlds, which is the anchor stowed forward but not in the forepeak. However, your concern is with older boats where the anchor line is stuffed through a deck hole into the forepeak, kept on deck, or carried aft in some locker.

My personal preference is to not carry the anchor line in the forepeak. In the Chesapeake Bay where I sail, all kinds of sea creatures are brought in on my anchor line, and after a while the forepeak starts to smell like a fish dock, not to mention the moisture the wet line adds. But anchor line stowage is a personal preference. So, if you intend to use the forepeak, you'll have to take this into consideration when upgrading this section. Do make sure that water will drain properly.

My last idea for the forepeak is strictly cosmetic. Since the forepeak on a sailboat tends to take on the characteristics of a back hall closet at home, with more and more being crammed into it, a very pleasant forward cabin can be spoiled by this doorless hole in the middle of a bulkhead with all kinds of things trying to fall out. So, like the closet at home, add a door. See Figure 93. You can make it simple or elaborate, whichever you prefer. Even if it's nothing but painted plywood with some trim around the edges, two hinges, and a latch, it will hide the access hole. But whatever type of door you use, make sure it allows for ventilation. In Figure 93 the anchor design cut into the panel serves two purposes: decoration and ventilation. One more point, the hardware fittings should be compatible with what's used below decks.

General Storage

The size of the boat will dictate the amount of general stowage you'll have in the forward cabin. Just about all boats will have one or more drawers under the berths, and many of the boats in the thirty-five-foot range or larger will have small bureau arrangements with several drawers.

Your first order of business is to check these drawers to determine if they can be enlarged. The details of this subject were covered in Chapter 6, and chances are you may have included the forward cabin drawers along with the main cabin drawers. There is one big difference, however, between the forward cabin drawers and the main cabin drawers. The shape of the hull in the main cabin is somewhat uniform which means any drawer enlargement can be the simple construction of a rectangle. On the other hand, the hull shape in the forward cabin has started to take on a more curved shape. This may mean the normal enlargement of a drawer nets you very little added space. But if you're willing to take the time to build a drawer that's designed to take into account the shape of the hull, you'll add storage space that otherwise would have been wasted.

The forward cabin is all curves and triangles it seems. This effect is created by the hull shape, and the V berths and layout can give you some challenging places to utilize. One is the angle created by the V berths themselves. See Figure 94 for an example of one way to use this area.

The storage box noted in Figure 94 offers an added advantage as well as storage. Many boats have V berths that are slightly high off the deck and if you're not long legged could present a problem getting into. This coupled with tight head room means you have to mind your head at the same time you're trying to climb into a V berth. My added storage creates a nice footstool to help getting on as well as out of the V berth.

Figure 93. Door for forepeak, designed for decoration and ventilation

Figure 94. Storage locker between V berths

Let's go back to the drawers and look at a dead-space triangle created by V berths and how you could put the area to work. Note Figure 95. Usually the space below the drawer or drawers, whichever the case, and the cabin sole is used as a storage bin. This is the best use of this area because the hull is coming in at a sharp angle which makes a drawer impractical. I suggest that this storage section have only an access hole and not a door for two good reasons. One, the cabin sole is a small place in the forward cabin and a door can be awkward low down in a confined space, and second, it is important for ventilation purposes not to have a door. (I will elaborate on this below.)

The forward sections under the V berths will have storage with access covers in the plywood bunk surface. I suggest this area be painted after cleaning so the stowed item will stay clean. There are two important things for you to do to these under bunk sections. First make sure there are drain holes so water won't stand, and second, drill or cut some ventilation holes so there can be an air flow from the storage bins as already mentioned. Since these storage places are odd shaped, because of the hull, and difficult to use, they tend to house the little used gear and aren't opened very often. That's why you should have some ventilation and assurance that water cannot be trapped.

You may want to consider one or more partitions in the under bunk areas but do so only if you have a particular use in mind. This is

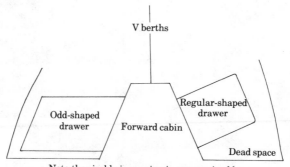

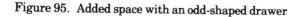

Note the sizable increasing in space gained by adding odd-shaped drawer instead of keeping regular-shaped drawer.

Figure 95. Added space with an odd-shaped drawer

a good place for the more bulky items, and partitions may be more trouble than they are worth. Again this is a personal preference on your part.

If you have a water or holding tank located in the forward cabin, of course you're going to have to take it into consideration. With the older full-keel boats, there was room in the bilge for the water tank; but in the case of the centerboard boat, there may not have been room in the bilge for the tank and it was placed under a bunk either in the forward cabin or the main cabin. Many older boats have added holding tanks which are generally placed in the forward section of the boat, so don't be surprised to see one. (Tanks will be discussed later.)

Bunk shelves are also an excellent addition over each of your V berths, and I recommend you add them. The shelf is easy to attach by screwing in a bracket to the forepeak bulkhead and another to the forward cabin bulkhead. The shelf can be cut to fit the hull curve following the procedure as noted in Figure 73 in Chapter 6. The front trim is the last thing to be added. Make sure the trim is at least three inches high. A shelf that nothing will stay on is useless, so have the front trim high enough to do the job. As far as the width of the shelf is concerned, make it as wide as you can without interfering with the use of the V berths. You can also add a partition or two to keep items from sliding fore and aft.

As for the existing over-bunk shelf, the best thing you can do is add higher trim to the front. Chances are what came on the boat will be on the small side. Don't forget the partitions if you feel they're necessary.

Our last item for storage is really a repeat of an idea from the main cabin, where I earlier discussed adding a recessed storage unit to the main cabin bulkhead. You can do the same thing with the forepeak bulkhead. A small storage unit can be mounted on one side or the other of the access door and projected into the forepeak several inches. I don't think the loss of space in the forepeak amounts to anything and the added storage space can always be used.

Hanging and Linen Lockers

The hanging and linen lockers are not actually a part of the foward cabin, but I feel they are more closely associated with the forward cabin so I'm including them in this chapter. I personally feel every boat should have both a linen and hanging locker if the boat is being used for overnight cruising. It's nice to carry shore-going clothes for those times when you want to get off the boat, and it's just as important to be able to get your hands on a towel easily.

The traditional location for these two lockers is between the main and forward cabins. Usually what comes from the builder is adequate, but there are some improvements you can make. Check the linen locker to see if you can add one or more shelves. Now this may involve removing what's there. For example, there might be two shelves but too far apart to make full use of the space. You can rearrange the existing two by adding one or more shelves. I've also found helpful shallow partitions on the shelves that hold the smaller items. After a good beat to windward it keeps the contents from piling up either at the back or next to the locker door to fall out when opened.

When it comes to the hanging locker, one of my pet peeves is that the hanger rod is never as high as it should be thereby allowing the bottom of the clothes on hangers to get wrinkled. Set your hanging rod as high as practical. Then look to see where you can add clothes hooks. You never have too many clothes hooks on a boat.

Be sure the lockers are clean, and before you paint the hanging locker give it a thorough going-over for any kind of protrusion that will damage clothes as they swing with the boat's motion. It can be something as simple as a screw coming a sixteenth of an inch through the bulkhead, or a fiberglass tag, or just the rough end of a piece of wood.

Don't wait and learn the hard way as I did by ruining a good coat. When you're sure everything is smooth, paint with a good enamel so that the area can be wiped clean.

Both of these lockers are used to house items which you'll use personally, and you certainly don't want any musty smell from your towel or jacket; so the ventilation of these lockers is a must. I suggest if they are side by side that air holes be drilled or cut so air can move from one locker to the other. Then add louvers both at the top and bottom. See Figure 96. Small louvers as shown in the example can be obtained from the marine store or mail order outlet. They are easy to install; just cut a hole and pop them in. I do suggest you use as large a louver as you can because what you're after is ventilation. I might

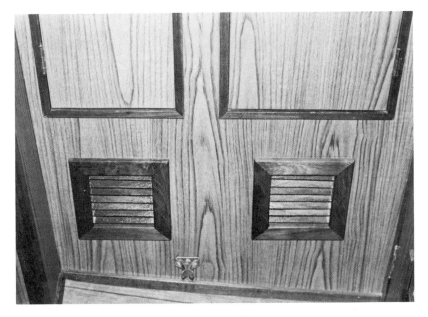

Figure 96. Ventilation louvers in hanging locker

add the louver makes a good insert for the forepeak access door and looks nice at the same time.

For the other topics such as ports, bunk cushions, lights, cabin sole, and cosmetic treatment of the exposed hull, refer to Chapter 6 on the main cabin. One final note here, however. Since the forward cabin is used for sleeping and dressing, it should be possible to have privacy. You should have some way to make the area private, be it a door or just a simple curtain.

Eight

GALLEY

The galley is part of the main cabin and is one of the reasons why the main cabin is the activity center below deck. The purpose or job of the galley is to provide the boat with a food storage and preparation area. I will discuss the special requirements needed to do this job while, at the same time, I'll take into consideration the upgrading and refurbishing projects that will be necessary.

Cleaning and Removing Galley Equipment

Although I'm sure you're tired of hearing me talk about it, your first chore is important, and bears repeating. Make sure the galley section is really clean, being sure to remove everything practical. For example, shelves or racks that are at the back of the countertop surface are places where years of out-of-sight messes occur, and you'll only discover them when you remove the storage units. Also, you may have dividers in dry storage lockers that should be removed. As you remove racks and shelves, you will be able to clean these units as well as under and behind them. Chances are these items will be showing their age, so I suggest you go ahead and refinish them before you put them back. As for refinishing, I think it's important that ongoing cleaning be kept in mind, so I suggest varnish or paint. Either will give you a hard surface that's easy to wipe clean.

The stove is next—be it a countertop type or the hanging model. You'll have no trouble here; it's just a matter of removing some screws, and out it comes. After the stove is removed, I suggest you take out the sink. The holding screws can be reached from underneath and are simple to remove. The only other thing to remember is to loosen the drain hose.

I'm sure the dirty rings on the countertop make it apparent why these two pieces of galley equipment should be removed. It's almost impossible to clean the old formica next to the sink and countertop stove in any proper manner, and removal is the best way to clear the decks, so to speak. Also it makes cleaning the sink and stove easier. Along with the sink goes the water pump and any other item that can be removed. You want to end up with empty lockers, and a countertop full of openings. Let me quickly add I will be considering the icebox later since it is deserving of special attention.

Countertop

Look at the condition of the countertop formica. Let's take the easy part first. You feel the formica is fine except it needs cleaning; there are no noticeable dings and knife marks. The color also is acceptable, so the bottom line is you'll keep what you have. As for cleaning, a standard household product like Ajax or Soft Scrub, warm water, and some elbow grease should take care of the stains. But, if the counter-top looks like it was used as a workbench, and no amount of cleaning will make it acceptable, you have no choice but to replace it. The color may enter into this decision as well. For the most part boat builders like colors that will go with anything, so they tend to use shades of white or beige. If you do decide to replace the formica, you may want to consider a color more to your liking; and believe me, there's plenty to choose from.

At this point, you can go one of two ways in replacing the formica. You can have it done by the boatyard, or you can have a carpenter or cabinetshop do the work. In case you don't know anyone to recommend a cabinetshop, you can fall back on the yellow pages. A good source to check to locate someone who does this type of carpentry is to call a lumber company that has a millwork shop and ask if they can recommend a finish carpenter.

On the other hand, if you decide to do the work yourself, I can guide you. Your first step is to remove all trim from the countertop. You want the entire perimeter trim free. I'll assume all other galley items have been removed as well. You want to end up with the old formica having nothing to hold it in place except the glue. Next, using a wide chisel no less than one inch, and wider if possible, start at one edge and slowly pry up the formica. Don't use a narrow chisel or a screwdriver; they seem to break the formica before the glue turns loose whereas the wider tool can distribute the load and have less chance of breaking the formica.

Don't expect the formica to come right off after you have gotten it started with the chisel. The material is brittle and will come off in pieces from one square inch to one square foot. The formica will also separate with the top color coming apart from the glued layer leaving the remaining material to be chipped away. All in all, removing the old formica is a messy job. Because the broken edges are very sharp I suggest you wear work gloves. Also wear some type of eye protection because the brittle material can send small fragments flying about.

I'm sure you'll find the formica had been glued to plywood so the chances are good that you pulled some plywood away with the formica, leaving a terrible looking surface to work with. Don't worry; just remove as much of the formica as possible with the chisel. Next, using a belt sander, level the surface making sure you don't leave any high spots where the formica was hard to remove. This surface should not be sanded smooth; it should be a little rough. Any deep depressions, say, an eighth of an inch or more, left when the plywood was pulled up, should be filled and sanded. Don't be concerned with the slight depressions.

Using cardboard or paper, make a pattern of the area to be covered, cutting out for any openings, but make the formica opening smaller than the actual one by at least one-half inch. Then trace the pattern on the back of the new formica.

It is more trouble to work on the back instead of the front, but it's important because when cutting formica, you use a saber saw with a metal cutting blade and when you work from the back, the teeth are coming into the colored surface. When the reverse is done, the teeth are pulling the color side away from the backing as they cut through the material. This pulling action on the color side can cause the color layer to break and chip, possibly ruining the formica. Also don't push the saber saw very fast; let it cut slowly. Make sure the formica is held firmly in place while sawing, or it might catch on the blade and jump about causing damage.

When it comes time to cut out your openings, leave at least one-half an inch overlap. The outside edges will be covered with trim so you can cut these lines as close as possible.

Once the formica is cut to size, apply the glue to both the countertop surface and the back of the formica. Holding the formica so contact is started at the back of the countertop, work the contact point from back to front. By doing it this way any slippage can easily be adjusted for on the front edge. If you start at the front and work towards a barrier at the back, any slight movement can cause the formica to hit the back edge before it's flat on the surface, creating a real problem. This is because the contact cement adheres instantly and does not allow you an opportunity to adjust the position of the formica. I suggest when you get ready to cement the formica down, you find an extra pair of hands to help.

After the formica is down, take a clean block of wood and with a hammer gently tap the entire surface to make sure firm contact is made. Trimming the edges is next, and the only way to do it right is to use a router with a formica edger. If you're not familiar with this tool, check your friends; if no luck there, ask around the boatyard for someone you can pay to do the job. I'm not talking about a big deal; to do the usual galley opening and locker covers will take no more than thirty minutes. If you want a really professional looking job, I suggest you use a router and nothing else.

Let me add one "don't." Don't leave the countertop locker covers in place and cover at the same time the countertop is done and expect to cut them out like you did the Nautolex deck covering in Chapter 6. You'll have to use a saw to cut the formica, and there's not enough room for the saw-blade action, as well as no way really to tell where you're cutting. The best method is to cover separately and trim with the router. I know this method will take a little more formica, but the end result is well worth it.

As for your material, any good lumberyard can supply you with the formica and contact cement. I suggest you use the glue recommended and follow the directions to the letter.

Now for some tips: a hacksaw blade is useful in hard-to-cut small places and works well when working on the color side because you're pushing the teeth into the color layer. As a matter of fact, you can do all your cutting in this manner if you want to take the time. You can use the belt sander to trim outside corners and edges so the wood trim will fit. If you have a spot where the contact cement does not adhere, heat the place with an iron, taking care not to overheat, and using the block of wood, hammer tap again. And last, the glue will require ventilation when using, so don't shut yourself up below deck or your head will start buzzing.

Another word of advice: if you've never put formica down before, take a small piece and practice. It's not hard to do and it helps knowing how the material handles.

The galley countertop will be the most difficult project. Your table and navigation desk is a piece of cake compared to the galley, in addition to the fact these items can be removed from the boat. Therefore, I suggest that you start here and work up to the galley.

Storage

Most galleys on the older sailboat have marginal to adequate storage space for the casual type of cruising. However, very few galleys have truly enough storage space. So I'd like to look at some ways to improve the storage capability of your galley.

The first thing to do is to check out the existing storage space with the idea of how can it be made to do a better job. For example, your galley will probably have a food locker with access through the countertop. Now if this locker is fourteen inches deep and full of 6-inch cans, there's a lot of space going to waste. It's fine to double stack everything and solve this problem until you have to remove half of the contents to find a particular item.

What you're looking for is the compromise point where the space is being used to the fullest and still provides easy access to most of the contents in the locker. Something I've found that does the best job here is plastic-covered metal racks. They can be hung around the locker sides as high as practical and enable you quickly to see what's in them. You can find these racks at variety and department stores with large kitchen sections. Like me, I'm sure you'll be amazed at all the shapes and sizes to choose from.

While on food lockers you may want to consider partitions to keep the contents from sliding around when the boat's motion gets lively. The material to use is quarter-inch plywood, and it's no trouble to install. I suggest you paint the locker before installing any racks or partitions. These items just make an awkward place harder to work. Therefore, paint first, then install the rack and partition. Also, paint the partitions before putting them in place, which leaves you with only touch-up painting to do in order to finish the project.

Your next storage topic concerns drawers. If the existing drawers can be extended, I suggest you do so. You may have already taken care of this when you checked your main and forward cabin drawers, but in any case don't overlook this.

When it comes to galley drawers, you may find yourself in the position of not having any. I found this hard to believe, but recently I was aboard several older sailboats that did not have any drawers for the galley. And I'm not talking about small boats, since one was thirty-seven feet. I wondered where all those utensils you need in the galley were kept.

So if you find yourself in this position, give your galley area careful thought and come up with a place to add one or more drawers. Frankly, this may involve another piece of galley equipment like the stove which I take up below.

The last storage units to try and improve are the special-use items like dish and glass racks. First, if what you have doesn't have partitions to keep things from sliding around, add them. I must admit in this case with all the various types of ready-made racks on the market, you may decide to either replace or add to what you already have with a new storage unit. Most of these storage racks are made of teak and look very good.

Stock boats in some cases make use of recessed storage areas at the back of the countertop. See Figure 97. This is a good idea because the "stuff" stays in place and is handy, but at the same time, it's often an eyesore. The solution to this is to add sliding panels and put the mess behind covers. Try to think of ways to store those awkward pieces and, just as important to me, keep them quiet.

The last thought concerns painting and varnishing. Give all lockers a good paint job using a light color. Lockers are hard enough to see into as it is, and a light color paint really helps. With time and use you'll also find the painted locker easy to freshen up simply by adding a coat of paint. Exposed wood, be it trim, racks, or whatever, should be varnished so the surfaces can be kept clean.

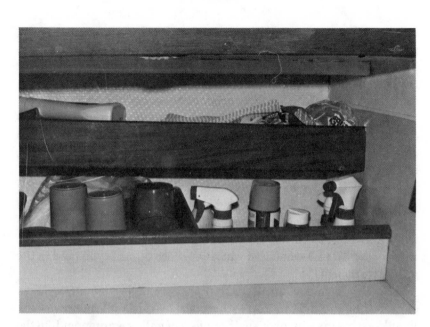

Figure 97. Exposed storage in galley

Stove

You may be lucky and have a new stove in which case this subject will not be useful. But if my experience is correct, your stove is more likely to resemble a rusty greaseball; and if this is the case, you have some work to do.

The most common type boat stove will use alcohol for fuel and come in two types: the two-burner countertop model and the oven model which is hung in an open area. Your first order of business is to see if the existing stove can be used. The only good way to clean up a stove properly is to take it out of the boat. The countertop model may already be out because of other galley refurbishing; if not, it's a simple matter to remove. The oven model is also easy to remove but awkward, and you may need help getting it off the boat.

You'll find that the usual heavy-duty household cleaners will do a good job of cleaning the stove. After cleaning, go over the working parts correcting all the obvious problems. Parts are easy enough to get either from your marine store or the stove manufacturer. After cleaning, you may prefer to have the stove checked over and worked on professionally.

Propane is another stove fuel rapidly gaining popularity with sailors. The stove you just cleaned could have been propane as well as alcohol, and at this point it makes absolutely no difference. So far all you've done is determine if the existing stove is suitable to keep and use. If the answer is yes, fine; you've saved some money.

But if the stove really looks bad or even after cleaning you would never quite trust it, you have no choice: it must be replaced and this decision opens up several new ideas to explore. The first thing to consider is precisely how do you intend to use the stove? What I'm really asking is what kind of cooking do you plan to do? Four-course dinners, or heating up a can of hash?

Bear in mind these questions are really a part of how you intend to use the boat which was detailed earlier. If you are only casually cruising on weekends, the stove will be used moderately and an oven, while nice, is not truly necessary. But if you plan to live on the boat for six months a year, your stove will be heavily used. And going offshore is another matter entirely. So, once you determine how you plan to use your boat, you can figure out what you need in a stove. You need to decide how the stove fits into your picture of intended boat use because this may offer you some options when it comes to upgrading or completely refurbishing your galley.

If you're going to replace your stove and it's the oven model, who says you have to replace it with another oven model? How about a countertop two-burner stove, and put the space used by the oven stove to work for you?

Note Figure 98 which shows a three-burner alcohol stove with oven in absolutely deplorable condition. Figure 99 shows the stove area after the stove has been removed. As the photograph clearly shows, you may expect to find a real mess that will have to be cleaned up. Figure 100 shows this area after it has been thoroughly scrubbed and cleaned. I might also add that, even after cleaning, paint may be needed to finish the job so that it looks presentable.

Figure 101 is a good example of how the space shown in Figure 100 can be used. A countertop covered with formica was added and a

Figure 98. Dirty alcohol stove with oven

Figure 99. Stove area before cleaning

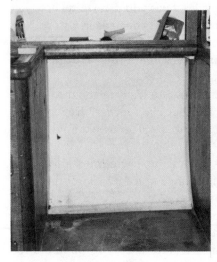

Figure 100. Stove area after cleaning

Figure 101. Stove area after refurbishing

two-burner alcohol stove installed. The hinged board to cover the stove when not in use is a nice added feature because it allows the stove top to do double duty as a counter space. The large area under the stove was then converted into storage space with various shelves and bins. This type of storage space is excellent for all those bulky kitchen articles that inevitably accumulate. The large formica covered door is a good idea, I think, because it allows you quick access to anything stored in this space. Of course you may prefer drawers, bins, or lockers, or maybe a combination of these, to make the best or most efficient use of this new galley space.

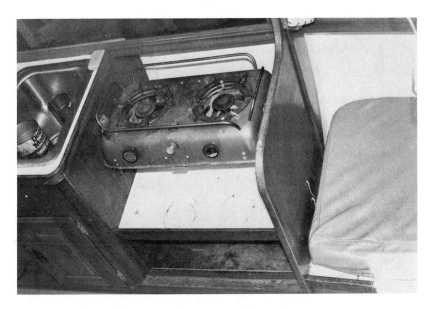

Figure 102. Dirty alcohol stove

Figures 102, 103, and 104 show a different way to do the same thing in a similar situation. In any case, the oven was deemed expendable, and storage space more important. Now, I'm not advocating all boat ovens should be tossed overboard. They're fine if you use them. What I'm saying is if you don't use an oven, why have one?

Figure 103. Stove area cleaned with shelves added

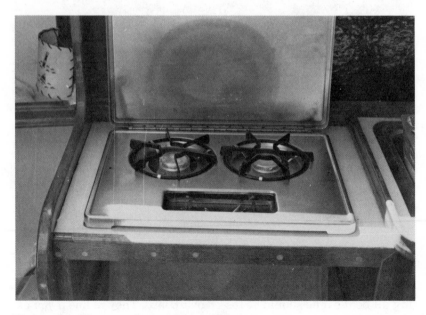

Figure 104. New propane stove installed

Another example has to do with the two-burner countertop stove. Again, you determine how you plan to use the boat and the galley, and if you decide the two-burner stove is all you need, look at another item. Why does the stove have to be permanently installed in the galley? The answer is: it doesn't have to be. This should lead you to think about the use of a portable stove which can be placed on the countertop when needed and stowed out of the way the rest of the time. After all, the stove is actually used a small portion of the day. The portable stove allows you to have more countertop space on one hand and the flexibility of using the stove in the cockpit. The drawbacks are storage when the stove's not in use and putting the stove together when you need it. This can be especially annoying if all you want is a hot cup of coffee. Think about a portable stove whether you want to replace the oven type or the standard two-burner countertop model.

The two types of stoves discussed so far have one basic drawback for use on a boat as they are not fully gimballed. The countertop model is not gimballed at all, and the oven model is installed only to swing in one direction.

Obviously, this does not create problems because almost all the boats used for casual weekend cruising do not have gimballed stoves, including mine. With very few exceptions what cooking is done is while at anchor or tied up to a pier. Don't think you have to have your stove gimballed unless, of course, you're going offshore for long periods of time.

When it comes to buying a new stove, you'll have to decide on what kind of fuel you prefer. For the most part pleasure boats use alcohol or propane, so I'll give you the pros and cons of each. First the old standby alcohol. It's easy to buy and fairly safe to use. The largest single feature that appeals to me about alcohol is the flames can be extinguished with water. Its greatest drawback is the low heat it puts out which means it takes longer to heat something. That first pot of coffee in the morning seems to take forever to perk.

Your next choice of fuel is propane. This fuel is easy to obtain, though not quite as available as alcohol in my opinion. Propane is heavier than air so any fuel that leaks will end up in the bilge which can be potentially dangerous. To put out a propane fire requires a fire extinguisher or smothering; water cannot be used as it can with alcohol. It's a clean burning fuel with a hot flame which is the main advantage propane has over alchohol—it makes cooking faster. Also, with propane you don't have to preheat the burners or keep the fuel under pressure; you just open the valve and light up the burner.

If you do opt for the propane stove, check out the camping supply stores before you buy, especially the ones that cater to the recreation vehicles because they will not only sell propane stoves but also all the tubes and fittings to hook it up. And just as important, you may pay less than at the marine store.

There are two safety tips I'd like to pass on. First, install the propane container in a box that drains overboard so if there ever is a leak, the propane won't end up in the bilge. Second, have a cutoff valve in the supply line in the tank compartment. This can be an electric shutoff valve as well as a manual one. The electric shutoff will allow you to have a switch near the stove and save you having to scramble for the manual one. This will allow you to shut off the fuel when the valves on the stove cannot be safely reached. And I would like to strongly emphasize that a fire extinguisher be located below deck and within easy reach of the galley. It is important, and I suggest you contact your boat insurance company to determine if any special requirements are necessary concerning the installation of a new stove. Don't discover the small print in your policy the hard way, after it is too late.

For those times when you would like something hot while underway and the boat is heeling, there is a small one-burner fully gimballed stove on the market which solves the problem nicely. Next, the small one- or two-burner camping stove that uses a small bottle of propane is perfect to use in the cockpit when you don't want to use the stove in the galley. If the idea about using a portable stove for all your cooking needs appeals to you, then you won't have to worry about an extra stove to be able to cook in the cockpit.

In any case whatever kind of stove you choose, it should be kept in good working condition, clean, and be conveniently located so it can be used safely. A stove that's awkward to use is unsafe in my opinion. And last, but certainly not least, the stove should look good and enhance the appearance of the galley.

Icebox

The icebox will be the single largest user of space in the galley. Most are top loading with the lid serving as a countertop area when closed. There are some boats with front loading iceboxes, but have the drawback that things are always falling out. If you have a front loading icebox, I suggest you make the change to top loading if possible. Two words can sum up the single most important attribute your icebox can have: *Well Insulated.*

One method that may prove helpful in checking insulation is first to measure the inside of the box, and then the outside in order to come up with some idea as to the thickness of the insulation cavity. Notice I said cavity because until you actually check out the insulation, you don't know how the cavity is filled. The next step is to find out what kind of insulation is used, and the best way to do this is to actually look at what's there. Check out the icebox from under the countertop, and don't forget to use a mirror to look into those places impossible to reach. What you're looking for is a place where you can see the insulation or where you can remove a panel to look at the insulation. If you have no luck here, then the only thing left is to drill an inspection hole.

If you're going to replace the formica anyway, open an inspection hole in the countertop. The hole is easy enough to plug and the new formica will hide all. In the event you have to open an inspection hole, I suggest you start with a three-quarter-inch drill bit. This gives you a large enough opening to see through and is a convenient size to plug. Use epoxy glue and a plug roughly the shape of the hole; it doesn't have to be a perfect fit. If for any reason you have to enlarge the inspection hole, the three-quarter-inch opening is suitable to take a saw blade.

Neither age nor manufacturer is a reliable guide to the quality of an icebox. Investigate the icebox insulation and find out for yourself what you have. There are three types of insulation you'll come across: small beadlike particles, foam, and stiff boards. The small particles and the foam are far better than the board because the boards leave air spaces which are often quite large.

At this point I would briefly like to take you back to the classroom. The principle of heat transfer states that the higher energy (hot air) always moves toward the lower energy (cold air). You can never stop this movement, but you can install a barrier to slow it down. The insulation in the icebox is nothing but resistance placed in the way of the heat to isolate the cold air as long as possible.

Insulation is used to take a given volume of air space and break it down into a very large number of tiny air spaces, which means the heat has to work longer at getting through. When water is introduced into this area and takes the place of the air space, you have a thermal bridge for the heat to travel directly to the cold air. Then ice melts much faster than you had planned on.

It's these thermal leaks that allow the cold to escape. Try to think of your icebox as a bucket of water and the air spaces as holes. The more holes, the faster the water runs out of the bucket; the more thermal leaks, the faster the cold runs out of the icebox.

So, our aim is to plug up those leaks. This is very difficult to do with board insulation. But the small particles of insulation and foam do this particular task very well.

If you have small particles or foam, then I'd say your icebox is well insulated. Since we're dealing with older fiberglass sailboats, the chances are you'll have the small particles or board insulation. One thing to check for if you do have the particles is the material packing down after being tossed about for years thus creating sizable air space. Of course, the solution is easy: just add some more insulation. Another telltale sign to look for is a wet or damp place on the outer wall of the insulation cavity. This signals that water from the icebox is leaking into the cavity.

If water is in the insulation cavity, your first job will be to cut access holes to expose the area. You'll probably never get the wet insulation dry, so it will have to be removed. In the case of board insulation, this is easy enough, but with the small beads the material is continually falling into the working area. Short of removing all of the insulation, the best thing you can do is put some type of retainer around the work area. Heavy cardboard does a good job because it can be trimmed to fit.

The next step is to locate and plug the leak. If the interior shell of the icebox is fiberglass, any good epoxy filler will do. When it comes to drying the wet place, you might have to help it along because chances are it's going to be in an area of poor air flow. So you'll have to add some heat. If it's summer, just moving air with a fan should do the trick. Another idea to use is a hair dryer. This is one of the handiest tools to have on the boat because it allows you to blow heat directly into a small area.

At this point you should know what you have in the way of an icebox, and if added insulation is called for. And when it comes to adding insulation, I recommend the foam type. In my opinion the foam type is the best under any conditions because its physical properties allow the material to flow and expand to fill every void. This means there are no air spaces at all to allow outside heat to attack the cold.

Foam can be purchased in two ways: one, the material comes in two parts and you mix before using; or two, you can purchase premixed cans which are small and more convenient to use.

There are some things to know about foam before you use it. When the two parts are mixed, you end up with a liquid with the consistency of a thick milkshake. You have only a matter of minutes to pour the material before the reaction sets in and the liquid begins to expand. It reminds me of bread dough rising. Anyway, the important part to remember is that foam exerts pressure as it expands and is capable of bulging the icebox liner or outer panels. I recommend you use the foam in steps. Just mix and pour a small amount, let cure, and then repeat until you've filled the void.

No matter how thick the mixed liquid is, foam will run downhill some before it begins to cure. You're going to have to retain the liquid in some manner, or you'll end up with a bilge full of foam. You can use tape, cardboard, or plywood. Another good retainer is board insulation; don't be surprised if you hear some snap, crackle, and popping when the foam starts to push against the board insulation.

The premixed foam that comes in cans acts in the same way as the kind that requires mixing. The big advantage is that the container (similar to a can of shaving cream) is so much easier to use. It allows you to reach the hard-to-get-to places. The drawback with the cans of foam is the cost; they're not cheap.

Your biggest problem when it comes to adding insulation to your existing icebox is how to get the material where you want it. This is where the can of foam really is useful. With one hand you can reach places that would be impossible with the pour-in variety. There are, of course, several ways to provide access for the foam, but it's going to require some boldness on your part. One method is to drill holes in the side and/or bottom of the inner wall of the icebox and then reseal with Marine-Tex. I know; I'm telling you to drill holes inside of your icebox which is like drilling holes in the bottom of the boat. But think about it for a moment. What better way to reach the insulation cavity from the top? When it comes to using foam insulation, always try and work from the top of the area you're filling.

You can drill holes at the top of the insulation cavity in the outer wall also to take care of the sides. If the formica is to be replaced, drill access holes in the countertop. However, it's the bottom cavity that will present the problem even when you can come in from underneath. The only sure way to add foam is to drill some holes in the bottom of the icebox.

Now for two pieces of advice concerning the foam insulation which you will find at most good marine stores. First read, believe what you've read, and then *follow* the directions. Second, experiment and become familiar with the foam before you actually do any work. It helps knowing what to expect.

Let's move on to other icebox topics that are important and at the same time fairly easy to do. Your icebox should have a drain. If it does, make sure it works. If not, then add one. A drain is simple to install with a small plastic thru-hull fitting and some plastic hose led to the bilge. Add a loop in the hose so water will stand and block air from flowing back into the icebox.

Make sure your countertop lid is thick enough to do a good job. You want a lid that looks like Figure 105, not a half-inch thick piece of plywood. Adding insulation to the icebox lid can be done in one of three ways. One, stick board insulation directly to the lid (see Figure 106); two, add a fiberglass shell and fill with foam (applying fiberglass over board insulation won't work unless you use epoxy resin since everyday polyester resin will dissolve the insulation); and three, add insulation and protect with wood.

Your icebox lid should have a good seal made of soft material so the lid seats well. Many times on older boats this seal will show its age. In this case, I suggest you replace it. New seal material can be found at your local hardware store or refrigeration supply firm.

My next suggestion is about a problem that affects all aft galley iceboxes—engine heat. It's ironic that the two extremes in temperature are located side by side. The answer to this situation is to increase the barrier between the hot and cold. Figure 107 shows a half-inch-thick rubber type industrial grade insulation that can be applied with contact cement. Board insulation will work well also

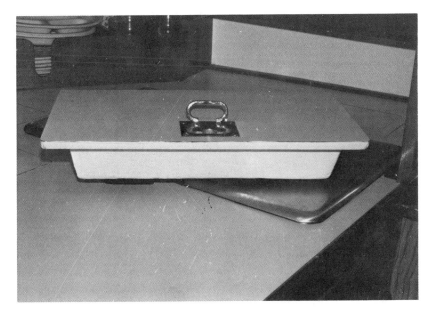

Figure 105. Proper icebox lid

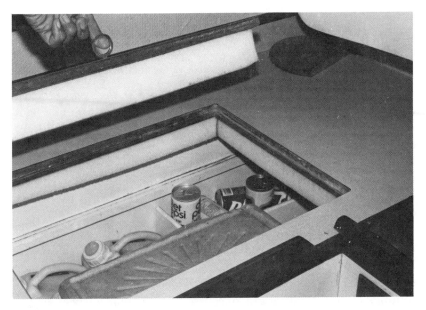

Figure 106. Icebox and lid with insulation added

Figure 107. Insulation between icebox and engine

though it does have a tendency to shed small particles when brushed against. Regardless of how you do it, add some type of insulation to help keep the engine heat from the icebox.

Refrigeration is our last topic. I must admit that refrigeration does seem to be the coming thing. More and more boats are having it installed; maybe in a few years it'll be as common as the auxiliary engine. Boat refrigeration on the scale we're talking about has certainly come a long way recently. On the market now are dependable units that don't take up much room, and that can be installed by the handyman owner. Moreover, they work, and they keep the icebox cold.

If you contemplate adding refrigeration, it will be extremely important to have a very well insulated icebox. The reason is simple. In the case of refrigeration you're responsible for supplying the power so the better the insulation, the fewer amps required. The two shortcomings of refrigeration are, of course, the need for a power supply and the cost.

If you're considering adding refrigeration, do your homework before you buy, not only from the technical standpoint. Determine where and how the equipment will be installed on the boat, keeping in mind you are going to have to maintain it which means you'll need access.

On the other hand, you may have bought a boat already equipped with refrigeration so you're going to be concerned with becoming familiar with the unit and making sure it's in good working order. The technical information is a must. If the data didn't come with the boat, contact the manufacturer or the local distributor.

You may prefer to call in a serviceman to check out the unit, and at the same time have him teach you some of the basics. There are a number of manufacturers with boat refrigeration equipment on the market. Just look in the boating publications and you'll find them with no trouble. I do have some advice on this subject. First, talk to several boat owners who have the type of unit you're interested in. Then after the homework is done, make your decision. Second, buy from a reputable firm that has a proven track record, even if you have to pay more.

Sink and Water System

The sink is the third and last major piece of equipment found in the galley, and it's just as necessary as the stove and icebox. Let's look at the cosmetic side first. Your sink will be stainless steel and more than likely will be in need of cleaning. If you're replacing the formica, you have the sink already out of the countertop. In the event you're not intending to add new formica, I suggest you still pull the sink out to clean it. This is necessary, I feel, because while the inside of the sink is easy to clean in place, the outside ring that rests on the formica is next to impossible to get really clean. The only way to do a proper job is to remove the sink.

The sink is one of those large shiny items that catches the eye, so it has to look good and complement the galley. Sinks at the same time have a tendency to get scratched and dinged up, especially if the boat has been raced, and the sink is located within handy reach of the companionway. Therefore, your sink may have some bangs and nicked places resulting from the winch handle being tossed with too much vigor. If you feel even after a good cleaning the sink doesn't measure up, replace it. You don't have to depend wholly on the marine store here; try a plumbing supply outlet or the recreation vehicle equipment firms. From my personal experience the recreational vehicle suppliers offer an excellent assortment of sinks and allied accessories.

Let me stress one point. Sinks on boats should be deep enough so water and other items won't jump out. Something around ten inches deep is ideal. As a matter of fact, if your present sink is fine in all respects but is on the shallow side, this is reason enough to replace it in my opinion.

The next topic is getting water to the sink, and here you have two choices: manual or pressure. Take the manual system first which is a very simple arrangement of a galley pump attached to a hose coming from the water tank. Chances are your galley pump will be the type that is hand-operated. In my opinion, this is one of the most inconvenient pieces of equipment on the entire boat because one hand is always occupied pumping. Just try to get your hands clean after a dirty job with this type of pump.

To solve this problem, I suggest you install a foot-operated galley pump. See Figure 108. This type of pumps allows you to use both hands in the galley and, at the same time, seems to provide more water per stroke than the hand type. Even if your hand-operated galley pump is in good working order, I suggest you replace it with the foot pump because of the added convenience.

There is one thing to be careful of when you add the foot pump. There has to be a pedal exposed in some fashion so you can get to it with your foot. Make sure you don't place the pump pedal where it'll be in the way. The best installation of a foot-operated pump I've ever seen was a large "mousehole" cut in the panel under the sink with the pump placed behind this opening. The pump pedal didn't protrude and was easily reached by putting your foot into the mousehole. Of course, this works fine if the pump is directly below the sink so you can get your foot in the hole as you face the sink. But suppose there's no way to install the pump under the sink? You'll run into this situation with the aft galley from time to time because of the engine.

The answer here is to place the pump to one side and pump with the side of your foot instead of the front of the foot. Now you're not going to be able to recess a side action pump because it would be very awkward to use. A good way to keep the pedal out of the way is to

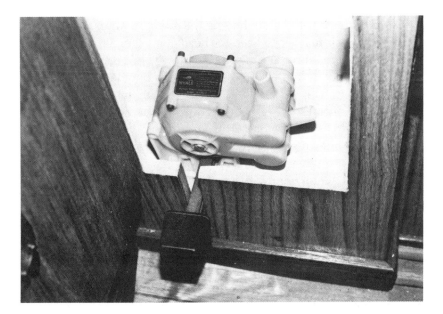

Figure 108. Galley foot pump

make sure it is four or five inches off the cabin sole. When you're looking at foot pumps, check to see if the pedal automatically returns to the up position when pumping is finished. By raising the pump a couple of inches, the pedal is high enough to keep from stumping your toe on it, and the few inches extra height doesn't affect the pumping motion at all.

Your second choice is a pressure system that uses an electric pump to supply the water and with it you will have a faucet just like you do at home. As with refrigeration, the pressure water system is gaining in popularity. You may even have bought an older boat that had a pressure system added by a previous owner. If this is so, you're way ahead of the game when it comes to upgrading the galley.

If you intend to add pressure water, you need an electric pump that is activated when the water is turned on and a common sink faucet. The pump can be found at marine or recreational vehicle stores and the faucet at your plumbing supply company although you may be able to get the faucet also at the recreational vehicle firm.

Some advice here before buying the pressure water pump. First, know what your needs will be in the head. For example, are you going to have only one faucet or are you intending to add a shower as well? Make sure your pump is the correct size to handle all your water needs, not just the galley sink. The pressure water system offers several nice options as well as a shower in the head. How about a spray nozzle to use in the sink. Frankly, pressure water is pleasant to have and the one area the ladies seem really to appreciate.

Don't let the installation worry you. It's simple and takes very little room; the man handy with tools will have no problem.

The next topic, the hot water heater, may offer a higher degree of difficulty. The hot water tank comes in several sizes. The smallest, around five gallons, seems adequate for the average thirty- to forty-foot sailboat that's used for casual weekend cruising. These tanks are made so they can draw heat either from a dockside electrical connection or the engine cooling water. Again, as with the pressure system, it's no big job to install. However, all is not a bed of roses. Just where you put the tank may be your main difficulty. It should be somewhere close to the engine if possible, but sailboats are designed to sail with the engine compartment having to do with what's available. The end result can be very close quarters indeed. Hot water heaters are found both at marine and recreational vehicle suppliers. As with refrigeration, buy a recommended product from a reputable manufactuer.

Now for the drawbacks to both the pressure system and the hot water tank. When you add the pump and a couple of faucets plus a shower, the cost of the pressure system adds up. Also, the hot water heater is a fairly expensive item. I hesitate to name figures because with the passage of time the numbers will be meaningless. You'll be able to put some figures together to answer the cost question with no trouble.

The second drawback is the amount of water you use. You quickly get used to turning on the tap and out comes the water just like at home, but the big difference is that the boat has a limited supply. I've known people who could cruise for a week with a fifty-gallon water tank. Then they added pressure hot water and had to fill up every three days. It's perfectly all right to use lots of water as long as you watch your tank and don't run out at an awkward time. In short, you're going to have to monitor your water more carefully.

The last drawback is that the pressure hot water system is more complicated than the simple manual water pump, meaning you'll spend time and money taking care of the maintenance. But when all is said and done, frankly the pressure hot water system is quite nice. If you want it, can afford it, and have the room for the equipment, I would add it. Nothing upgrades a boat like hot water from a tap.

Now let's take a look at what the water is kept in. A good many of the older sailboats, especially the ones built in the 1960s, will have a metal water tank, probably made out of stainless steel. Later on, the builders went to fiberglass tanks, cost being the main reason.

You're not really concerned with the location of the tank. Full keel boats will have the tank in the bilge, and centerboard boats will place the tank under a bunk either in the main or forward cabin. This is not a hard and fast rule, but generally speaking you'll find it so.

Your main interest is upgrading the water tank and making sure it will give good service. As with everything else in this book, your first task is to clean it.

In the case of tanks, both metal and fiberglass, that have inspection ports, your job is easy because you can reach and see inside the tank. Remove all the debris that has collected over the years and then clean using soap and warm water. Take pains to rinse well, and this brings up the question of removing the water. The best way I've found, if you don't have pressure water, and you dread the idea of manually pumping out the tank, is to use a small pump attached to a drill motor.

After cleaning and rinsing, give the tank a good visual inspection. Here is where a mirror on a handle will prove most useful along with a flashlight. If the tank passes inspection, close and use it. But if the inside of the tank doesn't pass inspection for whatever reason, say, pockets of crud which are impossible to remove, you may have to consider replacing with a new tank.

For a tank without the inspection port, it goes without saying that this tank is more of a problem to clean and check. You're not going to be able to clean this tank in the usual way; everything will have to be done at "arm's length," so to speak.

Removing all the junk that's collected on the bottom of the tank over the years is the first priority. Just pumping water through the tank will not pick up these bits and pieces because the outgoing pipe is always above the bottom of the tank for the exact purpose of not sucking up any trash. Here I suggest the very thing to solve this problem: a one-half-inch soft copper tube, say around three feet long. The soft copper is easy to bend and you want to end up with something that looks like Figures 109 and 110.

After hooking up the tube and pump, insert the tube through the fill hole. Start pumping and move the tube around so you cover the bottom as well as all the corners. You can do this with a hand pump if you want to, but it's very hard to move the tube about at the same time you're trying to pump, so use a drill motor pump if you can.

Collecting the discharge water in a bucket is the best method, I think, because you can see what's being removed. By emptying the bucket from time to time, you'll be able to tell when all the trash has been picked up. Another good idea is to rock the boat a few times to keep the particles from staying in a difficult place to reach.

By now I'm sure you see why the copper tubing works better if bent. It allows you to reach more areas when you're having to work through a small opening. Also my tube shape is not the last word. You

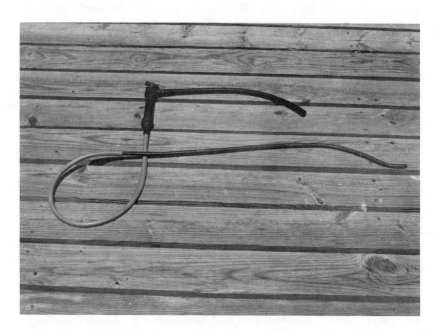

Figure 109. Pump and copper tube for cleaning tanks

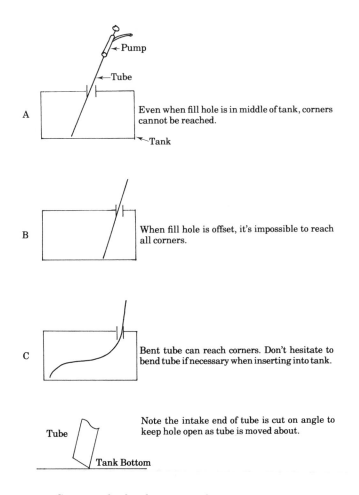

Figure 110. Copper tube for cleaning tanks

may have to do a little trial and error work here, depending on the shape of your water tank and location of the fill-up cap. Who knows? Maybe a straight tube or one with a slight curve will do, but by all means use the soft copper tube which can be purchased at any plumbing supply firm, because it will not flop about. If you try to use any type of flexible hose, you'll find you have very little control.

After cleaning the bottom, the only thing you can do to the tank is run some water tank solution through it, and hope for the best. If possible, you might want to consider adding an inspection port. Then you would have no problem cleaning the tank. But if there's no port and one can't be added, you're left with doing the best you can and letting it go at that.

If you decide to replace the water tank, you'll have three choices: one, metal, which can be expensive; two, fiberglass, which is cheaper and much easier to work with; and three, the nylon flexible tank, which will be the cheapest and most convenient way to go. Just remember one thing. Tearing out a water tank is a major job; either your cabin sole has to come up or a bunk has to be dismantled.

I'd suggest you consider using your water tank unless it is a pile of junk. Perhaps your objection to the existing tank centers on the taste or quality of the water for drinking purposes.

But the water on the boat has a great many other uses that the tank is perfectly suitable for. My suggestion is to carry your drinking and cooking water in separate containers which are freshly filled every time you use the boat, and this goes for a day sail too. It's no more problem to put a couple of gallon jugs of water on the boat than it is a case of soft drinks or beer.

My personal preference is the two-liter size of plastic soft drink bottles. They're easy to handle and use. I go so far as to keep one in the icebox so there's always cold water at hand. The bottles are convenient to stow and can take the punishment given out by a moving boat. When cruising for more than a weekend, I fill up the water bottles when we pick up ice. Remember—good tasting water gives you good tasting coffee, tea, and cocktails. Carrying your drinking water separately and using the tank water for all other needs is a method of living and making use of the old water tank which represents a savings of time, effort, and money. You may find it interesting to learn that there are new boat owners who carry some or all their drinking water separately.

Before we leave this topic of water tanks, a word about the hoses that supply the water from the tank to the sink. Inspect them for cracks, leaks, and loose connections and do what has to be done to put them into good working order. If the boat is over ten years old, all the original hoses should be replaced with clear plastic so visual inspections can easily be made.

While on the subject of hoses, let me touch on another subject. How do you tell how much water is in the tank? The old-fashioned dip stick is a good choice. Another method is to use the vent hose that allows air to enter the tank as water is pumped out. It can serve as a water indicator if you use clear plastic and mount the hose as low down as possible. The under bunk tanks lend themselves to this with little trouble because you can get at the tank in question. The bilge mounted tanks will be harder or even impossible to do. While it's not absolutely necessary to know how much is in the tank, it's handy information.

Let me touch on one other source of water before we move on: a hand or foot-operated pump that brings in outside water to the sink, be it salt or fresh depending on where you sail. This is a very good item to have when going offshore or when you're lucky enough to cruise in clean water. With the outside pump you have the choice to use your tank water for the important things while using the outside water for many of the other galley chores. The pump is easy to install. Just add the pump and hook up a hose to some existing thru-hull fitting, and you have it. I really feel, though, you don't need this outside water pump unless you're planning on living on the boat for months at a time.

Lights

Replace unsightly lights in the galley with dome lights and at the same time add extra dome lights where you particularly need light.

A bit of advice on the wiring for added lights. It's easy enough to tie the wiring into a power source; another light fixture is a good place. But make it a point to hide the wires in some fashion. Nothing gives the impression of "just thrown together" like exposed wires. Even a piece of wood with a groove looks fine if it's not possible to run the wire behind something. It shows the job was finished.

Light fixtures are on display all the time. Therefore if you plan to do very little to the galley in the way of large improvements, adding new lights is one way to give a visual (no pun intended) upgrading without spending much money, time, and effort.

One last thought: don't buy the cheapest thing you can find. You want a fixture that is both functional and that looks good to the eye.

The galley is an integral part of the main cabin which is where most of the living takes place below deck. As such, it's going to have to do its share of making the below deck area the pleasant place it should be. Before you begin working on the galley upgrading, do your homework and have a game plan of the projects, both immediate and future. Cranked into this game plan is how you intend to use the galley area. When you replace or add a piece of equipment, buy the best you can afford. This is a very important aspect of the upgrading and refurbishing process. A boat is supposed to look like a boat below, not a motel room. Therefore there's going to be all kinds of gear and equipment on display.

The bottom line is to make sure that you are proud of it.

Nine

THE HEAD

The head is one of the most important and necessary pieces of equipment on the entire boat. As a matter of fact, I would venture to say that it *is* the most important piece of equipment on board. Everyone appreciates the water closet that works flawlessly every time it's put to use. People on board also have a right to expect the head area to smell fresh, and to look pleasant as well.

To accomplish the task of providing this kind of a head you first need to take a look at the MSD (marine sanitation device) situation in your area. The Federal government, in general, and the Coast Guard, in particular, appear to be moving in the direction of getting out of the MSD regulation business. If this happens and the states begin enforcing their own MSD regulations, the recreational boater may have an illegal boat simply by crossing a state line unless the states work together.

This subject is far beyond the scope of this book. But since the bottom line on MSD's at the moment is that nothing seems certain about exactly what's going to be done, you have to work with the way the situation now exists.

Our main concern with MSD's is how they fit into the upgrading and refurbishing process. Since the head itself is the focal point of the head area, start with it. Again I'm assuming the head area has been thoroughly cleaned. Also, since the term *head* can mean toilet bowl as well as the section it is located in, I wish to define the head itself as the *water closet* and the area it is located in as the *head area*.

Water Closet

The only similarity between the marine water closet and the one in your home is that they both have bowls. The one at home uses water to remove the contents of the bowl. That's why there's a water tank on the back of the toilet bowl. When the flush lever is pushed, water is dumped from the tank into the bowl. This sudden flow of water then pushes the contents of the bowl over a hump that's out of sight at the back of the bowl. This hump also is what allows water to stand in the bowl after flushing. The hissing water sound after flushing is made by water refilling the tank. The entire arrangement is simple and easy to use, and effective because water is used to do the dirty work.

In contrast, the marine water closet removes the bowl contents with the help of a pump, a device which can cause a lot of trouble. After all, not much can go wrong with the bowl; it's only a collection place with two moving parts, the seat and lid. The pump, on the other hand, consists of moving parts that are constantly being used when people are on the boat.

Keep in mind we're talking about the old water closet. Currently, there are many new kinds of marine water closets on the market, but since you are dealing with the older fiberglass sailboat, chances are good the water closet you're working with is original equipment. See Figure 14.

Your first job is to remove the existing water closet with the intent of cleaning and rebuilding the pump. It makes no difference if the pump is working fine. You will want to remove the water closet for two very good reasons. One, you are dealing with personal hygiene, and you want to be sure the water closet is really sanitary. Second, it is in your best interests to know exactly how the pump is put together. Learn now, not while enjoying a beautiful anchorage.

Since working on a water closet can be somewhat distasteful, I have a suggestion that will help. Mix up about five gallons of warm soapy water using a good grease-cutting detergent. Fill the bowl, open the outgoing sea cock and pump about half of the soapy water out. Then refill the bowl clear to the rim where the small incoming water holes are, and let stand for ten minutes, giving the detergent time to act. Now pump the bowl dry and repeat at least two more times. The end result gives you a clean water closet to take apart making the work much more pleasant.

After this cleaning is done, remove the water closet which is relatively easy, just a matter of several bolts and hose clamps, and take ashore. You may even want to throw it in the trunk of your car to take home for more convenient working conditions.

Your next step is to take the whole thing apart, including the parts which are attached to the bowl itself. The bowl will be porcelain and very easy to clean with any brand of bathroom cleaner, but there's one place that should be given extra attention. At the top of the bowl is a section with small holes that goes all the way around the rim. This is where the incoming "clean" water enters the bowl before the water closet is used and flushed, and it readily becomes clogged and messy. After soaking the bowl in warm soapy water, I suggest you use a cloth patch on a wire along with the garden hose to clean the passage as well as you can.

Let's start on the pump. Rebuild kits for marine water closets are available at any good marine store and are not expensive, about thirty dollars. They will have drawings and instructions that are easy to follow, and you'll learn faster if you do it yourself. Remember, you can always find someone to help out if you get stumped, but keep in mind the pump is made of rubber parts quite simple to install. My point here is not only to end up with a rebuilt pump, but for you to know exactly what's going on inside the pump.

After cleaning and rebuilding, put the pump back together and paint—usually white or a light color looks best. The paint serves two purposes: makes things attractive, and any leaks can be quickly noticed against a background of fresh paint. I might add it's a simple matter to freshen up the water closet with a little touch-up paint.

Although water is flushed out of the water closet, it will run back in just as easily. Therefore, if the rim of the bowl is below the waterline, the water filling into the bowl could possible sink the boat. Note also that a bowl rim that's above the waterline at the dock can be below the waterline when the boat is heeled. Be sure you keep the seacocks closed when the water closet is not in use especially when sailing in heavy weather. To determine if the rim is above or below the waterline, take the discharge line away from the pump, hold it up, and open the sea cock. Then, lower the hose until you get water dribbling out. Try and mark the waterline on the hull or bulkhead so you'll always have a quick reference point. Once the waterline is established, you'll have no trouble checking the bowl rim. If the rim is below or close to the waterline, raise the water closet if possible. If this cannot be done, then I suggest you add a vented loop for the discharge line making sure it's higher than the waterline. The loop allows air to enter the discharge line but stops water from flowing back into the bowl. It's a good safety measure so use it if your boat does not already have one for below-waterline bowls.

There's one last item that also deserves attention on the water closet—the lid and seat. Replace with a new set, preferably one made of plastic which is easy to keep clean. Nothing detracts from the head area like an old, used toilet seat.

Holding Tanks

The bowl is the collector and the pump is the flusher, but where does the refuse go? There are three places: directly overboard; into a holding tank to be pumped out later; or into a waste and discharge unit to be treated before being pumped overboard.

Again, since you're dealing with the older sailboat that started life with the old-fashioned direct discharge water closet, and possibly had something added according to prevailing MSD regulations, you probably have a jury-rigged holding tank with a Y valve that lets you discharge directly overboard.

Let me state right here that when it comes to water closets, holding tanks, and MSD regulations the foremost thought you should have is protecting yourself legally. You don't want to be the unfortunate person whom the authorities decide to use as an example. I can help with the upgrading and refurbishing of the head area; but I'm afraid when it comes to protecting yourself from MSD regulations, you will have to check around your sailing area and follow the accepted method. From my experience the holding tank seems to be the best way to conform to the MSD regulations; concerning the actual tank, I can pass on information that will be useful.

If you already have a holding tank added to the boat, your problem is solved. You still need to check for leaks and to make sure the tank is clean and free of that barnyard odor, an odor that clings to everything and is difficult to get rid of. If you do have an odor problem, I suggest you visit a commercial janitorial supply firm and purchase some type of strong cleaner and an industrial grade deodorant. It may be possible to obtain both in one product. Don't waste your time and money on household products at the supermarket; they are simply not strong enough.

In the case you don't have a holding tank and plan to install one, you have two options, the regular tank made of metal, plastic, or fiberglass, or the flexible tank made of rubberlike material. My personal preference is the flexible tank because it doesn't take up very much room and can fit the odd-shaped space.

At this point you're going to have to determine if you really intend to use the holding tank or if it is to be a backup measure while you pump overboard. If you're going to use your tank some of the time, then I would recommend one that holds no more than five gallons which makes it possible to be carried off the boat to be emptied. At the same time the tank can be cleaned before returning to the boat helping to keep down odors.

Remember that since the older sailboats usually have shorter waterlines which make space a premium, you may have a problem adding a larger tank and will have to stick to the smaller one. On the other hand, if the tank is insurance, buy the smallest flexible tank you can and hook it up to a Y valve and go about your business (see Figure 111). Also you will want to give some thought here about how things look. Try and hide the holding bag in some fashion so it won't detract from the overall appearance of the head area.

If you wish to consider the unit that treats the waste before it is discharged, you can get all the information you need from any good marine catalog. If you do choose one of these newer types of water closets, there are several drawbacks to be aware of in respect to the older sailboat. First, you may not have the space to accommodate the unit; second, they are not cheap; third, the more complex the piece of equipment, the harder it is to maintain; and fourth, the treatment materials will be an ongoing expense.

Frankly, when it comes to sailboat equipment, I think the simplest is the best and especially when it comes to the water closet. I recommend a good quality, well-maintained hand-pumped water closet with or without a holding tank, whichever meets your particular needs.

Sink and Water Pump

Your sink will undoubtedly be stainless steel and on the small side.

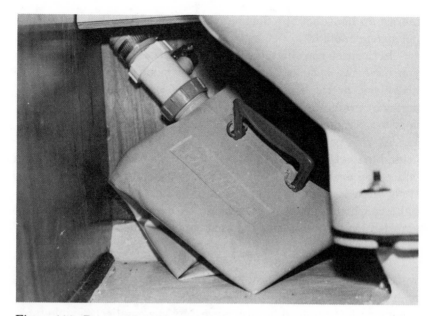

Figure 111. Removable holding container in head area

Just about the only upgrading you can do is to remove and clean it thoroughly, exactly as you did the galley sink. If you have reason to replace the sink, be sure to check the recreational vehicle suppliers first. Head area sinks not only have a tendency to be small but also shallow which makes the sink useless if the boat is moving about. So I'll repeat here what I said about galley sinks; i.e., replace with a deeper, more practical one, if possible. I say if possible because I recognize the fact the head area will be one of the tightest spaces on the boat, and you may not have room to upgrade the sink. However, I would like to stress one point. If at all possible, get rid of the hand-operated sink pump. The head area sink is used mostly for personal hygiene and not being able to wash both hands at the same time is a poor way to achieve this.

Countertop and Storage

The countertop surface will probably be in the same shape as the galley which means you clean it or replace it. However, there's a good chance you will not have any countertop surface. Many of the older fiberglass sailboats incorporated the head area into the passageway between the main cabin and the forward cabin which sometimes spreads things out. For example, the water closet to port with the sink to starboard, with the hanging locker thrown in just to make things cozy. Because of this blending together of this space, you'll have no counter space or what you do have will be very small. The problem that's created here is there's no place to put all the bathroom items that are used. This not only can be inconvenient but downright exasperating.

The solution is easy. Add a shelf in a convenient place and it doesn't have to be very large either. But it does have to have sides high enough to keep items from rolling off, say, at least two inches. Figure 112 is a good example of this type of shelf next to the mirror in the head area. Now don't think in terms of just one; add as many as practical. They're easy to make using plywood or solid wood for the bottom with trim (usually teak) purchased from a marine supplier on three sides. You attach them to the bulkhead.

Figure 112. Shelf in head area

Next let's take a look at head area storage in general. First, let me say you never seem to have enough so you'll make the best of what you have. You want to check and see if any sort of intermediate shelf can be added between existing locker shelves. Then consider if vertical partitions would be helpful. Possibly, there is some space where a small locker or bin can be added even at the expense of something else. Figure 113 shows a huge hanging locker, or I should say bin. Part of this space can be put to better use. You really don't need this much hanging space.

My last storage suggestion concerns all those spray cans like hair spray, deodorant, and shaving cream that seem to collect in the head area. These cans rattle and roll at the slightest motion of the boat unless you stuff towels, Kleenex, or T-shirts around them. The answer to this problem is to add some small racks just for the spray cans. The cans are now quiet and at the same time handy for use. Figure 114 shows racks that allow the can to lie flat. You can have

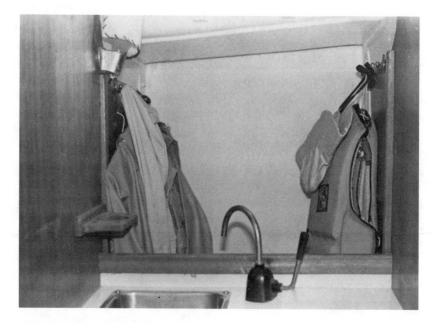

Figure 113. Large hanging bin

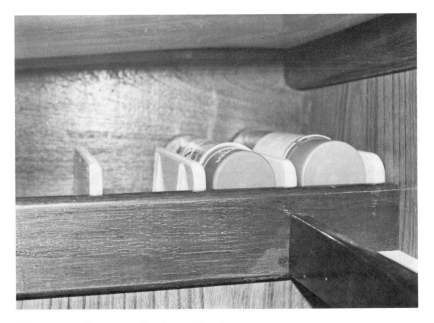

Figure 114. Spray can dividers in head area

vertical slots just as well. It depends only on the shape of the space which will hold the racks.

Before we leave the subject of storage, I want to touch on ventilation, not for the head area in general as this will be covered in the next chapter, but for areas behind locker doors. Try and add some form of air access in all your head area locker doors. One of the best ways to do this is with louver inserts. If this is not practical, then think about holes drilled in the form of some sort of decorative design. Nobody likes reaching for a fresh towel and have it come out of the locker with a sour smell.

Shower

One of the few things the new wide-body sailboats have over the older boats that I envy is a shower. Not many of the older boats that I'm familiar with came equipped with a shower, whereas today you can get a new twenty-seven-foot boat with the shower as standard gear. As a matter of fact with today's new boats, the exception is the boat without one.

If your older boat does not have a shower, it's easy enough to add; but you must have pressure water. So if you're going to use manual water pumps, you're out of luck for a shower. But don't worry, there's always the shower bag on deck. On the other hand, if you have or intend to add pressure water, then a shower is simple. What you want is called a phone-type shower head (see Figure 115). It is clipped to the bulkhead and you stand under it just as you would at home. But space in the head area makes things a little tight so it's nice if you can take the shower nozzle in your hand and direct the water where it's needed. The phone-type lets you do this.

The plumbing aspect of the shower nozzle is not complex. Just tie the nozzle hose to a line coming from your pump. Of course, if you

Figure 115. Phone-type shower

have that real luxury, hot water, this will have to be hooked up in the supply circuit.

While the incoming shower water is simple, the outgoing water is not. The new boats plan for a shower and the cabin sole of the head area is actually a collecting basin with a drain. On the older boats this is not the case. Chances are the same cabin sole that's in the main and forward cabins is used in the head area also, so you're going to have to do something to channel the water to the bilge from where it's pumped overboard. This is when the electric bilge pump is nice to have.

One idea is to cut a hole in the cabin sole and add a teak grate. While this is a good idea, it nevertheless allows some water to run over on the sole and travel about the boat, and you have the problem of keeping the shower curtain tucked in at the bottom. All in all the grate does look good, but unless you can keep the water and the curtain inside the grate section it's going to be somewhat messy.

Your next choice is some form of recess built into the cabin sole, most likely constructed out of fiberglass. This can be done, but it's going to take some careful thinking, and execution on your part, and you still have the problem of keeping the shower curtain tucked in. And if you don't use a curtain, you'll end up hosing down the entire head area.

I have an answer to this problem, that's simple, cheap and guaranteed to work. At a good variety store where they sell all kinds of household containers like buckets, trash cans, and kitchen storage units made out of rubberlike material, buy a container that's about sixteen to eighteen inches square with sides at least six inches high. Using a small plastic marine thru-hull fitting, say half-inch, make a drain hole in the bottom of the container. Then drill a hole in the cabin sole to receive the drain and place the container on the head area cabin sole with the drain inserted in the hole. Stand in the container, tuck in the shower curtain, and shower. After using, wipe the container dry and toss in the forepeak until needed again. Figure 116 is solid evidence this works. As for the shower curtain, again try the recreational vehicle supply firm. You should find something to do the job with no trouble.

I have one more suggestion concerning the shower that frankly is one of the handiest things you can have on the boat. When adding pressure water and the shower, install a shower hookup somewhere in the cockpit. I don't mean the whole shower arrangement but just

Figure 116. Cabin sole container for shower

the hookup so you can attach the hose and nozzle when you want to. This allows you the luxury of a pressure water shower in the cockpit when you have the anchorage to yourself. Also, after a rough day and the cockpit is covered with salt, it's nice to be able to hose it down. Of course you'll be using boat water to do this, but not much. A couple of gallons is all it takes to knock off salt. In my opinion adding a shower is one of the most positive upgrading projects you can do to your boat.

Cabin Sole and Lights

Just a word about these two subjects though they both have been covered in some detail in the chapters on the main and forward cabins. As for the cabin sole, I suggest you carry out the entire sole with the same material, i.e., have it the same in the head area as in the main and forward cabins. My reason is the older boat has a shorter waterline, hence a shorter cabin sole; and if it's cut up with different materials, it tends to make the sole appear even shorter whereas the same material, especially one with fore and aft lines, will make the cabin sole appear longer and more spacious. This may present a problem where carpet is used because you may not want to have carpet getting wet in the head area. You'll have to decide.

As far as lights are concerned, see Chapter 6, The Main Cabin. However, I do want to stress one point pertaining to the head area. This section has a tendency to be small and dark, yet it's the one place on the boat where you're expected to use a mirror. Combing your hair is bad enough in poor light, but try shaving or putting on makeup in a mirror full of shadows. My suggestion is to have one or two bright lights that give good illumination to the mirror.

Dressing Up the Head Area

My concern here is strictly with cosmetic projects. By far the most unsightly place on the boat is the plumbing required to make the water closet function. Brass turns green quickly, water always appears to be dripping off a hose or fitting, and the general dampness of the entire place seems to attract dirt and dust. Since there is little you can do to change things, don't even try.

Instead I suggest you cover it all from sight if at all possible. Figure 117 is a good example of hiding the ugly plumbing that goes with the water closet. It's nothing more than a formica-covered plywood shelf behind the bowl with the same material added on an angle to hide the sea cocks. Teak trim has been added both for looks and to let the shelf serve to hold various items when the boat is at anchor or tied up. Since every boat is different, exactly how you go about the project will have to be handled on an individual basis for a particular boat, but the principle remains the same; one or more panels or shelves is all that's needed.

Regardless of whether this section is hidden from view or not, I suggest everything that will take paint be painted. This will give the water closet a fresh, pleasant look. It's easy to keep clean and touch up to keep it always looking attractive.

Along with painting around the water closet, be sure to paint the inside of lockers and bins and even the overhead if it needs it. White or some light color does the best job. The head area needs light and the white or light-toned paints help with this tremendously. Be sure and use a good quality enamel paint that will take scrubbing.

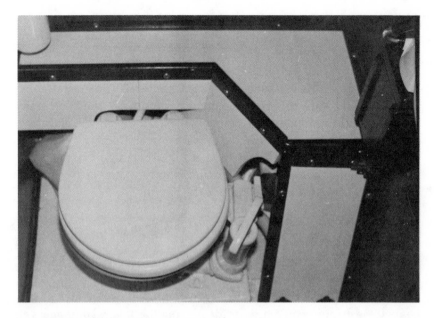

Figure 117. Panels to hide water closet plumping

Our last topic you've already heard about; hardware and fittings for locker fronts and privacy doors (see Chapter 6). I'll say here follow through in the head area with the same style of hardware used elsewhere in the boat.

Safety

Around the head area is where the doors will be located, and a great part of the time these doors are kept open so both air and people can move about with ease. In my opinion, one of the worst dangers on a sailboat is a door that slams shut unexpectedly when the boat takes a sudden heel. I'm talking about broken fingers and smashed up hands, so make sure you have some type of lock that will hold the door in place when the going gets rough. I think the barrel bolt is the best to use over a hook device. The barrel bolt can be locked in place (see Figure 118) where the hook could be knocked out. Anyway, secure the doors in some manner even if you have to use a piece of line looped over the handle.

Figure 118. Barrel bolt

In summing up this chapter, I want to stress safety as the most important single item. Be sure the water closet won't sink your boat; be sure a door will not slam on someone's hand; and be sure you have a handrail in the head area to hold on to when the boat starts jumping about.

The head area is a very necessary part of the boat, and there's absolutely no reason why it cannot be as attractive as the main and forward cabins. All it takes is a little work.

Ten

VENTILATION

Most older boats do not have very good ventilation when compared with what's being produced today. So even though this chapter is brief, I feel it's important enough as part of the upgrading and refurbishing project to be treated separately. By today's standards, companionways, opening ports, and hatches are small on the majority of the older fiberglass sailboats. I think this is partly due to designers wanting a safe, seaworthy boat, and the fact that the new generation of large opening ports and hatches were not available. But whatever the reason, the fact remains that what's designed to keep water out or even decrease the amount that can get below in a boat affects air in the very same way. And therein lies the problem: getting more air below. There's nothing as stuffy nor as miserable as a hot boat, so let's take a look at how to go about cooling things off.

Enlarging Existing Opening Ports and Hatches

Take a good look at every opening port and hatch with the idea of replacing with a larger one. Think back to the section on Ports, Chapter 6. Some of those ports may have really showed their age and may have been almost impossible to clean up. At this point you're in a position to accomplish two goals with one project, replace an old port with a new larger one at the same time improving the looks as well as the ventilation. The same goes for hatches. There are several firms making opening ports and hatches. You'll have no trouble at all obtaining the data you need from the marine supply firms or catalogs.

At this point I'd like to pass on some practical advice. If your deck is cored, be sure you seal the core before installing the new port or hatch. You also need to realize that in dealing with ventilation, it is the surface area of the opening that is significant. You don't have to increase the overall size very much to get a large increase in the surface area. For example, a port that has an opening of three by eight inches has twenty-four square inches of area. Notice what happens when the size is increased to four by twelve inches. You have forty-eight square inches which is twice the area, and yet you didn't double the size of the opening. You only increased the opening a few inches.

My point is you don't have to increase the overall size very much to end up with a large increase in the opening. Look what this does to a 16-inch-by-16-inch hatch which has 256 square inches when compared to an 18-inch-by-18-inch hatch with 324 square inches. The result is approximately a 25 percent increase in area which means 25 percent more air. Believe me, this would make a very noticeable difference below deck.

In my opinion when it comes to adding larger ports and hatches, I'd go with as large as possible as long as you don't detract from the overall appearance of the boat. This is more true with side ports than hatches. The side ports are always on display and have a lot to do with the way the boat looks while on the other hand hatches are flat, not seen as much, and so here you don't have to be quite as careful.

Adding New Opening Ports and Hatches

Along with enlarging existing openings you can install new ones as well. See Figure 119, a ten-by-ten-inch hatch. Just look around and you may be pleasantly surprised to see where a port or hatch could be added. Don't overlook the smaller places. Remember, some ventilation is better than none.

There are other advantages with the larger and added ports and hatches. You increase natural light below as well as provide more places to glance out which help dispel that closed-in feeling a sailboat can sometimes give below deck.

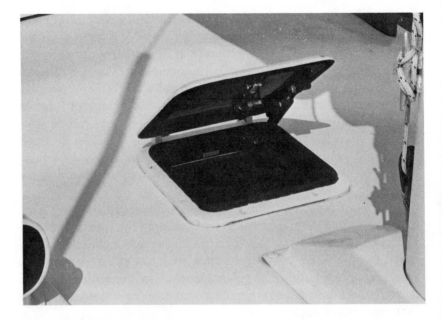

Figure 119. Ventilation hatch

Be careful, though, when cutting a new hole. Make sure there's nothing like wires, for example, in your way.

Windsails

Often the opening ports and hatches need some help, especially when the breeze is light or blocked. The answer here is the windsail which is a cloth funnel that directs air into the boat. Figures 120 and 121 are two styles of windsails which can be used. Figure 120 is the simpler version which costs less and comes from a marine supply firm. Figure 121 is more expensive and usually comes from a sailmaker who sizes it to fit the hatch.

I would suggest you have a windsail on your boat. It will make the difference sometimes between a pleasant time on the boat and that "can-hardly-wait-to-get-off" feeling.

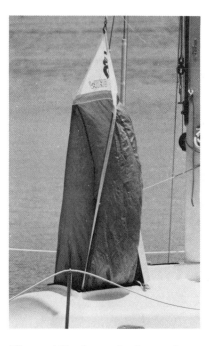

Figure 120. A standard or ready-made type of windsail

Figure 121. A custom-made windsail

Fans

Along with windsails to help things out, you can add fans as well. Installing a small fan in both the main and forward cabins is no trouble. See Figure 122. These fans have about a 6-inch diameter blade, run off the 12-volt battery, and use approximately 2 amps per hour, which is no big drain on your battery. Be sure you get the oscillating type so it can sweep around the cabin. Though this fan is small, remember a sailboat does not have a great deal of volume so the small fan can make a very dramatic difference on a hot day.

On my boat the fan is often used while under way. For example, when running downwind in a light breeze there's not much wind across the deck and even less below, so when someone goes below, say to fix lunch, the fan is snapped on and quickly makes the galley very pleasant. Also, many times both of our fans have run all night at

Figure 122. Bulkhead fan

anchor creating a very nice night from one that would have been stuffy otherwise.

These twelve-volt fans are sold by marine and recreational vehicle supply firms and are not expensive for what you get, something in the neighborhood of thirty to forty dollars.

I would also suggest you carry an 8- or 10-inch oscillating 110-volt fan that can be plugged in to shore current. Marinas are hotter than swinging on the hook, so a 110-volt fan that can move some air is really necessary sometimes. If you're really serious about moving air when shore current is available, get yourself an 18- to-20-inch floor fan. This type is great to lay across an open hatch and blow a huge volume of air below deck.

Since we're talking about mechanical help to keep cool, I feel a word about air conditioning should be mentioned. More and more sailboats are adding AC units since the manufacturers have come out with smaller units. They are, however, expensive and a place on the boat must be found to accommodate the unit. Granted, they are nice on a hot day when tied up at the marina; so as far as air conditioning is concerned, it's a judgment based on your preference.

Since I've talked about AC units, I'll touch on heaters as well. Very few boats have heaters down my way (Virginia) while farther north I imagine they're quite common. If you intend to add heat, you'll have a variety of choices, and the installation is easy. However, let me give two pieces of advice. One, buy a heater with a good track record from a reputable manufacturer, and two, pay close attention to how the unit is vented.

Dorade Vents

If your boat came equipped with Dorade vents, then fine; but if not, then I recommend you not add them. Frankly, they seem to introduce so little air down below that they are not worth the trouble. I'm sure they help some when the boat is closed, but there are cheaper ways to ventilate the boat when not in use. For example, add slots to the crib boards. I particularly like the idea shown in Figure 123 for allowing air to enter through a hatch. One word of caution here; make sure the hatch is secured in some manner to keep the unwanted out. Low profile vents placed in a hatch cover on the deck will allow air to circulate and any good marine supply firm or catalog will offer a good selection. See Figure 124.

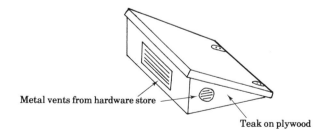

Figure 123. Hatch vent schematic

Figure 124. Hatch vent

In summing up this chapter, I suggest you start with windsails and fans, then go to enlarged and/or new hatches and finish with enlarged and/or added opening ports, if you feel your ventilation continues to be inadequate. No matter how you do it, it's important to get the air moving below to be comfortable when on the boat.

Eleven

THE AUXILIARY ENGINE
AND ELECTRICAL SYSTEM

In this chapter I will cover the auxiliary engine and the electrical system mainly within the framework of upgrading and refurbishing. Although some ongoing maintenance which the handyman sailor should be able to handle will be discussed, there will be no deep technical matters covered, either for the engine or electrical system. Bear in mind you are dealing with the older fiberglass sailboat, and the chances are very good that the engine that came in the boat is the original gas engine which has or has not been rebuilt. Even if the boat was repowered several years back, it could have been done so with a gas engine. The diesel has started to take over the auxiliary job, but it will be a number of years before all the gas engines are replaced. And even at that, the old gas Atomic Four won't and shouldn't give up without a good long fight. So you'll probably be working on an older model gas engine; if not, count yourself way ahead of the game.

I'm not a mechanic or electrician and what little I know about the subjects of mechanics and electricity has come the hard way. So if you don't feel comfortable with either the engine or electrical system, don't be discouraged. You're not alone; I think most sailors fall into this category at one time or another.

This may be your first experience with an inboard engine and as such you should try and learn all you can so you'll be in a better position to maintain your engine. I hope some of the following suggestions and information will prove helpful. At the same time, it is important to realize your own limitations and not hesitate to call in a mechanic before you add to the problem.

Engine and Engine Compartment

I suggest you read this section even if you have a brand new power plant. There are several areas to be covered that apply to engines and engine compartments in general, not just to older gas or diesel engines.

Using the Engine Manual. The very first thing you want to do is have a manual for the engine. On many older boats this has often been lost or misplaced and forgotten. If the boat doesn't come with a manual, make a point to contact the engine dealer or manufacturer just as soon as you buy the boat. Once you have a manual, *read it!* Become familiar with the information, and then use it. Another suggestion is to obtain a service book which is much more detailed than the standard operator's manual, even if you don't plan on becoming an engine mechanic. This service book should stay on the boat. It is in your best interest to know there is a service book handy when you call in a professional mechanic. Don't depend on the mechanic providing one. And how about an engine problem at some out-of-the-way place where the mechanic has only limited experience with your type of engine? The service book at this point is worth its weight in gold.

Cleaning the Engine and Engine Compartment. Chances are your engine and the area surrounding it need cleaning up. Start with the engine itself. Use sandpaper, scraper, and a wire brush to remove any rust and scale. At the same time it helps if you can hold a vacuum cleaner hose close to the place you're working and suck up the particles as they come loose. This keeps the rust and scale from adding to the mess around the engine. The best way to do this is to remove everything from the block, for example, the alternator or spark plug wires if a gas engine. Give yourself as much room as possible to work. I would suggest you leave the spark plugs in the gas engine in place and clean around them in order to keep trash from the cylinders. Frankly, the diesel is easier to clean because you don't have to worry about an ignition system.

This scraping and brushing will be tough to do, so don't expect to knock it out in five minutes. If the engine has a lot of oil or grease, it is best to wash it down with a grease cutter before you start on the rust. A grease cutter can be purchased at any auto parts store. Don't worry about the solvent going in the bilge; it's going to be hard to keep it out. (I'll cover this dirty bilge water below.) Don't forget to clean up the parts that you removed at the same time.

Once the engine is as clean as you can get it, begin on the surrounding compartment. Here you'll encounter mainly grease, oil stains, and bits of trash. What you need to do is to vacuum up everything you can, then finish with warm soapy water and a good household grease cutter like 409 and plenty of elbow grease. Do a final rinse with a hose.

As I mentioned at the beginning of the book about cleaning the entire boat before working on individual projects, I repeat my recommendation that the engine-cleaning project be done at the time the entire boat is cleaned. It makes sense to do it when you have the cleaning materials at hand. Also you want to determine what condition your engine is in as soon as possible. This is important because any needed parts can be placed on order while you pursue other projects.

By now your bilge is full of dirty engine water and you do not want to pump it over the side. I recommend you pump your bilge into a bucket so the oily water can be properly disposed of. Also, I don't think it's a good idea to run this mess through your bilge pump. A small hand or drill-operated pump is all that's needed.

As far as I'm concerned, this is the dirtiest job associated with refurbishing the older fiberglass sailboat. But, it should be done both to see exactly what you have and to help make easier the ongoing maintenance required to keep an auxiliary engine in good running condition.

Checking Over the Engine. With a clean engine and most likely some parts removed, it is a perfect time to check the engine for the obvious problems. Look at the fan belts for wear. Check every wire you can find with eye and hand for any broken places; pay attention to connections, especially ignition wires. If you know something about points, check them out; if not, don't even try. Let the mechanic take care of them. With wrench and screwdriver, make sure every nut and screw is tight, and don't be surprised if a couple are loose. Screws and nuts will work loose on the marine engine and checking them should be an ongoing maintenance item. Check the head nuts using a torque wrench, working to the numbers specified in your manual.

Assuming the engine will run, put everything back in place and crank it up. Now you want to check for water, oil, and gas leaks, and here the clean engine will start to pay dividends. You should easily be able to spot any problem. Take a good look at the water pump and use your hand to feel around for water or dampness.

Next look at your gauges to see if they're functioning, and if so, are they correct? Also note a lack of gauges. A short story that vividly illustrates what can happen when you don't have a temperature gauge follows.

A sailor I know was crossing the mouth of the Potomac River at Chesapeake Bay under power. Everything was going along very pleasantly (except the wind was light, and on the nose) until he glanced below and saw his cabin sole hatch covers floating about in several inches of water! The problem was sea grass had somehow been sucked up in the cooling water intake, passed through the water pump, and created a block at the thermostat. The engine overheated and blew off a hose at the water pump which then proceeded to fill up the thirty-two-foot boat.

As for the outcome of this situation, the good news is first—the problem was found and corrected, the boat pumped dry, and the trip continued. As for the bad news—the drastic overheating of the engine started a series of problems which culminated in major engine work and the necessity of buying a new head. Everything that happened was directly attributable to not having a temperature gauge. With a gauge, the heat buildup would have been known and correct action could have been taken before the situation became serious. So, if you don't have a full set of accurate gauges on your engine, I strongly recommend you add them.

Checking the Fuel System. The fuel system is made up of a tank, fuel line, fuel pump, and fuel line filters. With the gas engine you also have a carburetor and with a diesel, injectors. Your main interest here is with the tank, fuel line, fuel pump, and filters. The carburetor and injectors fall into the domain of the mechanic, I feel, and will not be detailed. What you need to look at is how to purge the fuel system of years and years of accumulated trash and water. Let's first tackle the tank itself which will be your largest collector of trash and water. Remember the bent copper tube used to clean the bottom of the water tank? You'll be able to use it again. Only this time a word of caution.

When the water tank bottom was cleaned, you had the choice of the hand pump or the drill motor pump. This time use only the hand pump. *Do not* use the drill motor pump as the drill creates sparks, and you're working with a combustible liquid, not water.

Make sure you have at least three or four gallons of fuel in the tank, and with the hand pump start pumping the fuel into a clean bucket, moving the copper tube like a probe around to all the corners you can reach. A good way to do this is to get a second person so one can pump while the other can concentrate on moving the tube. From experience, it's hard to do both by yourself.

After your bucket is full, sit back, rest, and let the fuel settle for a couple of minutes; then pour the fuel back into the tank except for the bottom two or three inches which will hold the trash and water. Next pour this small portion of fuel into another container. It's important to remove the junk from the bottom of the receiving bucket so you can note how much you bring up each time. Repeat this process remembering to rock the boat, and move the tube around until you feel like you have removed a large part of the trash and water. It's one of those tiring jobs; but when you see what comes out of the tank, I'm sure you'll think the effort well worth it.

Don't forget to check your tank to see if there's some other way to purge it. There may be a drain hole in the bottom, for example, but most of the time fuel tanks are very hard to get at, so the pump and tube may be your best bet. And while you're at it, check for leaks, using your nose as well as your eyes. The tank vent should be located and checked while you're below deck.

I would like to add that many older boats can have a steel fuel tank that with age has started to rust. No matter how much cleaning you do there will be a steady accumulation of material to create problems. In this case, the best thing to do is to replace the tank, because the rust will eventually cause a leak, and a leaking fuel tank is no joke. In the case of a fuel tank leak that is not something easy like tightening a fitting, I suggest you contact a firm that handles this type of repair.

The fuel pump bowl is the next item to clean; and it is a simple job, that is, if you can get to it. This, by the way, should be a routine task. I check my fuel pump bowl at least twice during the boating season.

Your next place to investigate is the filter. In many of the older boats you'll have a well-made filter and water separator which are easy to clean. Check them a couple of times a season also. If you don't have a filter between the tank and fuel pump, I suggest you add one or have it done. Any good marine yard or supplier will be able to fix you up.

Last, you want to see exactly how the fuel flows from the fuel pump just to make sure the line is clear. Unhook the line at the carburetor, place a container under it, and turn the engine over and watch how the fuel is pumped out. This will tell you firsthand if the engine is getting a good supply of fuel. If not, you'll have to go back through the fuel lines for the stoppage. You may even consider replacing the fuel lines.

After doing all these tasks, you now have a clean fuel system which you're going to have to maintain periodically to keep the trash and water from collecting. As for the carburetor, unless you're qualified, call the mechanic.

I have three suggestions that can help keep down the trash and water that are introduced when the tank is filled. These suggestions have proved very helpful for my engine which, by the way, is an Atomic Four.

1. Buy your fuel from a service station if possible. I use two 5-gallon cans and pick up the gas to take to the boat. Of course, I can't do this on a trip, but I do it when using the boat close to home. I also leave just a little gas in the can after pouring so if there's some trash, I'll not dump it into the tank.
2. Use one of the dry gas compounds which are now on the market to remove water from gas on a regular basis. This helps with the condensation that takes place when the boat sits for days and days.
3. Try and keep the tank filled up. I know this is sometimes inconvenient; but if you plan for the boat to sit for a while, do so. It really helps with the condensation.

Clean fuel is a must for any engine but especially so for the marine engine, and you are the only person who's going to see to this. Plan on taking care of your fuel system so the engine will work well for you.

Checking the Cooling System. In my opinion the cooling system is by far the largest supplier of problems connected with the marine engine. The reason for this is simple; the coolant used, in this case, water, is contaminated, i.e., the water comes from outside the hull and can have chemicals that deposit themselves in the form of scale and slowly close up the water passages. This is especially true of salt water. Along with this there are all sorts of things floating in the water. The sea grass clogging the thermostat was a good example.

Actually, a boat's system is exactly the opposite of your car's cooling system. The car's engine uses a closed system with a special liquid circulating throughout to remove the heat. The hot coolant passes through a heat exchanger (the radiator) where the heat is removed by air as the car moves. The coolant then returns to the engine for another load of heat. The closed system where the heat is dissipated by air is ideal as long as the heat exchanger can pass through the air at forty miles an hour. However, it's not going to work at six knots—the speed of your boat. So on a boat you have to get rid of the heat in some other fashion, and the handiest and most convenient material to use is what the boat sits in, water. Even when you have a closed system, like the car engine, you have to use a "radiator" that uses outside water to exchange the heat; and while the engine's system has fewer problems, the heat exchanger has all the trouble inherent in using outside water.

At this point you know what to expect, so how do you minimize the problems? The answer is to keep as many things as possible from entering the system at the entry point, and then keep the water passages clean so that scale and trash never have a chance to accumulate.

There's really nothing complicated about the marine engine cooling system. You have the entry point which will be a sea cock, a lever type, not a gate valve. (Remember, sea cocks were discussed in Chapter 3.) Next, there is the water pump which provides the pressure to push the water through the engine. You also have the thermostat that opens and closes with heat to allow the cooling water to be discharged from the engine into the exhaust system and overboard. Finally, hoses are used to tie all these parts together. To make things clear, I'll discuss each part in turn.

Sea Cock. This is a simple device that you're familiar with but I would like to stress two points. First, consider replacing it if you are not sure of its age. Think back to my story in Chapter 3 when the water intake broke with a gentle tug; so if in doubt, replace. Second, make sure your sea cock has a strainer. If the one on the boat does not, this is a good reason to replace the sea cock. I'm truly amazed at the number of boats which don't have a strainer on their engine water intake. And, how about the intake sea cock for the head or your outside water pump in the galley? You don't want these systems clogged any more than the engine. A strainer on the intake sea cock of my friend's boat would have kept the sea grass incident from ever happening in the first place. The strainer is your first line of defense in keeping foreign material out of your cooling system. You still need your temperature gauge, but the gauge will never stop a problem; it will only tell you there is a problem.

Water Pump. The majority of water pumps consist of a shaft turned by the engine that in turn rotates an impeller. The impeller is a small paddle wheel made of a rubberlike material which actually does the job of pushing the water through the engine. The impeller operates in a metal housing that causes a great deal of friction. Any time you have flexible material rubbing on metal, you can expect it to be a regular maintenance item. Impellers do come apart. See Figure 125.

Because impellers have to be changed, they are usually accessible behind a removable plate on the pump. Just take off the plate, pull the shaft with the impeller attached from the pump housing, replace the impeller, reinsert the shaft, and close up the plate. Nothing to it as long as you can get to it. Frankly, you may find it is more convenient to remove the whole water pump to replace the impeller. That is what I did. The pump is only held in place with two bolts that are easy to reach.

Since the water pump impeller is one of the major sources of cooling system problems, it should be replaced every year before the boating season gets underway. This is not only my suggestion, but the advice also of marine mechanics I know. After all, you're only talking about maybe an hour's time and something around ten dollars for the impeller.

Here I have some practical information that should prove helpful concerning impellers and water pumps. When buying impellers, the

Figure 125. Damaged impeller

pump model number will dictate what particular impeller to use. At the same time, it is important to know what type of liquid the impeller will be pumping. For example, oily water and salt water do not use the same impeller. Next even though the model numbers match, there's no guarantee the impellers are the same.

I've found this difference to be in the width only. The shaft hole and overall size will be a perfect match when you compare the old and new, but pay attention to the depth or thickness. I've found this to vary as much as a sixteenth of an inch.

This doesn't create any trouble if the new impeller is less in width; but if it is larger, it can shorten the life of the impeller. What happens is this. The extra little bit of width causes the cover plate to push against the side of the impeller thereby creating more friction which shortens the life of the impeller.

I learned all this the hard way. I did my usual spring replacement and two months later started having the symptoms of water pump problems. So I pulled the pump, checked the impeller, and found that two blades had broken off. Needless to say, I was concerned because usually you can depend on a year's trouble-free use of a new impeller. I gave everything a thorough checking, including the damaged and new impellers, and that's when I noticed the damaged one was thicker. I remembered back a couple of months earlier when I screwed the cover plate in place over the now-damaged impeller and thought at the time it seemed to take a lot of pressure to snug it down. Then I realized what the problem was. The impeller has enough friction when all is right; but apply added friction from the side and there's no way for the impeller to stay together.

So the bottom line here is check the thickness of the new replacement. And if it's a little larger, take this into account when putting the cover plate back in place. All you have to do is add a thicker gasket where the cover plate meets the pump housing. What you want to do is make sure the impeller doesn't project out beyond the gasket and when turning the screws the cover is not meeting any resistance from the impeller.

The symptoms of water pump trouble I will pass on to you. Your temperature gauge will start to read above normal operating temperature and then hover somewhere higher than it should. If the engine is being run hard, the temperature will continue to creep up; if the engine is slowed down, the temperature will drop, but still remain higher than normal. What has happened is that the impeller has lost a blade or two which not only impairs the efficiency of the impeller, but the loose blade or blades get in the way just making things worse.

It's simple to check this out. Remove the hose on the discharge side of the pump, crank up the engine for a few seconds, and notice how much water is being pumped. A damaged impeller will discharge a small volume of water and it will come out in squirts and fizzles. An undamaged impeller will throw a large stream of water just as steady as if it were coming from your garden hose.

A word of advice and caution when you remove the damaged impeller. Get all the parts and reconstruct the impeller before you install the new one. What you're doing is accounting for all the pieces to make sure some of the loose parts haven't been carried into the cooling system to create future problems.

If you cannot find all the parts, chances are good the lost pieces will be lodged in a right angle turn that your water pump should have on the discharge line before the hose is attached. If your water pump doesn't have a right angle before the hose attachment point, I suggest you add one because it's in your best interest to keep bits and pieces out of the engine cooling system.

The last thing about the water pump to be aware of is the grease cup. Keep it full of grease and turn every eight hours or so to keep the shaft lubricated. While the water pump is simple to look after, it does require attention. With a little effort on your part, you'll quickly become familiar with it.

Thermostat. Your thermostat is a heat-sensing device that opens and closes in order for the engine to operate within a given range of temperature. It is not good for an engine to run at too low a temperature, so the thermostat's job is to regulate the temperature by controlling the flow of water. Every so often the thermostat will need replacing, but most of the time just taking it out and cleaning it every year is all that's necessary. However, you can sometimes have problems with the older engines that have had scale buildup. A piece of scale can break away and lodge in the thermostat. If bits of trash block the thermostat, too much water is allowed to pass, in which case the temperature runs below normal; or you can block all or some of the water which gives you higher than normal temperature all the way up to overheating. So when you have a heating up problem, check the thermostat after you check the water pump. While you have the thermostat out, make sure it's opening and closing as it should be by placing it in a pan of water that's being heated. Use a thermometer to check the water temperature when the thermostat opens so you can determine if it's working in the proper heat range, around 140° for salt water and 180° for fresh water. Of course, if the thermometer does not open, then you've located the problem.

Temperature Gauge. The temperature gauge has to have a sensor to pick up the water temperature. So when you check the system, or any time you do any maintenance work, for that matter, remove and clean the sensor. You want the gauge to be as accurate as possible.

Hoses. Hoses tie together all these separate parts. They are not expensive, so I would suggest you replace all your hoses. This way you won't have to worry about them. And buy good quality from an industrial supply house. It only costs a little more to get the best.

Standpipe. This is the part of the exhaust system that keeps water from flowing back into the engine. Because of age, it can give trouble in the older boat. A little water is always left in the standpipe, and after a few years small leaks can occur that allow this water to seep back into the unused engine. Check for leaks; and unless you're good with pipes, I'd suggest you bring in a marine mechanic for any repair work.

I know when you put all these pieces of equipment together, it may tend to become confusing. Don't worry. With a little homework and using your manual, it'll all fall right into place for you.

I would now like to address the cooling system in general terms. First, there's no reason whatsoever why you, the handyman sailor, cannot learn to take care of your engine cooling system if you want to. There is absolutely nothing complicated, just remember: one, the engine heats up only when the cooling system has a blockage or a breakdown, and two, the blockage or breakdown *is* in the system and *can* be tracked down.

Since you're dealing with the older boat and hence most likely an older engine, I'm approaching everything from that standpoint. Your first task in checking the cooling system is to inspect the impeller and thermostat. Second, take off the water jacket where the water enters the block, and remove the pipe that allows water to pass from the block and head into the manifold, in short, removing everything you can connected with the cooling system except the head and manifold.

Next using a straightened coat hanger or any fairly stiff wire filed to a sharp edge on the end, rod out all water passageways you can get the wire into. This goes for the engine as well as the items removed. Now for the really messy part. First, take the parts ashore and blow water through them to make sure all the bits and pieces are removed. A garden hose with a pistol grip nozzle is the best thing to use for this. Next take the hose on board the boat. Cover everything as well as you can with plastic (garbage bags work fine) in the engine compartment and proceed to put water through the manifold and engine. You want to remove any trash and at the same time see that the water passes freely. Two pieces of advice here. Pack old towels or something similar around the bottom of the engine to keep as much trash as possible out of the bilge. Since it is not necessary to have tremendous pressure on the hose, start with low pressure and have someone standing by to increase the pressure until you're getting the job done and not wetting down the entire aft end of the boat. Don't forget to pump the bilge as you'll really be dumping in the water.

You'll never get all the junk out of the water passages; don't even try. What you're after is to establish the fact that the cooling water can flow freely throughout the system. The next thing you're doing is becoming familiar with the cooling system by the hands-on method which, in my opinion, is the most effective way of learning.

After you're comfortable with the cooling system, troubleshooting becomes a simple process of elimination when you notice your heat gauge start to rise. The manual will have instructions to follow, and I will add a couple of suggestions. Check your water pump first. If okay, this tells you two things: the sea cock is allowing water in and the pump is pushing the water. Next check the thermostat; if in order, then the blockage is in the hoses or water passages. Chances of blockage being a hose are slim because the diameter is large compared with most of the engine water passages. Most of the time the stoppage when the sea cock, pump, and thermostat are working will be a collection point in the engine passages. By collection point I mean a place where all the water has to pass through sooner or later, for example, where the water leaves the engine block and enters the manifold. These collection points often have turns in the passage making it easy to trap trash.

One of the most frustrating blockages is the blown head gasket. I'm told what happens is pressure from the explosion chamber is allowed to enter the water passage and create a blockage. Once I had an overheating problem and tore down the cooling system twice but still couldn't locate the problem. I called in a mechanic; and after hearing what had been done, he announced the engine had a blown head gasket. He pulled the head, and the path of the water could easily be seen. This is, as I understand it, not a very common occurrence, but it's good to be aware of. Just remember if the engine overheats, it is because the cooling water is blocked for some reason. All you have to do is find the blockage. I'm assuming you're handy with tools and are inclined to work on your engine. There's nothing wrong if you're handy with tools, but the engine is not your thing. In this case, do what you feel comfortable with and have a mechanic take care of the other areas. I might add this goes also for the engine in general, not just for the cooling system.

Controls, Stuffing Box, and Shaft. You have a lot of moving parts associated with the controls. Check over the throttle and choke connections, both at the cockpit and engine locations. Make sure there are no screws or nuts loose, and that the cables work freely. It's a good idea to lubricate if the controls seem hard to move. Check the gear shift hookup for any loose nuts and screws and lubricate also if things are binding.

The shaft connection behind the engine needs to be checked for any loose bolts. This won't be easy. You're working behind the engine, and things can start to get tight here. However, it's a piece of cake compared to the stuffing box. Here you want to be sure the hose is in good condition. Give it a poke with a screwdriver, and then try to twist it with your hand. If it needs replacing, you'll know it. Remove the large nut, and look at the packing with a mirror. If you plan to replace, use a piece of stiff wire with a hook to pull out the old packing and replace with new. Any good boatyard will have packing and the cost is only a couple of dollars. When you get it all back together, you're going to have to check to make sure it's loose enough to allow water to drip into the bilge. The tendency here is to make things too tight. After running the engine a few minutes, check to see if water is dripping every couple of seconds and at the same time feel the stuffing box. Slightly warm is okay, but hot is not good, so loosen things up until you get the proper flow of dripping water and the stuffing box itself is cool to slightly warm. This is accomplished by trial and error, but after a couple of times you'll get the hang of it.

Oh, yes, these stuffing box nuts are large so look around for a couple of wide-jawed wrenches to use. A stuffing box wrench is available on the market; get one if you can.

Engine History. I think it's a good idea to determine exactly what the work history is on the engine. Don't hesitate to ask the previous owner, then visit the yard that did the work and ask if you could copy the invoices or work sheets. At the same time track down the mechanic or mechanics and see if any history can be obtained. It will be ideal if all this can be done at the same location at the same time. It's a tremendous help when dealing with the older engine to know exactly what's been done to it.

Engine and Bilge Ventilation. Make sure your engine and bilge area have ventilation, both the blower and the fore and aft deck-mounted clamshell type with ventilation hose attached. Safety is involved here which makes this very important.

The Mechanic. When it comes to the real insides of the engine, I suggest you call in a mechanic unless you're competent. When you're ready to call in a mechanic, ask your sailing friends and the boat owners you come in contact with if they know of a mechanic who does part-time work at night or weekends. Another good source for an after-hours mechanic is the wholesale distributor of engines and parts.

Anyway, before taking your boat to an expensive yard, check around and see if you can locate a mechanic. There is, however, one drawback. When working with an individual like this you have no one to turn to if the mechanic's work is not satisfactory. What a reputable boatyard offers is good work which they back up; if you feel better going this route, by all means do so. Of course, you may have no choice if the yard you use for hauling or where you keep the boat doesn't allow any outside help to come in and work.

One more suggestion—regardless of who does what to the engine, make it a point to watch and learn everything you can even if it means making a pest of yourself. The mechanic will soon forget you worried him, and he's not going to be with you when the engine won't start when you're two days from home. It'll be up to you then; and the more you know, the better.

Painting the Engine and Engine Compartment. After you and your mechanic are through going over the engine and it's running "smooth as silk," your next job is to paint the engine and the area around it.

There's one very important reason to paint the engine and the surrounding area, and it's not looks either. Granted it's more pleasant for the engine to look clean instead of like a rusty greaseball. But the real reason is so anything that is not working properly is easily seen. For example, water leaks show up quickly on a painted engine block; hot spots where the cooling water is not circulating as it should show up by turning the paint to a brown-black color. Oil leaks disappear against a rusty block but stand out on paint. The same goes for the area around the engine. Sometimes there's a leak in a hard-to-see place, and it shows up in the surrounding area.

The color you choose is not significant, but be sure to use an engine paint so it will stand the heat. The time to paint is when the engine is all apart; if you cannot do it then, it can be done when all is back together. Just use a small half-inch brush and take your time. Remember, it doesn't have to be perfect; a few runs will not hurt anything. Do the engine itself first because you'll be dropping paint on the surrounding area. Don't paint spark plugs or electrical connections. The best rule is to only paint the metal.

General Thoughts Concerning the Engine. Here are some ideas I have found helpful.

1. Put a light in the engine compartment. Remember when I suggested you save the old cabin lights? This's a good place for one.
2. Change the oil as noted in the manual. Carry spare oil in plastic bags to lessen chance of an oil spill in the boat. Many older engines started out using nondetergent oil, and I suggest you continue with nondetergent oil if this is the case. The new high detergent oils can break loose accumulated sludge that can clog passages and maybe cause damage. If not on the shelf at your local auto parts store, they can order it for you. You may want to discuss this with a marine mechanic.
3. Use an additive called Marvel Mystery Oil which is added both to the crankcase oil and the gas. It is helpful in keeping valves from sticking, I have found.
4. Change the spark plugs every season.
5. Carry a good selection of spare parts: plugs, extra hose, any type of belts, ignition parts, gaskets and seals, and anything else you can think of.
6. Always check the auto parts store first when buying parts; often you can get what you need at a better price.

7. Consider using a sound-deadening material in the engine compartment. A good boatyard or an industrial hose and insulation firm may be able to supply you with the necessary material.

8. Add some form of insulation to any icebox surface that's in the engine compartment to help keep the engine heat from the icebox. This idea can be incorporated with sound deadening.

9. Have a complete set of tools for the boat and leave them there. That way you'll always have what you need on hand. Also consider hanging a paper towel rack in the engine area; you'll soon wonder how you got along without it.

10. Open one or more access doors to vent the heat out of the engine area, especially if you have an aft galley, when running under power in hot weather and no one's below. All this heat is bottled up exactly where you don't want it, next to the icebox and your food lockers. I go so far as to take the lids off countertop lockers so heat from below is not trapped. The best way to help get rid of engine heat on my boat is to open the forward hatch, then the engine access door, then prop up the lazaret hatch which gives a flow of air from front to back. If your lazaret hatch won't do the job or you don't have one, then use a seat locker. Believe me, it makes a big difference when you get to where you're going in hot weather and do not have all that heat trapped under the galley.

11. Rub your wet hands with table salt and rinse to remove gas smells. Also keep on board a hand cleaner used by mechanics. You can buy it at your local auto parts store.

12. Don't throw away that old cockpit cushion or lifejacket. Save it and use it to lay across the engine when you have to crawl about on top of it to reach something way in the back.

13. Have a set of long jumper cables made up so you can jump start your engine from a boat alongside. Remember, no matter how many batteries you have, it's still possible for them to be flat when needed.

14. Run the engine; it's been designed to operate, not sit idle. Try to crank it every week and run until warmed up, say twenty to thirty minutes. Don't just run it for five minutes when

leaving the slip and then raise the sails. Go ahead and power for a few minutes more. It's my understanding from people who know that it is the least used engines that give the most trouble.

In summary I wish to point out that my approach for the auxiliary engine was what I consider the worst case—an old gas engine. Also the two areas that seem to give the most trouble, fuel and cooling, are in my opinion, the simplest areas for the handyman to become proficient with. You don't have to be a mechanic to service these two systems so it makes sense, in my opinion, to become knowledgeable about them.

But the entire thrust of this book is upgrading and refurbishing, and one of the most positive projects you can do is repower with a new diesel. This probably will be your single largest outlay of money during the refurbishing project, but it will be money well spent. This is one place you'll have no trouble getting your money back if and when you decide to sell the boat.

The Electrical System

You'll be happy to know this time you don't have to bring out the soap and water. Just about the only thing required will be a screwdriver. Your first task is checking all the electrical fixtures, such as lights, radios, and instruments to make sure everything is working. Next check all the connections you can get at including the inside of the switch panel. What you're looking for is loose connections and corrosion. If any is noted, clean up with fine grade sandpaper. As a matter of fact, it's not a bad idea to clean up all your connections whether corroded or not.

The wires themselves should be looked at for any breaks or frayed places. It's not uncommon on a boat for a wire with a little play in it to rub the insulation off with the boat's motion. It's not going to be easy checking the wires because often they'll be almost inaccessible, if not completely so. You'll just have to do the best you can. Use a mirror on a handle to help you look into those hard-to-get-at places; and where you're not able to see at all, use your hand to examine the wires.

After this, go over the battery cables, connections, master switch, and last try to determine the age and condition of the battery or batteries. If the battery or batteries are not recent, this can be difficult. Check each cell to determine the charge. An inexpensive cell checker can be purchased at your local auto parts store.

At this point you have a good idea of the shape of the electrical system, so let's get into upgrading. Here upgrading and making repairs are rolled into the same project which will become clearer as we move along.

Take a look at all the items which don't work and you wish to have on the boat, for example, a VHF radio or a depth finder, and decide if they're worth fixing or if you prefer up-to-date equipment. My suggestion is if the particular item is not working and showing its age it's probably not worth fixing. One of the problems will be finding parts plus the added headache of the manufacturer possibly being out of business.

You're going to have to work out exactly what you intend to repair and what you plan to replace with new equipment. Light fixtures fall into this category as well as spreader lights covered earlier. Instruments are another good example of items that are repaired or replaced.

Adding new equipment has to be taken into consideration along with repairs and replacement of existing pieces. Installing a tape deck, FM radio, fans, pressure water, or a VHF radio if one did not come on the boat are among the pleasant ways to upgrade your sailboat. For short-handed sailing, an Autopilot is also very handy.

Let me say fixing or adding any of the above requires no special skills or knowledge beyond locating a source of power to run the unit and turning some screws to remove and attach. Electrical equipment is a self-contained package that's easily removed and sent out to be repaired, or a new unit can be installed. Unless you're qualified, don't even think about trying to fix something electrical; chances are you'll just add to the problem.

If you do add this equipment, I recommend you consider enlarging your switch panel. Your existing panel may have enough circuits to accommodate the new installations, but after years of use something may be ready to break. Frankly I would feel better with a new and up-to-date looking panel. You're not talking about a lot of money, and it certainly gives that positive upgraded appearance.

Adding Another Battery. There's a good chance your older boat came with only one battery. In this case I recommend adding another. With one battery you're always on edge about using too many amps and not being able to start the engine; furthermore, if you plan on installing some new electrical equipment, you'll be increasing the load even more. Two batteries will solve the problem and give you peace of mind when the fan, tape deck, and all the lights are on when swinging on the hook. See Figure 126.

First you have to determine where the new battery will go. For convenience, I suggest it be next to the existing battery if at all possible. The battery should be in a battery box and everything firmly held in place. The last thing you want rolling around when the boat is bouncing about is a battery. While on this subject make sure the existing battery box is secured also; don't find out the hard way it's not.

Before you go out and buy the necessary new cables, make some measurements. What may look about right to the eye suddenly be-

Figure 126. Second battery installation

comes too short when it has to make a couple of turns. Take the trouble to determine the lengths you need.

A new battery switch will be needed to handle two batteries. Any good marine supply firm or catalog will be able to supply you with a switch which meets all the required safety standards. You may also want to add an instrument that tells you the charge condition of the battery. It's really helpful to know if one battery is low compared to its partner.

If you'll be using a twelve-volt battery, size everything to this; if not, do so for the voltage you plan to use. For sailboat usage, twelve volts is usually the norm. When it comes to the battery itself, get a marine battery. The marine battery is designed to put out power over longer periods at a slower rate and then be charged back up. The auto battery is designed to give a sudden burst of power for a very short time. I'm not saying the auto battery won't work in a boat; it will— but not as well as the marine battery.

If your original battery is not up to the job, this is a good time to replace it. The actual hookup is simple since the original battery cables are already in place. With the added battery the only difference is you're adding another set of cables. However, if you're not sure of yourself, call in some help, either a knowledgeable friend or a mechanic. And if you do, pay attention to what's done for future reference.

Cosmetic Side of the Electrical System. Not only is electrical equipment expected to work, but it also should look good and complement its location below deck. To me nothing looks as unfinished as the exposed back of an instrument with wires running across the bulkhead. See Figure 127. Many instruments provide a cover box; if not included, a small box (Figure 128) can be built to do the job. If you have a whole bank of instruments in one place, consider adding a panel to cover all the instrument backs at the same time. Instead of leaving wires exposed, cover them with a piece of hollowed out wood trim. See Figure 129. Sometimes it's possible to run wires inside the headliner, under a countertop, or behind the front edge of a shelf. Give this some thought and hide those wires.

Shore Power. If you plan to do any cruising at all, you're going to need shore current. There'll be plenty of times when you're tied up at

Figure 127. Exposed instrument wires

Figure 128. Instrument box

Figure 129. Trim to hide wires

a marina, and frankly it's very nice to use an electric frying pan, perk coffee, and have a huge fan running if it's hot.

Chances are your boat will have shore power connections and so you need to determine what shape they are in. Start with the deck fitting, then check the wires and outlets which will be the same as your 110-volt outlets in your home. From my experience if what you have is original equipment, you have an outdated deck fitting plus only one or maybe two outlets below decks.

It's a simple enough matter to install a new shore power inlet fitting and add an extra outlet or two below deck if you need them. When you add the new power inlet fitting, you're going to have to add the power cord with the proper connector so everything fits together when you want to plug in at the dock.

Any good marine store or catalog firm will be able to supply all the necessary equipment except the actual 110 outlets. These you'll find at your local hardware store. Again they're easy to install; just cut a hole and run the wires. Put them anywhere you feel they're needed. One suggestion: have one in the head area because when tied up at a marina with the prospect of dinner out, you'll possibly want access to curling irons and hair dryers. Also, have one close to the engine area so you can plug in a light or hand-held power tool. Usually an outlet in the galley will serve for this if it's an aft galley arrangement; but if a side galley one may not be convenient.

In short, up-to-date shore power is an important part of upgrading your boat. Don't let this electrical work overwhelm you. If you can peel insulation from wires and use a screwdriver, you can put it all together. If you're still somewhat uneasy about your work, get someone who is knowledgeable to assist you. Of course, you may have been lucky enough to have bought a boat with an updated shore power system.

Let me give you a sobering thought concerning your electrical system in general. Many boat fires seem to come from some kind of electrical short, and they can happen just as easily when you're on the boat or away from it. The difference is that when you're aboard, something can be done immediately because detection is quick. But when no one is on board there is the possibility you can lose your boat. Therefore, cut no corners, use no questionable materials, and make sure everything is up to required standards.

Grounding System

Although it's not a part of the electrical system that supplies power to all the electrical units on the boat, it is in the category of electricity and needs to be addressed. I'll admit sitting in the middle of an electrical storm in a sailboat is not my idea of fun. As a retired army friend of mine said, "It's like being on the receiving end of an artillery barrage because you never know where the next one is going to hit." Therefore, it's a good feeling to know your boat is grounded. If it is grounded, there will be one or more wires attached to a chainplate and angling down toward the bilge. They are usually attached to the engine so the shaft can be used to allow the energy to reach the water.

If you cannot find a grounding system after checking, I suggest you contact the builder if possible to see if he can give you any information. In the event you don't have this system, you have two choices. One, you can install one, and here I suggest you contact a good boatyard for help—either for information or to have the job done. Two, carry a cable with a spring-loaded clamp on one end. You secure it to the backstay with the other end in the water whenever there is a chance of lightning. Also, it's a good idea to leave it attached when the boat is not in use. I personally know of only a very few boats to have been hit by lightning; but when dealing with something as deadly, it pays to take no chances.

In closing this chapter, I wish to add that the engine and electrical system are areas where you can put in hours and hours of work and no one but you will know what's been done. Your real sense of accomplishment with the engine and electrical system comes when you hit the starter button or flip a switch and everything works exactly as expected.

INDEX

Index